A Guide to the Birds of the Southeastern States

with photos by
Barth Schorre
Vernon E. Grove Jr.
David F. Parmelee
VIREO (Academy of
Natural Sciences,
Philadelphia) and
Kevin Winker

A Guide to the Birds
of the Southeastern States

Florida, Georgia, Alabama, and Mississippi

John H. Rappole

University Press of Florida
Gainesville · Tallahassee · Tampa · Boca Raton
Pensacola · Orlando · Miami · Jacksonville · Ft. Myers

A record of cataloging-in-publication data is available from
the Library of Congress.
ISBN 0-8130-2861-2

The University Press of Florida is the scholarly publishing agency
for the State University System of Florida, comprising Florida A&M
University, Florida Atlantic University, Florida Gulf Coast University,
Florida International University, Florida State University, University
of Central Florida, University of Florida, University of North Florida,
University of South Florida, and University of West Florida.

University Press of Florida
15 Northwest 15th Street
Gainesville, FL 32611-2079
http://www.upf.com

To my good friends and former colleagues of the Georgia Museum of Natural History "Rod and Gun Club":

Bud Freeman, Laurie Vitt, and Lloyd Logan; ex officio members Bonnie Rappole, Mary Freeman, Joe and June Meyers, Ron and Laura Odom, William Guthrie, Jim and Linda Kundall, and Connie Logan; and in memory of our beloved and esteemed director, Josh Laerm

Souls that have toiled, and wrought and thought with me—
That ever with a frolic welcome took
The thunder and the sunshine . . .

—Alfred Lord Tennyson, "Ulysses"

Contents

Figures

Acknowledgments

I thank Noel Parsons, former editor-in-chief of Texas A&M University Press, for agreeing to undertake this project. Several of the most outstanding wildlife photographers in North America donated slides for this book, including Barth Schorre, Vernon E. Grove Jr., David F. Parmelee, and Kevin Winker. Doug Wechsler, Academy of Natural Sciences, Philadelphia, was extremely helpful in providing additional photos from the academy's VIREO photo collection, and in reviewing all photos accompanying species accounts for errors.

Certain sections of this guide (for example, some species and range descriptions) are taken from *Birds of Texas: A Field Guide*, by John H. Rappole and Gene W. Blacklock (1994). Material from that work reprinted herein is used with the kind permission of my coauthor, Gene W. Blacklock. Bruce H. Anderson, Jerome A. Jackson, and David W. Steadman provided extraordinarily thorough and helpful reviews of the manuscript, for which I am very grateful. Any remaining errors, however, are my responsibility alone.

Dr. and Mrs. A. W. Rappole provided guidance and hospitality during our photo tours of the region, as did Bruce and Mary Ann Rowan. Finally, I thank my wife, Bonnie, for her invaluable encouragement and support throughout the long evolutionary history of the project.

Color Tab Index to Bird Groups

Introduction

Forty people million can't be wrong! That's the number who come to the south-eastern United States (Figure 1) each year from purple mountains, painted deserts, dusty cornfields, concrete canyons, and various frozen wastes to enjoy the region's undeniable attractions. Tourism is the largest single generator of revenue, with an annual economic impact exceeding 35 billion dollars.

This trend started early. Visitors have wondered at the marvels of the Southeast for nearly half a millennium. Juan Ponce de León, then governor of Puerto Rico, was the first to visit in historical times, landing on the Florida coast near the mouth of the St. Johns River on March 27, 1513, Easter Sunday, naming it "La Florida" in honor of Easter (The Feast of Flowers). Like many who have visited since, he was searching for the fountain of youth.

Subsequent exploration and settlement of the region were undertaken principally by the Spanish during the 1500s. Ponce de León returned to Florida in 1521, attempting to establish a colony on the Gulf Coast, but as other would-be settlers would find over the next two centuries, his presence was not welcomed by the indigenes, and the colony died out. A similar fate was shared by the colony established in Tampa Bay in 1528. In 1539, Hernando de Soto led an expedition across the area that is now the Florida Panhandle, Georgia, Alabama, and Mississippi in search of gold. The first permanent colony in continental North America, originally called San Augustin, now Saint Augustine, was established at the mouth of the St. Johns River in 1565. Over the next hundred years, France, England, and Spain contended for control of the Florida region, which extended north to the Savannah River and west to the Mississippi River (thus including most of the area defined herein as the Southeast).

James Oglethorpe was ceded rights to the region between the Savannah and Altamaha rivers (most of present day coastal Georgia) in 1732 by the King of England, and he subsequently established a colony at the mouth of the Savannah River later in that same year. In 1763, Spain granted official ownership of the region to England, but control of the Florida peninsula was returned to Spain in 1783 in exchange for the Bahamas. Spain sold West Florida (parts of the Panhandle, Alabama, and Mississippi) to France in 1795, a region claimed by the United States subsequent to the Louisiana Purchase. American squatters invaded Spanish Florida increasingly in the early 1800s, and Spain finally sold

Figure 1. Map of the Southeast region.

the Florida peninsula to the United States in 1819 for a little more than four million dollars.

Georgia was one of the original thirteen colonies, its boundaries extending from the Savannah River on the north to the St. Marys River on the south and west to the Mississippi, thus including most of present-day Alabama and Mississippi. Mississippi became a state in 1817, Alabama in 1819, and Florida in 1845.

Ornithological History

The region has an illustrious ornithological history, and was famous from early times as a place filled with strange and exciting creatures. Catesby's beautiful paintings of its birds, published over the years from 1731 to 1748, fired the imagination of many living elsewhere in the United States and Europe, as did the vivid descriptions contained in William Bartram's 1791 "Travels." Audubon, during his 1831 visit, waxed poetic, stating, "Here I am in the Floridas . . . a country that received its name from the odours wafted from the orange groves . . . and which from my childhood I have consecrated in my imagination as a garden of the United States" (Audubon 1832).

Modern ornithologists have found that the Southeast lives up to its billing. The region is extremely rich in birds, with a disproportionate number of exotic species found nowhere else in the United States. A total of about 627 species of birds has been recorded for the southeastern region, roughly 376 occurring *regularly* (common, uncommon, or rare). Complete descriptions and accounts for each of these birds are contained in this book, while the 251 species that are considered casual (occur a few times per decade), accidental (not expected to recur), hypothetical (not documented), or extinct are listed in appendix 1. Most of these strange birds are escaped exotics (e.g., the Burrowing Parrot), seen once or twice before disappearing. However, an unusually large number have become established as breeding populations in the Southeast, mostly in Florida, where such species as Eurasian Collared-Dove, Yellow-chevroned Parakeet, and Red-whiskered Bulbul can be seen fairly easily if you are in the right place at the right time.

Apparently, the region was even richer in avifauna during prehistoric and colonial times. Fossils document the presence of California Condors, Jabirus, and an extinct species, the Gray-necked Wood-Rail (*Aramides cajanea*). Early explorers found flamingos and whooping cranes, and the naturalist William Bartram reported the presence of a peculiar bird, not reported before or since. He describes the species, which he names the Painted Buzzard (*Vultur sacra*), in excruciating detail, including some very noteworthy characteristics:

> a large portion of the stomach hangs down on the breast of the bird, in the likeness of a sack or half wallet, and seems to be a duplicature of the craw, which is naked and of a reddish flesh colour; this partly concealed by the feathers of the breast, unless when it is loaded with food (which is commonly, I believe, roasted reptiles) [from prairie fires], and then it appears prominent. (Bartram 1928:138–139)

Unfortunately, this description does nothing for the great botanist's reputation as an ornithologist. A. H. Howell, in his book *Florida Bird Life*, is going easy on Bartram when he states, "we are forced to the conclusion that Bartram in this case drew on his imagination or repeated some tale related to him by others." (Howell 1932:8). The description, however, is far too detailed for such an explanation, leaving the reader to draw his own conclusions. In any event, if you see this bird, be sure to have reliable witnesses.

Excellent summaries of the ornithological history of the region can be found in Burleigh's (1958) *Georgia Birds*, Howell's (1932) *Florida Bird Life*, and Imhof's (1976) *Alabama Birds*, while more recent treatments of the region's avifauna are presented in *Birds and Birding on the Mississippi Coast* (Toups and Jackson 1987), *Birder's Guide to Alabama and Mississippi* (Vaughan 1994), *A Birder's Guide to Georgia* (Hitt and Blackshaw 1996), *Florida Bird Life* (Sprunt 1954), *Florida's Birds* (Kale and Maehr 1990), *Florida Bird Species* (Robertson and Woolfenden 1992), *The Birdlife of Florida* (Stevenson and Anderson 1994), and *A Birder's Guide to Florida* (Pranty 1996).

Geologic Provinces

Six geologic provinces are found in the Southeast (Figure 2). These include the following: (1) Coastal Plain, (2) Piedmont, (3) Blue Ridge, (4) Ridge and Valley, (5) Appalachian Plateau, and (6) Interior Low Plains. Of these, the Coastal Plain is far and away the dominant physiographic feature of the region, cover-

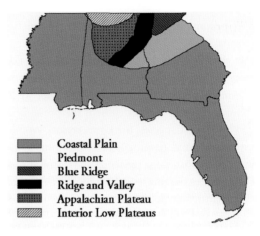

	Coastal Plain
	Piedmont
	Blue Ridge
	Ridge and Valley
	Appalachian Plateau
	Interior Low Plateaus

Figure 2. Geologic provinces of the Southeast region.

ing the southern half of Georgia and Alabama, and most of Mississippi and Florida. Characterized by its relative flatness, the Coastal Plain stretches 2,200 miles along the edge of the continent from Massachusetts to the Mexican border, forming the shifting boundary between land and ocean.

The Piedmont is the easternmost of the four provinces that form subcategories of a single geological feature—the Appalachian Highlands (Piedmont, Blue Ridge, Ridge and Valley, and Appalachian Plateau). The hills of the Piedmont extend west from the Fall Line to the base of the Blue Ridge Mountains in north Georgia and the mountains of the Ridge and Valley of northwest Georgia and northeast Alabama.

The Blue Ridge is a long and narrow province consisting of a single ridge or series of parallel ridges and valleys running generally from southwest to northeast 550 miles from Carlisle, Pennsylvania, to north Georgia.

North and west of the Blue Ridge is a wider series (up to 80 miles) of higher ridges and deeper valleys that also run southwest to northeast; these constitute the Ridge and Valley province, which extends 1,200 miles from the St. Lawrence River at the Canadian border to central Alabama.

West and north of this province are the steep hills of the Appalachian Plateau, covering just the northern tip of Alabama. A sixth province, the Interior Low Plateau, occurs only in north-central Alabama.

In practice, when describing the distribution of birds in the region, I refer to only three landform divisions: (1) coastal plain, as described above; (2) piedmont, including the area shown as Piedmont in Figure 2 along with the Interior Low Plateau, Appalachian Plateau, and lower portions of the Ridge and Valley; and (3) mountains or highlands, including the Blue Ridge and higher portions of the Ridge and Valley. Subdivisions within these units are also referred to at times in range descriptions (e.g., upper and lower coastal plain) (Figure 3).

Climate

Four major climatic zones occur in the Southeast, and I use the so-called life zone classification system developed by C. Hart Merriam, based principally on climatic characteristics, to refer to them: (1) Austral or Austroriparian—characterized by hot summers, mild winters, and moderate precipitation, and found throughout the Coastal Plain except for the southern tip and Keys of Florida; (2) Carolinian—characterized by hot summers, cool winters, and moderate precipitation, and covers the Piedmont region and valleys of the southern Appalachians; (3) Alleghenian—characterized by warm summers, cold winters, and moderate precipitation, and covers most of the Appalachian Highlands; and (4) Tropical, found only in southernmost Florida in our region—characterized by hot, rainy summers and mild winters.

Habitats

Obviously, from the above descriptions, there is little in the way of spectacular geography in the Southeast—no lofty peaks, ridges, or mesas. Indeed the highest point in the state of Florida is 345 feet. Nevertheless, there is a wonderful diversity of plant and animal communities or "habitats" that occur here. Specific associations or communities of plants and animals constitute a habitat for a given species, and, with experience, one can learn to recognize these communities and know which birds to expect in them. However, there are differences among the classifications provided by biologists. For instance, C. Hart Merriam recognized four major life zones, based principally on climate, for the Mid-Atlantic, while the plant ecologist Küchler (1975), has described 17 principal habitat types, nearly double the number found in the Mid-Atlantic region: (1) mixed mesophytic forest; (2) Appalachian oak forest; (3) oak-hickory-pine

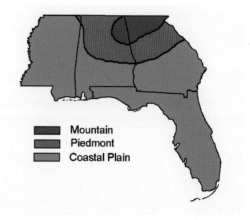

Figure 3. Landforms of the Southeast as used in the Abundance and Distribution category of Species Accounts.

Figure 4. Marine, coastal waters, and shoreline habitat. Bush Key in the Dry Tortugas is one of the most exciting birding localities in North America. Breeding populations of Brown Noddy, Sooty Tern, Magnificent Frigatebird, Roseate Tern, and Masked Booby are found here, as well as common to occasional visits of White-tailed Tropicbird, Red-footed Booby, Brown Booby, Bridled Tern, Northern Gannet, Sandwich Tern, and Black Noddy.

forest; (4) southern mixed forest; (5) cedar glades; (6) oak-hickory forest; (7) blackbelt; (8) southern cordgrass prairie; (9) live oak–sea oats; (10) sand pine scrub; (11) palmetto prairie; (12) everglades; (13) cypress savanna; (14) subtropical pine forest; (15) marl-everglades; (16) mangrove; and (17) southern floodplain forest. The difference in the number of groupings selected derives largely from considerations of scale. At one end of the spectrum, one could place all creatures on the planet in a single habitat called Earth, while at the other, we could assign the space occupied by each individual organism as its own particular habitat.

In the habitat categories presented below, I have attempted to define plant associations that are easily recognizable, and possess characteristic bird communities.

Marine, Coastal Waters, and Shoreline (Figure 4)

The coastal marine habitat can be broken into five major subdivisions, each with its own characteristic group of avian species: (1) pelagic (open ocean) and bays, (2) beaches and dunes, (3) live oak hammock, (4) mangrove, and (5) estuaries, salt marshes, and tidal flats. Typical pelagic species include gulls, terns, grebes, and sea ducks (inshore and bays) and petrels, shearwaters, and gannets (offshore). Some of the beach and dune species are American Oystercatcher, Wilson's Plover, Least Tern, Willet, and Royal Tern. Live oak hammock species include Northern Parula, Painted Bunting, Carolina Wren, and White-eyed Vireo. Mangrove species include Mangrove Cuckoo, Black-whiskered Vireo, Yellow Warbler, and Gray Kingbird. Salt marsh and tidal flat species include Little Blue Heron, Snowy Egret, Great Egret, Tricolored Heron, Clapper Rail, Black Skimmer, and Gull-billed Tern.

Freshwater Wetlands (Figure 5)

Lakes, ponds, wet prairies, impoundments, rivers, and marshes comprise freshwater wetlands. The defining characteristic is the presence of fresh water, which stimulates the growth of such plants as cattails (*Typha*), sedges (*Carex*), and bulrushes (*Scirpus*). In many parts of the coastal plain, freshwater wetlands are threatened habitats, perhaps because they tend to limit human economic activities, and so are dammed, dredged, drained, channeled, and filled out of existence. Many that remain serve principally as conduits for waste. Protected wetlands have spectacular communities with such birds as Limpkin, White Ibis, Roseate Spoonbill, Wood Stork, and Snail Kite.

Grassland and Dry Prairies (Figure 6)

Most native grasslands are gone from the Southeast, but remnants remain, especially in central Florida and Mississippi. Some characteristic species of Mississippi grasslands include Northern Bobwhite, Eastern Kingbird, Loggerhead

Figure 5. Freshwater wetlands habitat. Bottomlands of the Tombigbee River are accessible from Choctaw National Wildlife Refuge in southwestern Alabama, where 18 species of waterfowl can be seen at various times of the year.

Figure 6. Grassland and dry prairies. Large portions of central Florida are grazing land for cattle, and some parts of these grasslands at least have the structure of the prairies once native to the region, such as this site along Arbuckle Creek Road, near Lorida in Highlands County. Crested Caracaras, Burrowing Owls, and Grasshopper Sparrows are among the species that can be found in this habitat type.

Shrike, Eastern Meadowlark, and Eastern Bluebird; Florida's dry prairies harbor Grasshopper Sparrows, Burrowing Owls, Crested Caracaras, and exotic Eurasian Collared-Doves.

Appalachian Oak Forest (Figure 7)

Appalachian oak forest characterizes much of the mountainous region of North Georgia, and has a number of breeding species that occur only as transients or winter residents elsewhere in the region, including Scarlet Tanager, Baltimore Oriole, Black-throated Blue Warbler, Rose-breasted Grosbeak, Veery, Dark-eyed Junco, and Least Flycatcher.

Broadleaf Deciduous and Mixed Forest (Figure 8)

The piedmont is covered primarily with the broadleaf deciduous and mixed forest habitat type. Several of Küchler's (1975) forest communities are lumped within this designation, including mesophytic forest of maple, beech, oak, tulip poplar, and horse chestnut found in much of the Appalachian Plateau of northern Alabama. The avian communities of these different plant associations share 80%–90% of their species, which are the typical birds of the "eastern deciduous forest," e.g., Wood Thrush, Eastern Towhee, Ovenbird, Downy Woodpecker, Red-shouldered Hawk, and Red-eyed Vireo.

Figure 7. Appalachian oak forest. Just another fabulous autumn afternoon along Wildcat Creek in the Georgia mountains where many species considered more characteristic of northeastern states can be found as summer residents.

Figure 8. Broadleaf deciduous and mixed forest. Watson Mill Bridge State Park on the South Fork of the Broad River is located in the heart of the Georgia piedmont. Campers share the habitat with Carolina Chickadees, Hooded Warblers, Barred Owls, Blue Jays, Tufted Titmice, and raccoons (if you forget and leave the chips out).

Figure 9. Pine forest and savanna. There are some habitat types that even a passing familiarity with birds helps bring to life. Most people whiz by spectacular stands of longleaf pine savanna on I-95 without a thought—just another bunch of pine trees. But a person who has heard the beautiful trill of a Bachman's Sparrow in these pines or discovered the long-sought for, tell-tale "bark rain" of a foraging Red-cockaded Wood-pecker feels very differently about this unique southeastern habitat. The magnificent longleaf stands of St. Catherine's Island, Georgia, of-fer just these types of experiences.

Pine Forest and Savanna (Figure 9)

Much of the uplands of the Coastal Plain is covered in pine forest and savanna, a habitat that includes distinctive subcategories: longleaf pine savanna, pine flatwoods, and sand pine scrub, each of which has some distinctive species. Longleaf pine savanna is home to the Red-cockaded Woodpecker and Bachman's Sparrow, two southeastern specialties, as well as Carolina Chicka-dee, Eastern Screech-Owl, and Mourning Dove; Pine Flatwoods are home to Brown-headed Nuthatch, Pine Warbler, Red-bellied Woodpecker, Northern Cardinal, and Great Horned Owl; Sand Pine Scrub is a habitat unique to Flor-ida, harboring the endangered Florida Scrub-Jay.

Mesic Hammocks (Figure 10)

Mesic hammock habitats are found only in South Florida in the Southeast. Dominant trees include live oak, cabbage palm, southern magnolia, loblolly pine, laurel oak, swamp chestnut oak, basswood, musclewood, and in southern-most Florida such tropical plants as mahogany, gumbo limbo, tamarind, poi-sonwood, and pigeon plum. Some of the exciting bird species that can be found in this tropical forest include White-crowned Pigeon, Smooth-billed Ani, Short-tailed Hawk, and, in winter, several wood warblers, e.g., Prairie Warbler,

Figure 10. Mesic hammock. Five minutes in downtown Fort Lauderdale makes you think that it couldn't provide much in the way of habitat for anything but people and rats, but that impression is incorrect. A little searching turns up Hugh Taylor Birch State Park at the corner of Sunrise Boulevard and Atlantic, a tiny gem of a mesic hammock in a thoroughly urban setting. Rarities sighted here include Bahama Mockingbird, Short-tailed Hawk, White-crowned Pigeon, Red-crowned Parrot, Smooth-billed Ani, and LaSagra's Flycatcher. Bring your DEET.

Palm Warbler, Black-and-white Warbler, Ovenbird, Northern Waterthrush, and Yellow-throated Warbler.

Southern Floodplain Forest (Figure 11)

The southern floodplain forest type includes cypress forest and hardwood swamps, once the dominant habitat of lowlands throughout the coastal plain of the Southeast. These great bottomland forests formerly choked every river with tangled swamps and bayous along the coastal plain from Virginia to east Texas, but now persist only as remnants. Southern floodplain forest has a distinctive breeding bird community that includes Swainson's Warbler, Yellow-throated Warbler, Swallow-tailed Kite, Chuck-will's-widow, Anhinga, and Yellow-crowned Night-Heron.

Agriculture/Residential (Figure 12)

Unfortunately, many of the beautiful and unique habitats of the Southeast have been converted to the universal agriculture/residential habitat types: a cornfield looks pretty much the same in Georgia as it does in Iowa, or Ecuador for that matter, and plowed soil is plowed soil, no matter where you find it. These habi-

Figure 11. Southern floodplain forest. St. Catherine Creek National Wildlife Refuge in southwestern Mississippi offers ready access to the largest floodplain on the continent— that of the lower Mississippi River, and there are no waiting lines. Wading birds, shore-birds, and waterfowl abound.

tats share common species in many parts of the world, such as European Star-lings, House Sparrows, and Rock Pigeons. Still, some species native to the region's aboriginal grasslands and woodlands can be found in "improved" pas-tures, orchards, suburban lawns and gardens, and similarly altered environ-ments—for example, Northern Mockingbirds, Ruby-throated Hummingbirds, Yellow Warblers, Song Sparrows, and American Crows.

Migratory Movements

More than 70% of the species that occur in the Southeast region are migrants whose populations shift in distribution from place to place according to the seasons. Some, such as our eastern deciduous forest birds, spend only four or five months in the northern and central portions of the Southeast, and then depart for winter homes in the tropics. Typical representatives include cuckoos, swallows, flycatchers, thrushes, tanagers, warblers, and vireos. Members of other species, e.g., loons, grebes, and many ducks, breed far to the north, and are found in our region only during the winter months. Herons and egrets have summer resident populations in the mountains and piedmont and permanent resident populations in the coastal plain, and a large number of shorebirds and songbirds occur in the Southeast as transients only, on their way in fall from breeding grounds in Canada and the northern United States to wintering grounds in the Caribbean and Middle and South America, and on the reverse trip in spring.

The Atlantic Ocean serves as a barrier to many species, causing large numbers to collect along the shore and to follow the coastline. As a result, these areas are excellent places for viewing migrating herons, egrets, waterfowl, shorebirds, and hawks as they parallel the coastline on their migratory flights. Often hundreds of birds will pass along the beaches or just offshore during the course of a single day during peak migratory periods. Songbirds also back up in coastal habitats during migration—mostly young birds lacking experience in preparation and navigation. Some immature Broad-winged Hawks funnel south along the coast all the way to the southern tip of Florida, where they remain for the winter, instead of proceeding on south with broadwing populations to wintering grounds in Middle and South America. Similarly, members of several species of wood warblers choose to winter in the mesic hammocks and mangroves of the Everglades rather than make the trans-Gulf journey to Middle or South America where the majority of their populations winter. For other species, the western Atlantic is an important pathway. Major seabird migrations occur offshore in the western North Atlantic, and can be viewed by chartered boat or cruise ships.

One of the more interesting aspects of migration in the Southeast is the fact that many species that are common breeding birds in the eastern United States

Figure 12. Agricultural and residential. Freedom Lake Park in St. Petersburg is great for pigeons and grackles, as you can see. Less aggressively manicured sites at the park have yielded some interesting observations—Limpkin, Snow Goose, Monk Parakeet, Budgerigar, Eurasian Collared-Dove, and Muscovy Duck.

evidently pass over Florida during migration. Examples include the Rose-breasted Grosbeak and Scarlet Tanager, which breed throughout the eastern United States south to the Georgia mountains, and winter in Middle or South America. Presumably they fly over Florida or the western North Atlantic, taking the most direct route south to their wintering sites, because normally few are seen in Florida in transit, and most of these are recorded on northward migration in spring along the Florida Panhandle or Gulf Coast of Alabama and Mississippi.

Another striking characteristic of Southeastern migration is the tendency for many of the transient species to follow a different route north during spring migration from the one taken south in fall. These birds tend to be more numerous in fall in eastern portions, e.g., coastal Georgia (but not peninsular Florida, which they presumably fly over), and more numerous in spring in western portions, e.g., coastal Mississippi, including such species as Peregrine Falcon, Swainson's Thrush, Philadelphia Vireo, Tennessee Warbler, and Blackburnian Warbler.

The elliptical shape of their migration route is most likely dictated by wind and weather patterns in the Atlantic, Caribbean, and Gulf regions at different seasons. In general, migrants follow the most direct route between origin and destination. However, speed and direction of winds, and such hazards as storms and broad stretches of open water can favor significant course alterations. In fall, fronts coming from the north with strong, northerly winds can favor a direct route over Florida and the Caribbean to Middle or South America. In spring, southeasterly trade winds over the Caribbean favor a more westerly swing. In addition, the probability of meeting fronts coming from the north, which can prolong the overwater flight significantly, also favor a flight along the western and northern coast of the Gulf, where landfall in the event of a norther is at least an option.

Using the Guide

Each account begins with the species' common name followed by the scientific name in italics. Nomenclature follows the American Ornithologists' Union *Check-list*, 7th ed. (1998) and revisions up to 2004.

The size of the bird is given in parentheses: L = length from tip of the bill to tip of the tail in inches; W = wingspread in inches.

A description of the adult male in breeding plumage follows. Other plumages are described where necessary, for instance, immature (First Basic, i.e., first winter after hatching) and female plumages when they differ markedly from the breeding male. The plumage description necessarily involves the use of a few arcane morphological terms that are illustrated in Figure 13.

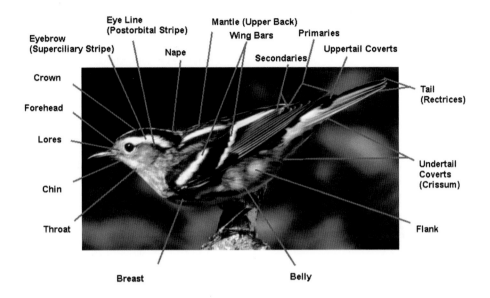

Figure 13. Bird parts as referenced in the text.

At least one photo depicting each species is provided. Although photos can be misleading in terms of plumage coloration, they capture an essence of the way the bird carries itself that is peculiar to that particular species, a quality that is very difficult to capture in a painting. In addition, photos often place the bird in a fairly typical habitat.

Habits

The category of Habits is included only when some peculiarity of the bird's behavior can be useful in identifying the species, e.g., "hangs upside down while foraging," or "flicks tail." Only behaviors likely to be displayed within the region are described. Other characteristic behaviors, such as those used as displays on the breeding ground for species that do not breed in the region, are not described.

Voice

The Voice section usually consists of two parts: (1) description of the song, which is usually given only by the male during the breeding season, and (2) the call, which is normally given by both sexes at any time during the year. For the song description, a more or less "typical" song is described, based on field notes, recorded songs, or, where necessary, descriptions in the literature (author credited). It should be remembered that songs may vary not only regionally but individually. Also one person's interpretation of what a song sounds like will differ from another's. To some people "chip" is "ship" or "tschip" or "slip." Songs are not described for species that do not sing in the region.

Similar Species

In the category of Similar Species, details of other species are described and compared when they are similar in size, pattern, and coloration.

Habitat

Those habitats most often used by the bird in the Southeast and on its North American breeding grounds are given. No attempt is made to describe tropical habitats used by birds when they are away from our region. Transients are found in a variety of habitats in which they would not normally forage, and no attempt is made to catalog all such habitats.

Abundance and Distribution

The abundance, principal time of occurrence, and range for the bird in the Southeastern region are presented here. Usually only regular (common, uncommon, rare) occurrences of the bird within the region are reported. All species that have been recorded as breeding in the region are marked with an asterisk (*) following a statement of their residency status.

The meanings of the abundance categories used are as follows:

Common: Ubiquitous in specified habitat; high probability of finding several individuals (>5) in a day.

Uncommon: Present in specified habitat; high probability of finding a few individuals (<5) in a day.

Rare: Scarce in specified habitat, with only a few records per season; low probability of finding the bird.

Casual: A few records per decade.

Accidental: Not expected to recur.

Hypothetical: Recorded for the region, but not accepted by the state records committees.

A few special terms are used in describing range of birds in the Southeast. The landforms used in range descriptions have been defined above (coastal plain, piedmont, mountains/highlands) (Figure 3). These divisions often serve to dictate avian distributions, and are referred to extensively for that purpose in the text. Florida lacks physiographic variation—the entire state falls within the lower coastal plain. Nevertheless, bird distribution varies sharply within the state as a result of other factors. Therefore, it has been found useful to divide the state into sections as defined by Pranty (1996) as follows: (1) Panhandle, (2) North Florida, (3) Central Florida, (4) South Florida, and (5) the Keys (Figure 14). The Keys are further subdivided into (1) Upper Keys, (2) Lower Keys, and (3) Dry Tortugas. At times, North, Central, and South Florida are referred to collectively as "peninsular Florida."

Where to Find

Some species are ubiquitous, and for these it is almost silly to provide a specific locality. There is an old story about a bird-watching newspaper columnist who, when called and asked, "What's this bird in my yard?" answered, "House Sparrow." Good guess. Some birds are everywhere, but for most species, you will have a much better chance of finding them if you are given a particular place. In the Where to Find section at least three localities are provided when possible from different parts of the region. Directions to all localities are provided in appendix 2, a directory of birding sites in the Southeast. When considering sites for listing, I have attempted to choose those that are well-known, public-use areas requiring relatively little familiarity with the region to find. Nevertheless, there are some localities listed that will require fairly adventurous navigating. Another caveat is that there is no guarantee that the bird will be there when you get there. The locality information is derived principally from published accounts in the "bird-finding" guides that have been written on various parts of the region. In most cases, I have tried to pinpoint the best places and time of year in which to find the bird. But there are many species that simply are not found anywhere with any degree of regularity, and even in well-known regions there are places that have escaped the notice of bird-watchers. To obtain further information on the best places to find birds, the reader should consult bird-finding guides, which may have ten or fifteen widely distributed localities where a bird may be found. The principal sources for bird-finding sites are listed in appendix 2 and in the references.

Range

Total (world) range of the bird is provided in abbreviated form, based on information from the American Ornithologists' Union *Check-list*, 7th ed. (1998).

Maps

A distribution map is provided for every species found regularly in the Southeast, showing where the bird can be expected to occur by season (summer, winter, and fall/spring transient).

Species Accounts

Ducks, Geese, and Swans
Order Anseriformes
Family Anatidae

Heavy-bodied waterbirds with short legs, webbed feet, and broad, flat bills.

1. Black-bellied Whistling-Duck
Dendrocygna autumnalis
(L-21 W-36)

A long-necked, long-legged duck; neck and breast a rich, tawny buff; black belly; gray head with brown crown; dark streak running from crown down nape to back; red-orange bill and legs; dark wings with broad white stripe; dark tail. **Immature** Similar to adult but head is entirely gray (no brown crown), bill and feet are gray, breast is brownish, and belly is grayish.

Voice A shrill, whistled "per-chee-chee-chee."

Similar Species The Black-bellied Whistling-Duck has a black belly, orange bill, and extensive white in wings visible in flying bird. The similarly shaped Fulvous Whistling-Duck has buffy belly, gray bill, and white in the tail but not in the wings.

Habitat Ponds, lakes, marshes, grasslands, croplands.

Abundance and Distribution Rare, local, but apparently increasing resident* in western Florida, mainly Sarasota County.

Where to Find Myakka River State Park, Florida.

Range Breeds from south Texas, northwestern Mexico, and South Florida south through Middle and South America to Peru and southern Brazil.

SUMMER
MIGRATION
WINTER
PERMANENT

2. Fulvous Whistling-Duck
Dendrocygna bicolor
(L-20 W-36)

A long-necked, long-legged duck; body a rich, tawny buff; mottled black and tan on back; dark streak running from crown down nape to back; whitish streaking on throat; white on flanks; gray bill and legs; dark wings; dark tail with white base.

Voice A shrill, whistled "ker-chee."

Similar Species The Black-bellied Whistling-Duck has a black belly, orange bill, and extensive white in wings visible in flying bird. The similarly shaped Fulvous Whistling-Duck has buff belly, gray bill, and white in the tail but not in the wings.

Habitat Lakes, marshes, flooded rice fields, ponds.

Abundance and Distribution Uncommon to rare and local resident* in Central and South Florida (Everglades); rare to casual along the coastal plain elsewhere in the region, mainly in fall and winter.

Where to Find Crews Lake County Park, Florida; Savannah National Wildlife Refuge, Georgia; Dahomey National Wildlife Refuge, Mississippi.

Range Breeds locally from southern California, Arizona, Texas, Louisiana, and Florida south in coastal regions to Peru and central Argentina, West Indies; also in the Old World from East Africa, Madagascar, and India.

3. Greater White-fronted Goose
Anser albifrons
(L-28 W-57)

Grayish brown body; barred with buff on back; speckled with black on breast and belly; white lower belly and undertail coverts; pinkish bill with white feathering at base, edged in black; orange legs; in flight, white rump and gray wings are key. **Immature** Lacks white feathering at base of bill and speckling on breast and belly; pale legs and bill.

Voice A tremulous, high-pitched "ho-ho-honk."

Similar Species Other dark geese of the region have white heads or chin straps clearly visible in flight.

Habitat Lakes, marshes, grasslands, croplands.

Abundance and Distribution Uncommon to rare winter visitor (Oct.–Mar.) along the northern coast of Georgia, southern Mississippi, and southern Alabama; increasingly scarce southward and inland in the region; not recorded in the Keys.

Where to Find Harris Neck National Wildlife Refuge, Georgia; Fairhope Park, Alabama; Vicksburg National Military Park, Mississippi.

Range Breeds in Arctic regions; winters in temperate regions of Northern Hemisphere.

4. Snow Goose
Chen caerulescens
(L-28 W-57)

A medium-sized white goose with black primaries; red bill with dark line bordering mandibles; red legs. **Immature** Patterned like adult but with gray bill and legs and grayish wash on back. **Blue Phase** Dark gray body with white head, neck, and belly; red legs and bill. **Immature** Dark brownish gray throughout with white chin and belly; dark legs and bill.

Voice A shrill, high-pitched "honk."

Similar Species White phase Snow Goose has dark line on mandible edges ("grin patch") that Ross' Goose lacks; Snow Goose bill is longer than head while Ross' is shorter. The immature Greater White-fronted Goose has no white on chin and has pale legs and bill (not dark as in blue phase immature).

Habitat Lakes, marshes, grasslands, croplands.

Abundance and Distribution Uncommon to rare winter visitor (Oct.–Mar.) along the northern coast of Georgia, southern Mississippi, southern Alabama, and the Florida Panhandle; increasingly scarce southward and inland in the region; casual in the Keys.

Where to Find Rum Creek Wildlife Management Area, Georgia; Eufaula National Wildlife Refuge, Alabama; Mississippi Sandhill Crane National Wildlife Refuge, Mississippi; St. Marks National Wildlife Refuge, Florida.

Range Breeds in Arctic Canada; winters in the west along the Pacific Coast from southwestern Canada to central Mexico, and in the east from Chesapeake Bay south through the southeastern United States to northeastern Mexico; also east Asia.

5. Brant

Branta bernicla

(L-24 W-39)

A small goose; dark above, barred with brown; white upper tail coverts nearly obscure dark tail; white below with gray barred flanks; black breast, neck, and head with white bars on side of throat; dark bill and legs. **Immature** Lacks barring on throat.

Habits Feeds by dabbling for seagrasses in shallows of bays and estuaries.

Voice A rolling, guttural "krrrronk."

Similar Species Black breast contrasting with white belly, and white upper tail coverts distinctive even in flight.

Habitat Bayshores, estuaries.

Abundance and Distribution Rare winter visitor (Nov.–Feb.) along the north Georgia coast.

Where to Find Savannah National Wildlife Refuge, Georgia.

Range Breeds in high Arctic; winters along northern coasts of Northern Hemisphere.

6. Canada Goose

Branta canadensis

(L-26–48 W-54–84)

Subspecies of this goose vary considerably in size; grayish brown above; grayish below; black neck and head with white chin strap; white rump, belly and undertail coverts; black tail.

Habits These geese often fly in large Vs.

Voice A medium or high-pitched, squeaky "honk," given at different pitches by different flock members.

Similar Species The Brant has black across breast and lacks white chin strap of the Canada Goose.

Habitat Lakes, estuaries, grasslands, croplands.

Abundance and Distribution Common (north) to rare (south) winter resident (Oct.–Apr.); permanent resident* populations are increasing rapidly, mainly as a result of introductions; casual in the southern tip of Florida and the Keys.

Where to Find Yazoo National Wildlife Refuge, Mississippi; Piedmont National Wildlife Refuge, Georgia; Wheeler National Wildlife Refuge, Alabama; Buck Lake, Tallahassee, Florida.

Range Breeds across northern half of North America; winters from northern United States south to northern Mexico, farther north along coasts; also introduced in various Old World localities.

7. Tundra Swan
Cygnus columbianus
(L-52 W-81)

Very large, entirely white bird; rounded head; black bill, often with yellow preorbital spot. **Immature** Brownish gray with orangish bill.

Voice A mellow "hoonk," repeated.

Habitat Lakes, bays.

SUMMER
MIGRATION
WINTER
PERMANENT

Abundance and Distribution Uncommon to rare winter resident (Nov.–Feb.) along the northern coastline of Georgia; scarcer southward and inland in the region; not recorded in the Keys.

Where to Find Savannah National Wildlife Refuge, Georgia; Yazoo National Wildlife Refuge, Mississippi; Eufaula National Wildlife Refuge, Alabama.

Range Breeds in Arctic regions of Northern Hemisphere; winters in coastal boreal and temperate areas.

Figure 14. "Yazoo" means "place with many ducks" in Cherokee (I'm making this up). Actually, I do not know what it means, but Yazoo National Wildlife Refuge in western Mississippi is, in fact, a great place for ducks as well as many other waterbirds and species typical of the Delta's ponds, swamps, marshes, sloughs, and bottomland hardwoods.

8. Muscovy Duck

Cairina moschata
(L-25–30 W-50–55)

A large, iridescent, black duck; broad white patches on upper wing; wing linings white; red knobs at base of bill. **Female** Duller; smaller; often lacks bill knobs.

Habitat Tropical rivers and swamps; nests mainly in tree cavities.

Abundance and Distribution An exotic species from the New World tropics that has become a locally common to rare resident* on the lakes, ponds, and canals of Florida, apparently derived from feral domestic stock. Rare to casual and apparently increasing elsewhere in the region along the coastal plain.

Where to Find Freedom Lake Park, St. Petersburg, Florida.

Range Lowlands of northern Mexico south through Middle and South America to northern Argentina.

9. Wood Duck

Aix sponsa
(L-19 W-29)

Green head and crest streaked with white; red eye, face plate, and bill; white throat; purplish breast; iridescent dark bluish back; beige belly with white flank stripes. **Female** Deep iridescent blue on back; brownish flanks; grayish belly; brownish gray head and crest; white eyering and postorbital stripe; white chin.

Voice A high, whistling "aweek aweek aweek," etc.

Similar Species The shrill flight call, relatively short neck, large head, and long square tail are distinctive for the birds in flight.

Habitat Mainly rivers and swamps.

Abundance and Distribution Common to uncommon resident* in swamplands nearly throughout; rare to casual in the Keys.

Where to Find Mathews Brake National Wildlife Refuge, Mississippi; Piedmont National Wildlife Refuge, Georgia; Choctaw National Wildlife Refuge, Alabama; Lake Woodruff National Wildlife Refuge, Florida; Lower Suwannee National Wildlife Refuge, Florida.

Range Breeds across southeastern Canada and the eastern half of the United States, and in the west from southwestern Canada to central California, also Cuba and Bahamas; winters in southeastern United States south through northeastern Mexico, and in the west from Oregon, California, and New Mexico south through northwestern Mexico.

10. Gadwall

Anas strepera
(L-20 W-34)

A dapper, medium-sized duck; gray above; scalloped gray, black, and white on breast and flanks; brownish head; white belly; black hindquarters; chestnut, black, and white patches on wing. **Female** Brown body mottled with buff and dark brown; orange bill marked with black; white wing patch, which, when visible, is distinctive.

Voice A nasal "ack."

Similar Species Female Mallard has mottled (not white) belly, white tail, and lacks white patch on wing.

Habitat Lakes, estuaries, ponds, bays.

Abundance and Distribution Common (north) to rare (south) transient and winter resident (Oct.–Mar.). A few birds remain through the summer.

Where to Find Panther Swamp National Wildlife Refuge, Mississippi; Rum Creek Wildlife Management Area, Georgia; Choctaw National Wildlife Refuge, Alabama; St. Marks National Wildlife Refuge, Florida.

Range Breeds in boreal and north temperate prairie regions; winters temperate and northern tropical areas of Northern Hemisphere.

11. Eurasian Wigeon

Anas penelope
(L-19 W-32)

Medium-sized duck; gray above and on flanks; pinkish breast; chestnut head with creamy forehead and crown; white belly; black hindquarters; white and black patches on wing; green speculum. **Female** Brown body mottled with buff and dark brown; grayish bill; black wing patch; green speculum.

Similar Species Female Eurasian Wigeon has gray axillaries visible in flight (white in female American Wigeon) and a brownish head (paler in American Wigeon, contrasting with brown back).

Habitat Estuaries, lakes, marshes, crops, fields.

Abundance and Distribution Rare winter visitor (Nov.–Mar.), mainly along the Atlantic coast of the region.

Where to Find Savannah National Wildlife Refuge, Georgia; Merritt Island National Wildlife Refuge, Florida.

Range Breeds in northern Eurasia; winters in temperate and subtropical Eurasia, but regular along coasts of North America.

12. American Wigeon
Anas americana
(L-19 W-33)

Medium-sized duck; gray above; purplish brown on breast and flanks; white crown and forehead; broad, iridescent green stripe through and past eye; densely mottled black and white on cheek, chin, and throat; pale blue bill with black tip; white belly; black hindquarters; green speculum. **Female** Brown body mottled with buff and dark brown; grayish bill; black wing patch; green speculum.

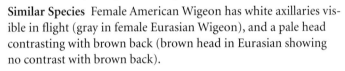

Voice A wheezy "whip" or "wheep."

Similar Species Female American Wigeon has white axillaries visible in flight (gray in female Eurasian Wigeon), and a pale head contrasting with brown back (brown head in Eurasian showing no contrast with brown back).

Habitat Lakes, estuaries, bays, ponds, crops, fields.

Abundance and Distribution Common transient and winter resident (Sept.–Apr.) nearly throughout, though uncommon to rare in some areas such as the western Florida Panhandle and the Keys. A few birds remain through the summer.

Where to Find Vicksburg National Military Park, Mississippi; Blackbeard Island National Wildlife Refuge, Georgia; J. N. "Ding" Darling National Wildlife Refuge, Florida; Choctaw National Wildlife Refuge, Alabama.

Range Breeds from northern North America south to the northern United States; winters along Atlantic and Pacific coasts, and inland from southern United States to northwestern Colombia; West Indies.

13. American Black Duck
Anas rubripes
(L-23 W-36)

A large duck; dark brown body, mottled with light brown; violet speculum; reddish legs; yellowish or

greenish bill; light brown head and neck finely streaked with dark brown.

Voice A relatively high-pitched "quack," repeated.

Similar Species The female Mallard has a white tail (dark brown in American Black Duck). The Mottled Duck has a buffy, unstreaked chin and throat (streaked in American Black Duck and female Mallard).

Habitat Rivers, lakes, ponds, estuaries.

Abundance and Distribution Uncommon to rare winter resident (Oct.–Apr.) in Georgia, Alabama, Mississippi, the Panhandle, North and Central Florida; casual or absent in South Florida and the Keys.

Where to Find Cumberland Island National Seashore, Georgia; Wheeler National Wildlife Refuge, Alabama; Yazoo National Wildlife Refuge, Mississippi.

Range Breeds across northeastern North America south to North Carolina; winters in the eastern United States south to the Gulf states.

14. Mallard
Anas platyrhynchos
(L-23 W-36)

A large duck; iridescent green head; yellow bill; white collar; rusty breast; gray scapulars and belly; brownish back; purple speculum; black rump and undertail coverts; curling black feathers at tail; white tail. **Female** Brown body mottled with buff; orange bill marked with black; white outer tail feathers; blue speculum.

Voice A nasal "quack" (male) or series of "quack"s (female).

Similar Species The female Mallard differs from the American Black Duck in having a white tail (dark brown in American Black Duck), and from the female Gadwall in having a mottled (not white) belly, white tail, and no white patch on wing. The Mottled Duck has a buffy, unstreaked chin and throat (streaked in American Black Duck and female Mallard).

Habitat Ponds, lakes, marshes, estuaries, bays.

Abundance and Distribution Common (north) to uncommon or rare (south) winter resident (Nov.–Mar.); rare and irregular in Central and South Florida; locally uncommon to rare as a permanent resident* throughout the region.

Where to Find Piedmont National Wildlife Refuge, Georgia;

Wheeler National Wildlife Refuge, Alabama; Lower Suwannee National Wildlife Refuge, Florida; Morgan Brake National Wildlife Refuge, Mississippi.

Range Breeds across boreal and temperate regions of the Northern Hemisphere; winters in temperate and subtropical regions.

15. Mottled Duck
Anas fulvigula
(L-22 W-35)

A large duck; dark brown body, mottled with light brown; violet speculum; reddish legs; yellowish or greenish bill; light brown head and neck finely streaked with dark brown.

Habits Often in pairs.

Voice A nasal "quack" or series of "quack"s.

Similar Species The Mottled Duck has a buffy, unstreaked chin and throat (streaked in American Black Duck and female Mallard); female Mallard has a white tail (dark brown in Mottled and American Black ducks).

Habitat Ponds, lakes, bays, rice fields, marshes.

Abundance and Distribution Common resident* in Central and South Florida; uncommon to rare or casual (Panhandle) and along the Gulf coast of North Florida, Alabama, and Mississippi; casual or absent in the Keys.

Where to Find Harris Neck National Wildlife Refuge, Georgia; J. N. "Ding" Darling National Wildlife Refuge, Florida; Kaliga Park, Florida; Blakely Island, Alabama; West Ship Island, Mississippi.

Range Resident in Florida and the coastal plain of the Gulf states to northeastern Mexico.

16. Blue-winged Teal
Anas discors
(L-16 W-25)

A small duck; brown mottled with dark brown above; tan marked with spots below; light blue patch on wing; green speculum; dark gray head with white crescent at base of bill. **Female** Mottled brown and dark brown above and below; tan undertail coverts spotted with brown; yellowish legs.

Voice A high-pitched "eeeee" (male); a series of soft "quack"s (female).

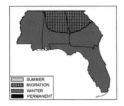

Similar Species The female Blue-winged Teal often shows some light blue on wing, has yellowish legs (not grayish); the female Green-winged Teal has smaller bill than other teal and white (not spotted) undertail coverts.

Habitat Lakes, estuaries, marshes, ponds.

Abundance and Distribution Common transient (Aug.–Oct.; Mar.–May) throughout; uncommon to rare winter resident (Nov.–Mar.) in the coastal plain, most numerous in Central and South Florida and the Keys; rare summer resident* (May–Aug.) in Florida and rare to casual elsewhere in the region along the Gulf Coast.

Where to Find Okefenokee National Wildlife Refuge, Georgia; Eufaula National Wildlife Refuge, Alabama; Fort Caroline National Memorial/Timucuan Ecological and Historic Preserve, Florida; Panther Swamp National Wildlife Refuge, Mississippi.

Range Breeds across boreal and temperate North America south to central United States; winters southern United States to northern South America, West Indies.

17. Northern Shoveler
Anas clypeata
(L-19 W-31)

A medium-sized duck with large, spatulate bill; green head; golden eye; black back; rusty sides; white breast and belly; black rump and undertail coverts; blue patch on wing; green speculum. **Female** Mottled brown and dark brown above and below; brown eye; orange "lips" on dark bill.

Voice A low, hoarse "kuk kuk."

Similar Species The heavy, flattened bill is distinctive.

Habitat Lakes, estuaries, bays, ponds.

Abundance and Distribution Common to uncommon transient and winter resident (Sept.–Apr.) along the coastal plain; common to uncommon transient (Sept.–Oct., Mar.–Apr.) and rare winter resident elsewhere; rare to casual in the Keys; a few birds remain in the region through the summer months.

Where to Find Wassaw National Wildlife Refuge, Georgia; Wheeler National Wildlife Refuge, Alabama; Merritt Island National Wildlife Refuge, Florida; Noxubee National Wildlife Refuge, Mississippi.

Range Breeds across boreal and north temperate regions (mainly in west in North America); winters along temperate coasts south to subtropics and tropics of Northern Hemisphere.

18. Northern Pintail

Anas acuta

(L-26 W-36)

A long-necked, long-tailed duck; gray back and sides; brown head; white neck, breast and belly; black rump, undertail coverts and tail with extremely long central feathers; speculum iridescent brown. **Female** Brownish mottled with dark brown throughout; grayish bill; pointed tail.

Voice A high-pitched "quip" (male); a series of "quack"s (female).

Similar Species The female resembles other female dabblers but shape is distinctive (long neck and relatively long, pointed tail).

Habitat Flooded fields, swales, shallow ponds, bays.

Abundance and Distribution Uncommon to rare transient and winter resident (Sept.–Mar.) along the coastal plain and piedmont of Alabama, Mississippi, and Georgia; uncommon transient (Sept.–Oct., Feb.–Mar.) in the highlands; uncommon to rare winter resident (Oct.–Mar.) in Florida.

Where to Find Fort Pulaski National Monument, Georgia; Merritt Island National Wildlife Refuge, Florida; Yazoo National Wildlife Refuge, Mississippi; Eufaula National Wildlife Refuge, Alabama.

Range Breeds in Arctic, boreal, and temperate grasslands and tundra; winters in temperate, subtropical, and tropical areas of Northern Hemisphere.

19. Green-winged Teal

Anas crecca

(L-15 W-24)

A small, fast-flying duck; chestnut head with broad iridescent green stripe above and behind eye; gray body; beige breast with black spots; white bar on side of breast; white tail; black rump and undertail coverts. **Female** Mottled brown and white above and below; whitish undertail coverts; green speculum.

Voice A high-pitched "teet" or a nasal "kik quiik kik kik."

Similar Species The female Green-winged Teal has a smaller bill than other teal and white (not spotted) undertail coverts; the female Blue-winged Teal often shows some light blue on wing and has yellowish (not grayish) legs

Habitat Lakes, estuaries, marshes, ponds.

Ducks, Geese, Swans

Abundance and Distribution Common transient and winter resident (Sept.–Apr.) in North and Central Florida and along the coastal plain and piedmont of Alabama, Mississippi, and Georgia; uncommon to rare winter resident in South Florida and the Keys; common to uncommon transient (Sept.–Nov., Mar.) in the highlands.

Where to Find Wassaw National Wildlife Refuge, Georgia; Eufaula National Wildlife Refuge, Alabama; Morgan Brake National Wildlife Refuge, Mississippi; Sawgrass Lake County Park, St. Petersburg, Florida.

Range Breeds in boreal and Arctic areas; winters in temperate and subtropical regions of Northern Hemisphere.

20. Canvasback

Aythya valisineria
(L-21 W-33)

A medium-sized, heavy-bodied duck with steeply sloping forehead; rusty head; red eye; black breast; gray back and belly; black hindquarters. **Female** Grayish body, brownish neck and head.

Voice A gabbling "kup kup kup," etc.

Similar Species The sloping forehead is distinctive for both sexes; female Redhead has bluish bill with black tip (Canvasback is all black); also Canvasback female shows contrast between brown head and gray body that is lacking in the all-brown female Redhead.

Figure 15. Alabama's Eufaula National Wildlife Refuge on the Chattahoochee River is an excellent inland site for migrating shorebirds.

Habitat Lakes, bays.

Abundance and Distribution Uncommon to rare transient and winter resident (Nov.–Mar.) along the coastal plain of Alabama, Mississippi, Georgia, the Panhandle, North and Central Florida; uncommon to rare transient (Nov., Mar.–Apr.) and rare winter resident in the piedmont and highlands; rare transient and winter resident in South Florida; not reported from the Keys.

Where to Find Sapelo Island National Estuarine Research Reserve, Georgia; Wheeler National Wildlife Refuge, Alabama; Noxubee National Wildlife Refuge, Mississippi; Lake Adair, Orlando, Florida.

Range Breeds across northwestern North America south to California and Iowa; winters locally from southern Canada south through the United States to southern Mexico.

21. Redhead
Aythya americana
(L-20 W-33)

Rusty head; red eye; bluish bill with white ring and black tip; black breast; gray back and belly; dark brown hindquarters. **Female** Brownish throughout; bluish bill with black tip.

Voice A soft, catlike "yow," repeated.

Similar Species Redheads lack the sloping forehead of the Canvasback; female Redhead has bluish bill with black tip (Canvasback is all black); also Canvasback female shows contrast between brown head and gray body that is lacking in the all brown female Redhead.

Habitat Bays, lakes, ponds.

Abundance and Distribution Uncommon to rare transient and winter resident (Nov.–Mar.) along the coastal plain of Alabama, Mississippi, Georgia, the Panhandle, North and Central Florida; uncommon to rare transient (Nov., Mar.–Apr.) and rare winter resident in the piedmont and highlands; rare transient and winter resident in South Florida; not reported from the Keys.

Where to Find Wheeler National Wildlife Refuge, Alabama; Wolf Island National Wildlife Refuge, Georgia; Lake Adair, Orlando, Florida.

Range Breeds in western Canada, the northwestern United States, and locally in the Great Lakes region; winters central and southern United States south to Guatemala; also Greater Antilles.

22. Ring-necked Duck
Aythya collaris
(L-17 W-28)

A smallish duck with characteristically pointed (not rounded) head; black back, breast and hindquarters; dark head with iridescent purple sheen; gray flanks with white bar edging breast; golden eye; white feather edging at base of bill; white band across dark bill. **Female** Brown body and head; white eyering; bill with whitish band.

Voice "Caah," repeated.

Similar Species The pointed head shape of Ring-necked Ducks is distinctive. Scaup have rounded heads; male scaup have light (not dark) backs; female scaup have distinct white face patch at base of bill (dark in female Ring-necked Duck).

Habitat Lakes, ponds.

Abundance and Distribution Common transient and winter resident (Oct.–Apr.) nearly throughout; rare in the Keys; a few birds remain through the summer*.

Where to Find Seminole State Park, Georgia; Choctaw National Wildlife Refuge, Alabama; Lower Suwannee National Wildlife Refuge, Florida; Pearl River Waterfowl Refuge, Mississippi.

Range Breeds across central and southern Canada, northern United States; winters along both United States coasts, southern United States south to Panama, West Indies.

23. Greater Scaup
Aythya marila
(L-19 W-31)

Rounded head; gray mottled with black back; black breast and hindquarters; dark head with iridescent green sheen; gray flanks; golden eye; bluish bill with dark tip. **Female** Brown body and head; white patch at base of bill; bill bluish gray.

Voice A soft cooing or rapid, whistled "week week week" (male); a guttural "caah" (female).

Similar Species Male Greater Scaup has green sheen on a more rounded head (male Lesser has purple sheen on a more pointed head); Lesser Scaup has white band on secondaries only, Greater Scaup has white band on primaries *and* secondaries (both sexes, visible only in flight).

Habitat Large lakes, bays.

Abundance and Distribution Uncommon to rare transient and winter resident (Nov.–Mar.) in Alabama, Mississippi, Georgia, the Panhandle, North and Central Florida, mainly along the Atlantic coast; casual visitor in South Florida; not reported from the Keys; has summered*.

Where to Find Harris Neck National Wildlife Refuge, Georgia; West Beach Drive, Panama City, Florida; Lake Purdy, Alabama; Dahomey National Wildlife Refuge, Mississippi.

Range Breeds in Old and New World Arctic; winters along temperate and northern coasts and large lakes in Northern Hemisphere.

24. Lesser Scaup
Aythya affinis
(L-17 W-28)

A smallish duck; gray back; black breast and hindquarters; dark head with iridescent purple sheen (sometimes greenish); gray flanks; golden eye; bluish bill with dark tip. **Female:** Brown body and head; white patch at base of bill; bill grayish.

Voice A soft "wheeooo" or single whistled "weew" (male); a weak "caah" (female).

SUMMER
MIGRATION
WINTER
PERMANENT

Similar Species Male Lesser Scaup has purple sheen on a more pointed head (male Greater has green sheen on a more rounded head); Lesser Scaup has white band on secondaries only, Greater Scaup has white band on primaries *and* secondaries (both sexes, visible only in flight). The pointed head shape of Ring-necked Ducks is distinctive. Scaup have rounded heads; male scaup have light backs (dark in male Ring-necked Duck); female scaup have a distinct white face patch at base of bill (dark in female Ring-necked Duck).

Habitat Bays, lakes.

Abundance and Distribution Common transient and winter resident (Oct.–Apr.) nearly throughout; rare in the Keys; a few birds remain through the summer*.

Where to Find Sweetwater Creek State Conservation Park, Georgia; Eufaula National Wildlife Refuge, Alabama; Merritt Island National Wildlife Refuge, Florida; Yazoo National Wildlife Refuge, Mississippi.

Range Breeds in Alaska, western and central Canada, and northern United States; winters coastal and central inland United States south to northern South America, West Indies.

25. Surf Scoter
Melanitta perspicillata
(L-19 W-34)

Black with white patches on nape and forehead; orange bill with bull's-eye on side (white circle, black center); white eye. **Female** Entirely brown with white patches in front of and behind eye; dark bill.

Voice A guttural croak.

Similar Species Surf Scoter female has distinct white pre- and postorbital patches on otherwise brown head and brown throat; female White-winged Scoter has feathering almost to nostrils on bill (lacking on Black and Surf scoters); female Black Scoter has white cheek and throat contrasting with dark brown head and neck.

Habitat Marine, bays, lakes.

Abundance and Distribution Uncommon to rare winter resident (Nov.–Mar.), mainly along the northern Atlantic coast of the region; rare to casual winter visitor to Central and South Florida; absent from the Keys.

Where to Find Sapelo Island National Estuarine Research Reserve, Georgia; St. Vincent National Wildlife Refuge, Florida.

Range Breeds northern North America south to central Canada; winters mainly along coasts from Alaska to northwestern Mexico, and Nova Scotia to Florida, also Great Lakes.

26. White-winged Scoter
Melanitta fusca
(L-22 W-39)

Black with white eye and wing patches; dark bill with black knob at base and orange tip. **Female** Entirely dark brown (sometimes with whitish pre- and postorbital patches); bill dark orange with black markings; feathering on bill extends nearly to nostrils; white secondaries sometimes visible on swimming bird.

Voice A plaintive whistle or low growl.

Similar Species Female White-winged Scoter has feathering almost to nostrils on bill (lacking on Black and Surf scoters).

Habitat Bays, lakes.

Abundance and Distribution Rare to casual winter resident (Nov.–Mar.), mainly along the Georgia Atlantic coast.

Where to Find Wolf Island National Wildlife Refuge, Georgia; St. Marks National Wildlife Refuge, Florida.

Range Breeds in boreal and Arctic regions of the Old and New World; winters mainly along northern coasts, south to northwestern Mexico and Florida in North America.

27. Black Scoter
Melanitta nigra
(L-19 W-33)

Entirely black with orange knob at base of bill. **Female** Dark brown with whitish cheek and throat contrasting with dark crown and nape. **Immature** Patterned similarly to female but with whitish belly.

Voice A rattle-like "quack."

SUMMER
MIGRATION
WINTER
PERMANENT

Similar Species Female White-winged Scoter has feathering almost to nostrils on bill (lacking on Black and Surf scoters); female Black Scoter has white cheek and throat contrasting with dark brown head and neck; Surf Scoter female has distinct white pre- and postorbital patches on otherwise brown head and brown throat.

Habitat Marine, bays, lakes.

Abundance and Distribution Uncommon to rare winter resident (Nov.–Mar.), mainly along the Atlantic coast; casual in the Keys.

Where to Find Wassaw National Wildlife Refuge, Georgia; Merritt Island National Wildlife Refuge, Florida.

Range Breeds locally in tundra regions of Eurasia and North America; winters in northern and temperate coastal waters of Northern Hemisphere, south to California and Florida in the United States.

28. Long-tailed Duck
Clangula hyemalis
(L-19 W-29)

Dark head with white face; dark neck and breast; gray and brown on back; dark wings; white belly and undertail coverts; black, extremely long pointed central tail feathers. **Female and Winter Male** White head with dark brown cheek patch and crown; white neck; brown or grayish breast; white belly and undertail coverts; sharply pointed tail.

Voice "Ah ah ah-ah-ee-ah."

SUMMER
MIGRATION
WINTER
PERMANENT

Similar Species Combination of white head and all dark wings are distinctive, as is the call.

Habitat Marine, bays, large lakes.

Abundance and Distribution Rare winter resident (Nov.–Mar.), mainly along the Atlantic coast.

Where to Find Sapelo Island National Estuarine Research Reserve, Georgia.

Range Breeds in high Arctic of Old and New World; winters mainly along northern coasts of Northern Hemisphere, in United States south to California and Georgia.

29. Bufflehead
Bucephala albeola
(L-14 W-23)

A small, plump, short-billed duck; head white from top of crown to nape, the rest iridescent purple; black back; white breast, belly, and sides; gray bill; pink legs. **Female and Immature** Dark back; grayish white below; dark head with large white patch extending below and behind eye.

Voice A weak, nasal "eeh."

SUMMER
MIGRATION
WINTER
PERMANENT

Similar Species The larger male Hooded Merganser also has white back of crown and nape but the white is edged in black; also has golden eye (dark in Bufflehead), thin, pointed bill, rusty sides.

Habitat Bays, lakes, estuaries.

Abundance and Distribution Common to uncommon transient and winter resident (Nov.–Apr.) in Alabama, Mississippi, Georgia, the Panhandle, North and Central Florida; rare transient and winter resident in South Florida; not reported from the Keys; has summered*.

Where to Find Clarkson State Park, Mississippi; Rum Creek Wildlife Management Area, Georgia; Lake Guntersville State Park, Alabama; Lower Suwannee National Wildlife Refuge, Florida.

Range Breeds across Canada and extreme northern United States; winters from subarctic along both coasts of North America, and inland from central United States south to central Mexico.

30. Common Goldeneye

Bucephala clangula
(L-18 W-30)

Iridescent green head (sometimes purplish); golden eye; white patch at base of bill; black back and hindquarters; white breast, sides, and belly; black and white scapulars; white wing patch visible in flight. **Female** Gray body; brown head; white neck; golden eye; gray bill yellowish at tip (mostly yellow in some birds).

Voice A high-pitched, nasal "eeh."

Habitat Bays, lakes.

Abundance and Distribution Uncommon to rare transient and winter resident (Nov.–Apr.) in Alabama, Mississippi, Georgia, the Panhandle, and North Florida, mainly along the coast; rare to casual transient and winter resident in Central and South Florida and the Keys.

Where to Find Savannah National Wildlife Refuge, Georgia; Lake Guntersville State Park, Alabama; Yazoo National Wildlife Refuge, Mississippi; West Beach Drive, Panama City, Florida.

Range Breeds across boreal and north temperate regions of Old and New World; winters along northern coasts south to temperate and subtropical regions of the Northern Hemisphere.

31. Hooded Merganser

Lophodytes cucullatus
(L-18 W-26)

Head with white crest from top of crown to nape broadly edged in black, the rest black; golden eye; black back and tail; white breast with prominent black bar; rusty sides; sharp, black bill. **Female and Immature Male** Body brownish; head a pale orange with dusky crown; pale orange crest off back of crown and nape; upper mandible dark; lower mandible orangish.

Voice A trilled "crrroooo" (male); low grunt (female).

Similar Species Other female mergansers (Common and Red-breasted) are much larger and have dark russet heads, long orange bills, grayish bodies.

Habitat Ponds, lakes, estuaries, bays; for breeding sites, the bird prefers cavities located in heavily wooded bottomlands with swift, clear-running streams nearby.

Abundance and Distribution Common to uncommon transient and winter resident (Nov.–Mar.) in Alabama, Mississippi, Georgia, the Panhandle, North and Central Florida; rare transient and winter resident in South Florida and the Keys; rare to casual as a summer resident* in the region.

Where to Find Okefenokee National Wildlife Refuge, Georgia; Lake Guntersville State Park, Alabama; Noxubee National Wildlife Refuge, Mississippi; Chassahowitzka National Wildlife Refuge, Florida.

Range Breeds across central and southern Canada and northern United States, farther south in Rockies and Appalachians; winters mainly along coasts from southern Canada to northern Mexico, West Indies.

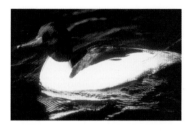

32. Common Merganser
Mergus merganser
(L-25 W-36)

Iridescent green head; sharp, red-orange bill; black back; gray rump and tail; white breast, sides and belly. **Female and Immature Male** Rufous, crested head; white chin; rufous throat and neck ending abruptly at white breast; gray back and sides; orange bill.

Voice A low "uu-eek-wa" (male); a harsh "karr" (female).

Similar Species The female Common Merganser lacks white wing patch that is evident in female Red-breasted Merganser; female Common has distinct boundary between white throat and rufous neck; female Red-breasted has a whitish neck and throat with no abrupt line between rufous neck and throat.

Habitat Lakes, rivers, bays.

Abundance and Distribution Uncommon to rare winter visitor (Nov.–Mar.) along the Georgia coast; rare to casual winter visitor along the coast elsewhere in the region.

Where to Find Wolf Island National Wildlife Refuge, Georgia; Cumberland Island National Seashore, Georgia.

Range Breeds in Old and New World subarctic and boreal regions south in mountains into temperate areas; winters from northern coasts south inland through temperate and subtropical zones of the Northern Hemisphere.

Figure 16. Cumberland Island National Seashore, Georgia.

33. Red-breasted Merganser
Mergus serrator
(L-22 W-32)

Iridescent green, crested head; sharp, red-orange bill; white collar; buffy breast streaked with brown; gray back, rump, and tail; black shoulder with white chevrons; white scapulars; grayish sides. **Female and Immature Male** Rufous, crested head; white chin and throat; gray back and sides; white wing patch.

Voice "Eeoww" (male); a harsh "karr" (female).

Similar Species Female Red-breasted Merganser has a whitish foreneck and throat with no abrupt line between rufous hindneck; female Common has distinct boundary between white throat and rufous neck; female Red-breasted has a white wing patch that the female Common Merganser lacks.

Habitat Bays, lakes, marine.

Abundance and Distribution Common to uncommon transient and winter resident (Nov.–Mar.) throughout the region except inland in Florida where rare to casual; rare to casual summer resident (Apr.–Oct.).

Where to Find Wassaw National Wildlife Refuge, Georgia; West Beach Drive, Panama City, Florida; Weeks Bay National Estuarine Research Reserve, Alabama; Gulf Islands National Seashore, Mississippi.

Range Breeds in Arctic and boreal regions of Old and New World; winters mainly along coasts in southern boreal and temperate areas.

34. Ruddy Duck
Oxyura jamaicensis
(L-15 W-23)

A small duck; chestnut body; stiff black tail held at a 45 degree angle; black cap; white cheek; blue bill.
Winter Grayish brown body; dark cap; white cheek.
Female Mottled grayish and white body; stiff black tail; dark cap and dark line below eye.

Voice A staccato, cicada-like "tsk-tsk-tsk-tsk quark."

Habitat Lakes, ponds, bays.

SUMMER
MIGRATION
WINTER
PERMANENT

Abundance and Distribution Common to uncommon transient and winter resident (Nov.–Mar.) nearly throughout, although casual or absent in the Keys; rare to casual as a summer resident* in the region.

Where to Find Sweetwater Creek State Conservation Park, Georgia; Eufaula National Wildlife Refuge, Alabama; Panther Swamp National Wildlife Refuge, Mississippi; McKay Bay Nature Park, Tampa, Florida.

Range Breeds locally from northern Canada through the United States to central Mexico, West Indies, and South America; winters coastal and southern United States south to Nicaragua and elsewhere in tropical breeding range.

Curassows, Guans, and Chachalacas
Order Galliformes
Family Cracidae

35. Plain Chachalaca
Ortalis vetula
(L-23 W-26)

A pheasantlike bird with long neck, legs, and tail; olive green throughout, buffier on belly; patch of naked, red skin at chin; long, broad tail tipped with buff.

Habits Terrestrial, flying to trees to feed on fruits or escape predators.

Voice An extremely loud, raucous "ca-ca-cow" given by several members of a group in alternating cadences producing a deafen-

ing cacophony at close range; also various chuckles, clucks, and cackles.

Habitat Riparian forest, thorn forest, thickets, second growth, swamps.

Abundance and Distribution Introduced resident* on Georgia barrier islands.

Where to Find Sapelo Island, Georgia (follow directions for Sapelo Island National Estuarine Research Reserve); Blackbeard Island National Wildlife Refuge, Georgia.

Range In lowlands from south Texas and northwestern Mexico to Costa Rica. Introduced on Sapelo, Blackbeard, and Little St. Simons barrier islands, Georgia.

Pheasants, Turkeys, and Grouse
Family Phasianidae

Terrestrial, heavy-bodied, mostly seed- and fruit-eating birds with short, curved wings for quick takeoff.

36. Ruffed Grouse
Bonasa umbellus
(L-17 W-28)

Body mottled brown and white; head with a crest; white line through eye; black shoulder patches; tail chestnut barred with black and white with a broad black subterminal band and white terminal band. **Female** Similar to male but black and white terminal bands are incomplete (central tail feathers grayish at tip).

Habits "Explodes" in a burst of sound when flushed.

Voice Male makes a distinct, loud booming sound with his wings; the booms gradually increase in frequency until they almost run together. The female gives various chickenlike clucks to the brood.

Similar Species Pheasant female has a relatively long, pointed tail, not square as in the grouse.

Habitat Deciduous and mixed woodlands, especially near aspen groves (feeding) and dense conifer stands (roosting).

Abundance and Distribution Rare resident* in the highlands of north Georgia and, formerly at least, Alabama (Howell 1928:119) and, perhaps, Mississippi; recently documented in northwestern Alabama.

Where to Find Brasstown Bald, Georgia; Rabun Bald, Georgia.

Range Boreal and north temperate regions of North America, south in mountains to northern California and Utah in the west and north Georgia in the east.

37. Wild Turkey
Meleagris gallopavo
(*Male*: L-47 W-63)

Quail

Dark brown body with iridescent bronze highlights; naked red head and neck; blue skin on face with dangling red wattles; hairy beard hanging from breast; tail dark barred with buff; tarsi with spurs. **Female** Naked facial skin is grayish; lacks beard and wattles.

Habits Males associate in groups of 2–3, females in larger flocks.

Voice A rapid, high-pitched gobble.

SUMMER
MIGRATION
WINTER
PERMANENT

Habitat Deciduous forest, oak woodlands.

Abundance and Distribution Locally common to rare resident* throughout the Southeast except for the Florida Keys, where absent.

Where to Find Panther Swamp National Wildlife Refuge, Mississippi; Tuskegee National Forest, Alabama; Blackwater River State Park, Florida; Laura S. Walker State Park, Georgia.

Range Formerly from southern Canada to central Mexico, now extirpated from many areas but being reintroduced.

Quail
Family Odontophoridae

38. Northern Bobwhite
Colinus virginianus
(L-10 W-15)

Brown and gray above mottled with dark brown and white; chestnut sides spotted with white; white breast and belly scalloped with black; chestnut crown with short, ragged crest; white eyebrow and throat. **Female** Tawny eyebrow and throat.

Habits Coveys fly and scatter in a burst when approached.

SUMMER
MIGRATION
WINTER
PERMANENT

Voice Familiar, whistled "hoo WHIT" (bob white), several other calls including a whistled "perdeek."

Habitat Brushy fields, pastures, grasslands, agricultural areas.

Abundance and Distribution Common to uncommon resident* nearly throughout the Southeast; scarcer in the highlands and absent from the Florida Keys.

Where to Find Natchez Trace Parkway, Mississippi; Laura S. Walker State Park, Georgia; Eufaula National Wildlife Refuge, Alabama; Tall Timbers Research Station, Florida.

Range Eastern and central United States south to Guatemala; isolated populations in Arizona and Sonora.

Loons
Order Gaviiformes
Family Gaviidae

Mallard-sized or somewhat larger waterbirds with tapered body and chisel-shaped bill. Legs set far back for swimming and diving. Awkward on land, loons require a considerable distance of flapping and running on water to become airborne. In flight, rapid wingbeats, humpbacked silhouette, and feet extending beyond tail are characteristic.

39. Red-throated Loon
Gavia stellata
(L-25 W-42)

Black mottled with gray on back; gray, rounded head; gray neck striped with white on nape; rufous throat; red eye; white below with barring on flanks; relatively thin, slightly upturned bill. **Winter:** Black back with indistinct white spots; head grayish with some white below eye; throat and underparts white.

SUMMER
MIGRATION
WINTER
PERMANENT

Similar Species White spotting on black back; lack of white patch on flank; thin, upturned bill and usual upward tilt of head separate this bird from other winter loons.

Habitat Marine, bays, lakes, rivers.

Abundance and Distribution Uncommon to rare winter visitor (Oct.–Mar.), mainly along the Atlantic coast of Georgia and northeastern Florida; rare to casual along the Gulf coasts of Florida, Alabama, and Mississippi, the Keys, and inland during migration.

Where to Find Tybee Island Beach, Georgia.

Range Breeds in the high Arctic; winters in coastal temperate and boreal regions of the Northern Hemisphere.

40. Common Loon
Gavia immer
(L-31 W-54)

Checked black and white on back; black head with a white streaked collar; white below with black streaking on breast and flanks; thick, heavy bill; red eye. **Winter:** Dark gray above; white below; dark gray crown and nape; white face and throat with a partial collar of white around neck.

SUMMER
MIGRATION
WINTER
PERMANENT

Similar Species The Common Loon in winter plumage can be distinguished from the smaller Red-throated Loon by heavy, chisel-shaped rather than thin, upturned bill, and lack of white spotting on back.

Habitat Marine, bays, lakes, rivers.

Abundance and Distribution Uncommon winter resident (Oct.–Apr.) principally along the coast; scarcer in south Florida and inland; rare to casual in summer.

Where to Find J. P. Coleman State Park, Mississippi; St. Marks National Wildlife Refuge, Florida; Cumberland Island National Seashore, Georgia; Lake Guntersville State Park, Alabama.

Figure 17. Mississippi's section of the Gulf Islands National Seashore has a range of coastal habitats including marsh, bay, and barrier island.

Range Breeds in northern North America south to northern United States; winters coastal North America and on large lakes inland south to Baja California, Sonora, and south Texas.

Grebes
Order Podicipediformes
Family Podicipedidae

Loonlike birds the size of a small to medium-sized duck; dagger-shaped bill and lobed toes are distinctive. Grebes are seldom seen in flight, though most species are migratory.

41. Pied-billed Grebe
Podilymbus podiceps
(L-13 W-22)

Grayish brown body; short pale bill with dark black ring; black throat; dark brown eye with white eyering. **Winter** Whitish throat; no black ring on bill. **Juvenile** Prominently striped in dark brown and white (Mar. to as late as Oct.).

Habits This bird has the curious facility of simply sinking when disturbed. Carries newly hatched young on its back.

SUMMER
MIGRATION
WINTER
PERMANENT

Voice A cuckoolike "hoodoo hoo hoo hoo hoo kow kow kow kow."

Similar Species The blunt, white bill (with dark ring in breeding plumage) is distinctive. Other grebes have sharp, dark (in Eared and Horned grebes) or horn-colored (Red-necked Grebe) bills.

Habitat Ponds, lakes, swales, marshes, estuaries, bays.

Abundance and Distribution Common to uncommon winter resident (Sept.–Apr.) throughout; uncommon to rare and local summer resident*.

Where to Find Panther Swamp National Wildlife Refuge, Mississippi; Arthur R. Marshall Loxahatchee National Wildlife Refuge, Florida; Rum Creek Wildlife Management Area, Georgia; Eufaula National Wildlife Refuge, Alabama.

Range Breeds across most of Western Hemisphere from central Canada south to southern Argentina; West Indies; winters in temperate and tropical portions of breeding range.

42. Horned Grebe

Podiceps auritus
(L-14 W-23)

Dark back; rusty neck and sides; whitish breast; black head with buffy orange ear patch and eyebrow; red eye. **Winter** Upper half of head dark with white spot in front of eye; cheek, throat, and breast white; nape and back dark.

Similar Species Winter Horned Grebe has white cheek and neck, not grayish as in Eared Grebe; also Horned Grebe has whitish spot in front of eye, which Eared Grebe lacks. Not all individuals of these two species are readily separable in winter plumage.

Habitat Bays, estuaries; larger lakes.

Abundance and Distribution Common to uncommon winter resident (Oct.–Mar.) along the coast; scarcer inland; rare to casual in the Florida Keys.

Where to Find Weeks Bay National Estuarine Research Reserve, Alabama; Canaveral National Seashore, Florida; Lake Lanier, Georgia; Gulf Islands National Seashore, Mississippi/Florida.

Range Breeds in boreal and north temperate regions; winters mainly along coast in boreal and temperate regions of the Northern Hemisphere.

43. Eared Grebe

Podiceps nigricollis
(L-12 W-22)

Dark back; black neck and rusty sides; whitish breast; black head with buffy orange ear tufts; red eye. **Winter** Dark gray throughout except grayish chin and ear patch, whitish on breast and throat.

Voice "Kip kip kip kuweep kuweep," etc.

Similar Species Winter Eared Grebe has grayish cheek and neck not as white as in Horned Grebe; also

Eared Grebe lacks whitish spot in front of eye, which is present in Horned Grebe. Not all individuals of these two species are readily separable in winter plumage.

Habitat Lakes and ponds (breeding); bays, estuaries, larger lakes (winter).

Abundance and Distribution Rare winter visitor (Sept.–Apr.); not recorded in the Keys.

Where to Find Wassaw National Wildlife Refuge, Georgia; Dauphin Island, Alabama; Noxubee National Wildlife Refuge, Mississippi; Okaloosa County Holding Ponds, Florida.

Range Breeds locally in southern boreal, temperate, and tropical regions of the world; in North America mainly in the west.

Fulmars, Petrels, and Shearwaters
Order Procellariiformes
Family Procellariidae

Dove- or crow-sized seabirds with long, narrow wings, short legs and tail, tubed nose, and hooked bill; rapid fluttering flight with frequent glides. Fulmars, petrels, and shearwaters as well as other pelagic species generally live at sea, coming to land only to breed, and then only to isolated, oceanic islands. However, tropical storms can blow them ashore or even inland on occasion.

44. Black-capped Petrel
Pterodroma hasitata
(L-16 W-37)

Brown above; white below; black cap; white forecrown; white collar; white rump; black tail; wings dark above, white with dark edging below. Some birds have a brown neck (rather than white) with brown extending down onto the breast.

Similar Species Gull-like in size, but with short neck and stubby, tube-nosed bill. Characteristic stiff-winged flap and glide behavior is distinctive.

Habitat Pelagic.

Abundance and Distribution Uncommon to rare offshore in the Gulf Stream. Highest density appears to be Apr.–Oct.

Where to Find Gulf Stream off the Atlantic coast of Central Florida.

Range Breeds in the Greater and Lesser Antilles; winters at sea in the Caribbean and western North Atlantic north to Cape Hatteras, North Carolina (following the Gulf Stream) and south to eastern Brazil.

45. Cory's Shearwater
Calonectris diomedea
(L-18 W-44)

Plump, large-bodied shearwater; gray brown above; brownish head; pale throat; white below; white wing linings with dark tips; pale bill.

Similar Species Greater Shearwater has contrasting sharp black cap and white throat; also has black (not pale) bill, white rump, and black smudge on belly.

Habitat Pelagic.

Abundance and Distribution Uncommon to rare in summer (Apr.–Aug.) offshore, mainly on the Atlantic side.

Where to Find Pelagic birding trips.

Range Mainly temperate and tropical areas of Atlantic Ocean, Caribbean and Mediterranean seas, and Gulf of Mexico.

46. Greater Shearwater
Puffinus gravis
(L-19 W-44)

Plump; dark gray above; white below with dark belly smudge; contrasting dark cap and white throat; white collar, base of tail, and wing linings; black bill; pinkish legs.

Similar Species Cory's Shearwater lacks the contrasting sharp black cap and white throat of the Greater

Figure 18. Ships that cruise Florida's offshore Atlantic waters en route to the eastern Caribbean, like the *Galaxy* shown here readying for departure from Charleston Harbor, provide terrific platforms for oceanic bird viewing—with all the comforts of home and then some.

Shearwater; also the Greater Shearwater has black (not pale) bill, white rump, and black smudge on belly.

Habitat Pelagic.

Abundance and Distribution Rare offshore, mainly on the Atlantic side in summer (May–Oct.).

Where to Find Pelagic birding trips.

Range Atlantic Ocean.

47. Sooty Shearwater
Puffinus griseus
(L-19 W-42)

Entirely dark brownish gray except for pale wing linings; dark bill and legs.

Habits Flaps and glides like other shearwaters; when foraging, drops from a yard or so above the water, wings out; often in large, loose flocks.

Similar Species Entirely dark body with pale wing linings contrasting with dark flight feathers and long bill separate the Sooty Shearwater from other shearwaters in the region, which are dark above and white below with shorter bills.

Habitat Pelagic.

Abundance and Distribution Rare offshore, mainly on the Atlantic side in summer (Mar.–Oct.).

Where to Find Pelagic birding trips.

Range Breeds on islands near Cape Horn and New Zealand during austral summer (Oct.–Mar.); disperses widely across the oceans of the world during migration; spends boreal summer mainly in oceans of Northern Hemisphere.

48. Manx Shearwater
Puffinus puffinus
(L-14 W-33)

A small shearwater; dark above; white below with white wing linings (primaries and secondaries) and undertail coverts; black bill; pink legs.

Similar Species Audubon's Shearwater has dark primary linings and undertail coverts.

Habitat Pelagic.

Abundance and Distribution Rare to casual offshore on the Atlantic side in winter (Aug.–May).

Fulmars, Petrels, Shearwaters

Where to Find Pelagic birding trips.

Range Atlantic Ocean, Caribbean and Mediterranean seas.

49. Audubon's Shearwater
Puffinus lherminieri
(L-12 W-27)

Black above, white below; primary linings and undertail coverts dark; pale legs contrast with dark undertail coverts.

Similar Species Small size and contrasting plumage (dark above, white below) separate this species from other shearwaters found regularly in the region. Manx, the other small shearwater, has white (not dark) primary linings, and mostly white (not dark) undertail coverts that extend to the end of the short tail.

Habitat Pelagic.

Abundance and Distribution Uncommon to rare offshore, mainly on the Atlantic side in summer (Apr.–Oct.). Most numerous off of the Florida Keys.

Where to Find Pelagic birding trips.

Range Warm temperate and tropical seas of the world.

Storm-Petrels
Family Hydrobatidae

Dark, swallowlike seabirds that feed by hopping and skipping over the waves.

50. Wilson's Storm-Petrel
Oceanites oceanicus
(L-7 W-16)

Dark grayish brown with white rump and undertail coverts; pale stripe runs diagonally on secondaries of upper wing; square tail; feet extend beyond tail.

Habits Skims and flutters over water surface, often dabbling feet in water.

Similar Species Dabbling behavior is distinctive. Leach's Storm-Petrel has slightly forked tail; feet do

not extend beyond tail in either Leach's or Band-rumped storm-petrels.

Habitat Pelagic.

Abundance and Distribution Rare summer visitor (Apr.–Nov.) offshore in both the Atlantic and Gulf of Mexico.

Where to Find Pelagic birding trips.

Range Atlantic, Indian, and southern Pacific oceans.

51. Leach's Storm-Petrel
Oceanodroma leucorhoa
(L-8 W-19)

Dark grayish brown; white rump with dark central stripe; slightly forked tail.

Habits Flight is erratic, with sudden alterations of speed and direction, low over water.

Similar Species Leach's Storm-Petrel has a dark central stripe across the white rump and slightly forked tail, which the Wilson's Storm-Petrel lacks. Also these two species are quite different in behavior. The Leach's Storm-Petrel glides and darts erratically over the water surface while the Wilson's Storm-Petrel skims and flutters, often dabbling feet in water.

Habitat Pelagic.

Abundance and Distribution Rare summer visitor (Apr.–Nov.) offshore in both the Atlantic and Gulf of Mexico.

Where to Find Pelagic birding trips.

Range Breeds on islands in the northern Atlantic and Pacific oceans; winters in temperate and tropical seas of the world.

52. Band-rumped Storm-Petrel
Oceanodroma castro
(L-9 W-18)

Dark grayish brown; white rump; square tail.

Habits Flight is shearwater-like with alternate flapping and gliding.

Similar Species See Leach's and Wilson's storm-petrels.

Habitat Pelagic.

Abundance and Distribution Rare visitor (Jun.–Dec.) offshore in both the Atlantic and Gulf of Mexico.

Where to Find Pelagic birding trips.

Range Tropical and warm temperate portions of Atlantic and Pacific oceans, Caribbean Sea.

Tropicbirds

Order Pelecaniformes
Family Phaethontidae

Graceful, long-tailed, narrow-winged, white seabirds of tropical oceans.

53. White-tailed Tropicbird

Phaethon lepturus
(L-28 W-36)

White with black patch running diagonally on wing from wrist; black on primaries; black around eye; extremely long central tail feathers (streamers); yellow bill. **Immature** White with black barring on back and head; no streamers.

Similar Species Yellow bill separates this from other tropicbird species; terns have forked tails—tropicbird tail is wedge shaped, even when lacking streamers.

Habitat Pelagic.

Abundance and Distribution Rare to casual summer visitor (Mar.–Jul.) in the Dry Tortugas, casual at other times of the year; also offshore, mainly on the Atlantic side.

Where to Find Dry Tortugas National Park; pelagic birding trips.

Range Tropical seas.

Boobies and Gannets

Family Sulidae

Boobies and gannets are large, heavy-bodied seabirds with long, cone-shaped bills, narrow, tapered wings, and webbed feet. They dive for prey from considerable heights.

54. Masked Booby
Sula dactylatra
(L-32 W-63)

White body; wings white with black primaries and second-aries; black wedge-shaped tail with elongated central feathers; orangish bill; dark legs; bare skin at base of bill and around eyes is dark. **Immature** Brown mottled with white on wings and lower back; brown head; white breast and belly; wings patterned white and dark brown from below.

Similar Species The combination of dark head, white upper back, and yellow bill separate the immature from other young boobies; Black tail, black secondaries, and yellow bill separate the adult Masked Booby from the adult Northern Gannet (white tail, white secondaries, gray bill).

Habitat Pelagic.

Abundance and Distribution Uncommon resident* in the Dry Tortugas; rare offshore in both the Atlantic and Gulf of Mexico.

Where to Find Dry Tortugas National Park, Florida; pelagic birding trips.

Range Tropical seas.

55. Brown Booby
Sula leucogaster
(L-29 W-48)

Brown back, wings, and hood; white breast and belly; yellowish bill and legs; white at base of wing lining extending in a wedge toward wing tip; bare skin on face is bluish; western birds have whitish heads. **Immature** Similar in pattern to adult but with brownish white rather than white underparts.

Similar Species Immature Masked Booby has mostly white wing linings (dark in immature Brown Booby) and yellowish (not bluish) bill.

Habitat Pelagic.

Abundance and Distribution Uncommon resident in the Dry Tortugas; may have bred; rare in the Florida Keys; rare offshore in both the Atlantic and Gulf of Mexico, scarcer northward.

Where to Find Dry Tortugas National Park, Florida; pelagic birding trips.

Range Tropical western Atlantic and eastern Pacific oceans.

56. Red-footed Booby
Sula sula
(L-29 W-60)

Brown body; white rump, undertail coverts, and tail; bluish bill; red legs; pinkish skin at base of bill. **White phase** White with black primaries and secondaries; black carpal patch. **Immature** Dark throughout with bluish bill and dark feet.

Similar Species This is the only red-footed booby, whether in white or brown phase. Immatures lack the wing lining patterns of other boobies.

Habitat Pelagic.

Abundance and Distribution Rare spring and summer visitor in the Dry Tortugas; rare to casual offshore in both the Atlantic and Gulf of Mexico from Mar.–Oct.

Where to Find Dry Tortugas National Park, Florida.

Range Tropical western Atlantic, Pacific, and Indian oceans.

57. Northern Gannet
Morus bassanus
(L-38 W-75)

Largest of the boobies; entirely white except for black primaries; rusty wash on head; bill bluish; feet dark. **Immature** Brown except for whitish belly and white spots on upper wing and back; bluish bill.

Habits Occasionally visible with a spotting scope from barrier islands as they dive for fish in the open Gulf.

Voice A series of crowlike "caw"s.

Similar Species Immature gannets lack white wing lining patterns of other boobies, and have a whitish belly (which immature Red-footed Booby lacks).

Habitat Pelagic and immediate offshore environment.

Abundance and Distribution Common to rare and irregular inshore and offshore in the Atlantic and Gulf of Mexico, mainly in winter (Oct.–May).

Where to Find Wolf Island National Wildlife Refuge, Georgia; Gulf State Park, Alabama; Gulf Islands National Seashore, Florida/Mississippi.

Range North Atlantic Ocean, Gulf of Mexico, Mediterranean Sea.

Boobies, Gannets

Pelicans

Family Pelecanidae

Extremely large, heavy-bodied waterbirds with long bill and gular pouch.

58. American White Pelican
Pelecanus erythrorhynchos
(L-62 W-105)

White body; black primaries and secondaries; enormous yellow or orange bill and gular pouch; often with a hornlike growth on upper mandible (breeding); orange-yellow feet.

Habits Does not dive from the air for fish like Brown Pelican. Forages by dipping for prey from the surface of the water, often in groups. Migrates in large flocks.

Voice Various coughs and croaks.

Similar Species Immature Brown Pelicans can appear a dusty brownish white, but the American White Pelican is bright white in all plumages.

Habitat Large lakes, impoundments, coastal waters.

Abundance and Distribution Common and local winter visitor (Sept.–Apr.) in Central and South Florida, less common in North Florida, the Panhandle, and coastal Alabama and Mississippi; rare in the Keys and inland in Mississippi, Alabama, and throughout Georgia. Some Florida birds remain through the summer.

Where to Find Cedar Keys National Wildlife Refuge, Florida; Everglades National Park, Florida; Cumberland Island National Seashore, Georgia.

Range Breeds locally at large lakes and marshes in central and western Canada south through western half of the United States; winters southwestern United States to Nicaragua, and from Florida around the Gulf of Mexico to Yucatan.

59. Brown Pelican
Pelecanus occidentalis
(L-48 W-78)

Grayish above; brownish below with dark chestnut nape and neck; whitish head tinged with yellow; enormous bill and gular pouch. **Immature** Entirely brownish gray.

Habits Dives from a considerable height to catch fish.

Voice Occasional croaks.

Similar Species The immature Brown Pelican can appear a dusty brownish white. The American White Pelican is bright white in all plumages

Habitat Marine bays, estuaries, lakes (Florida).

Abundance and Distribution Common resident* along both Atlantic and Gulf coasts; uncommon to rare inland in Central Florida; breeds at Lake Okeechobee.

Where to Find Blackbeard Island National Wildlife Refuge, Georgia; Bon Secour National Wildlife Refuge, Alabama; St. George Island State Park, Florida; Merritt Island National Wildlife Refuge, Florida.

Range Coastal Western Hemisphere from southern New Jersey to eastern Brazil including West Indies in east and California to southern Chile in west.

Cormorants
Family Phalacrocoracidae

Dark waterbirds the size of a small goose with tapered body, long, hooked bill, small gular pouch, and webbed feet. Cormorants generally fly in small flocks with necks extended.

60. Double-crested Cormorant
Phalacrocorax auritus
(L-32 W-51)

Entirely iridescent black; whitish or dark ear tufts during breeding season; gular pouch of bare orange skin. **Immature** Brown with buffy head and neck.

Habits Forages by swimming low in water and diving for long periods. Sits on snags and posts with wings spread to dry.

Voice Various croaks.

Similar Species The larger, heavy-bodied immature Great Cormorant shows a dark throat and upper breast and lighter belly. The smaller immature Double-crested Cormorant has lighter throat and upper breast contrasting with darker belly.

Habitat Estuaries, marine, lakes, ponds.

Abundance and Distribution Common winter resident (Oct.–Apr.) in peninsular Florida, the Keys, and along the Georgia coast; uncommon in winter in Alabama, Mississippi, the Florida Panhandle, and inland Georgia; common to rare in summer*. Mostly a transient (Apr.–Jun., Oct.–Dec.) in the Georgia mountains.

Where to Find J. N. "Ding" Darling National Wildlife Refuge, Florida; Reed Bingham State Park, Georgia; Bon Secour National Wildlife Refuge, Alabama; Cedar Keys National Wildlife Refuge, Florida; Dahomey National Wildlife Refuge, Mississippi.

Range Breeds locally across central and southern Canada and much of the United States, along both coasts from Alaska to southern Mexico on the west, and Newfoundland to Florida on the east; also Cuba; winters in coastal breeding range to Florida, south Texas, Greater Antilles, Yucatan Peninsula, and Belize.

Anhingas
Family Anhingidae

Dark waterbirds similar to cormorants but with serpentine neck, long, pointed bill, and long, wedge-shaped tail.

61. Anhinga
Anhinga anhinga
(L-35 W-45)

Snakelike neck and long triangular tail with thin white bars and terminal buffy band; long, sharp, yellow-orange bill; black body with iridescent green sheen; mottled white on shoulders and upper wing coverts. **Female and Immature** Light buff head, neck, and breast; lack white wing spotting.

Habits Often forages with only the sinuous neck and head protruding above water. Sits with wings spread to dry.

Voice A series of metallic "kaakk"s, some reminiscent of a cicada.

Similar Species Cormorants have hooked rather than stiletto-shaped bill; tail is shorter than that of Anhinga and lacks terminal buffy band.

Habitat Rivers, lakes, ponds.

Abundance and Distribution Common to uncommon resident* along the Atlantic and Gulf coasts, mainland Florida, and the

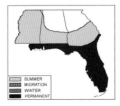

SUMMER
MIGRATION
WINTER
PERMANENT

Keys; common to uncommon summer resident*, uncommon to rare in winter, along the coastal plain of Georgia, Alabama, and Mississippi.

Where to Find Okefenokee National Wildlife Refuge, Georgia; Choctaw National Wildlife Refuge, Alabama; Harris Neck National Wildlife Refuge, Georgia; Jaycee Park, Lake Okeechobee, Florida; Noxubee National Wildlife Refuge, Mississippi.

Range Breeds from the southeastern United States south through the lowlands of the subtropics and tropics to southern Brazil, Cuba; winters throughout breeding range except inland in Gulf states.

Frigatebirds
Family Fregatidae

Dark, long-winged, fork-tailed seabirds of tropical waters.

62. Magnificent Frigatebird
Fregata magnificens
(L-40 W-90)

Black body; red, bare-skinned throat (inconspicuous unless distended); extremely long, narrow wings and long forked tail; long, hooked beak. **Female** White breast and belly, black throat. **Immature** Variable– white on head and underparts.

Habits Uses superior flying skill to rob gulls and terns of fish.

SUMMER
MIGRATION
WINTER
PERMANENT

Habitat Coastal marine.

Abundance and Distribution Common to uncommon resident in South Florida; breeds* in the Dry Tortugas; uncommon to rare summer resident (Apr.–Oct.), increasingly scarce northward along the coasts of Florida, Alabama, and Mississippi; rare to casual in summer along the Georgia coast; scarcer in winter.

Where to Find Everglades National Park, Florida; Dry Tortugas National Park, Florida; Gulf Islands National Seashore, Florida/ Mississippi; J. N. "Ding" Darling National Wildlife Refuge, Florida; Dauphin Island, Alabama.

Range Tropical and subtropical coasts and islands of Western Hemisphere, also Cape Verde Islands off western Africa.

Herons, Egrets, and Bitterns
Order Ciconiiformes
Family Ardeidae

Long-billed, long-necked, long-legged wading birds; most with long, thin bills.

63. American Bittern
Botaurus lentiginosus
(L-26 W-39)

A chunky, relatively short-legged heron; buffy brown above and below streaked with white and brown on throat, neck, and breast; dark brown streak on side of neck; white chin; greenish yellow bill and legs; yellow eyes.

SUMMER
MIGRATION
WINTER
PERMANENT

Habits A secretive bird; often, rather than fly when approached, it will "freeze" with its neck extended in an attempt to blend in with the reeds and rushes of the marsh.

Voice A deep "goonk glunk-a-lunk," like blowing on an empty coke bottle.

Similar Species Could be mistaken for an immature night-heron in flight, but dark brown primaries and secondaries contrast with light brown back and upper wing coverts; night-herons lack prominent dark streak on side of neck.

Habitat Marshes.

Abundance and Distribution Common to uncommon transient (Mar.–May, Sept.–Oct..) nearly throughout; common to uncommon winter resident (Sept.–May) in Florida and the lower coastal plain of Georgia, Alabama, and Mississippi; casual summer resident in mainland Florida; reportedly has bred; casual in the Florida Keys.

Where to Find Wassaw National Wildlife Refuge, Georgia; Lake Woodruff National Wildlife Refuge, Florida; Choctaw National Wildlife Refuge, Alabama; Grand Bay National Wildlife Refuge, Mississippi.

Range Breeds central and southern Canada south to southern United States and central Mexico; winters southern United States to southern Mexico and Cuba.

64. Least Bittern

Ixobrychus exilis
(L-14 W-17)

The smallest of our herons; dark brown with white streaking on back; tan wings, head, and neck; dark brown crown; white chin and throat streaked with tan; white belly; yellowish legs and bill; yellow eyes; extended wings are half tan (basally) and half dark brown.

Habits Like the American Bittern, this bird will often "freeze" with neck extended when approached.

Voice A rapid, whistled "coo-co-co-co-coo."

Similar Species Immature Green Heron is heavily streaked below and lacks buff shoulders.

Habitat Marshes.

Abundance and Distribution Uncommon to rare summer resident* (Apr.–Sept.) along the coastal plain; uncommon transient (Apr.–May, Sept.–Oct.) throughout; rare summer resident* in piedmont; uncommon to rare winter resident (Oct.–Mar.) in peninsular Florida; rare resident* in the Keys.

Where to Find Reed Bingham State Park, Georgia; Eufaula National Wildlife Refuge, Alabama; Dahomey National Wildlife Refuge, Mississippi; Kaliga Park, Florida.

Range Breeds in the eastern half of the United States and southeastern Canada; locally in the western United States, south through lowlands to southern Brazil, West Indies; winters through breeding range from the southern United States southward.

65. Great Blue Heron

Ardea herodias
(L-48 W-72)

A very large heron; slate gray above and on neck; white crown bordered with black stripes that extend as plumes (breeding); white chin and throat streaked with black; gray breast and back plumes; white below streaked with chestnut; chestnut thighs; orange-yellow bill; dark legs. **Immature** Dark cap; brownish gray back; buffy neck. **White phase** ("Great White Heron" of some authors) Entirely white or mixed white and blue with yellow bill and legs; this phase is extremely rare except in South Florida and the Caribbean.

Voice A low "krarrrk."

Habitat Lakes, rivers, marshes, bays, estuaries.

Abundance and Distribution Common to uncommon resident*
along the coastal plain throughout the region and in the Keys;
scarcer in the piedmont and highlands.

Where to Find *Blue phase*: Pearl River Waterfowl Refuge, Mississippi; George L. Smith State Park, Georgia; Lake Guntersville State
Park, Alabama; Big Lagoon State Recreation Area, Florida. *White
phase*: Dry Tortugas National Park, Florida; Everglades National
Park, Florida.

Range Breeds from central and southern Canada south to coastal
Colombia and Venezuela, West Indies; winters southern United
States southward through breeding range.

66. Great Egret
Ardea alba
(L-39 W-57)

Entirely white, with shaggy plumes on breast and back in
breeding season; long, yellow bill; long dark legs that extend well beyond tail in flight.

Voice Various "krrank"s and "krronk"s.

Similar Species The Great Egret has yellow bill and dark
legs; the smaller Snowy Egret has black bill, black legs, and
yellow feet; immature Little Blue Heron has two-tone bill
(dark tip, pale base), pale legs, and usually some gray
smudging on white plumage; Cattle Egret is half the size;
has short, thick yellow bill and yellowish legs that barely
extend beyond tail in flight.

Habitat Lakes, ponds, rivers, marshes, estuaries, bays.

Abundance and Distribution Common resident* along the
coastal plain throughout the region and the Keys; uncommon to
rare summer visitor, rare or absent in winter, in the piedmont and
highlands.

Where to Find Stephen C. Foster State Park, Georgia; Meaher
State Park, Alabama; Panther Swamp National Wildlife Refuge,
Mississippi; Jaycee Park, Lake Okeechobee, Florida.

Range Breeds in temperate and tropical regions of the world;
winters mainly in subtropical and tropical portions of breeding
range.

67. Snowy Egret

Egretta thula

(L-23 W-45)

Small, white heron; black legs with yellow feet; black bill; yellow lores; white plumes off neck and breast (breeding). **Immature** Has yellow line up back of leg.

Habits Occasionally arches wings to form a canopy while foraging; also puts foot forward and shakes it on bottom substrate.

Voice A crowlike "caaah."

Similar Species The Snowy Egret has black bill, black legs, and yellow feet; immature Little Blue Heron has two-tone bill (dark tip, pale base), pale legs, and usually some gray smudging on white plumage; Cattle Egret has short, thick yellow bill and yellowish legs that barely extend beyond tail in flight; the Great Egret has yellow bill and black legs.

Habitat Marshes, ponds, lakes, estuaries, bays.

Abundance and Distribution Common to uncommon resident* in Florida and along the coast throughout the rest of the Southeast; uncommon to rare summer visitor inland along the coastal plain; casual or absent elsewhere in the region.

Where to Find Stephen C. Foster State Park, Georgia; Bon Secour National Wildlife Refuge, Alabama; Fort Caroline National Memorial/Timucuan Ecological and Historic Preserve, Florida; Bogue Chitto National Wildlife Refuge, Mississippi.

Range Breeds locally across United States and extreme southern Canada south in lowlands to southern South America, West Indies; winters from coastal southern United States southward through breeding range.

SUMMER
MIGRATION
WINTER
PERMANENT

Herons, Egrets, Bitterns

Figure 19. The natives are friendly along the shore at Florida's Venice Beach, but keep an eye on your fish catch.

68. Little Blue Heron

Egretta caerulea
(L-23 W-39)

A smallish heron; dark blue body; maroon neck and head; two-tone bill, black at tip, pale gray or greenish at base; plumes on neck, breast and head; dark legs. **Winter** Mainly dark blue on neck with maroon tinge; no plumes. **Immature** Almost entirely white in first year with some gray smudging and blue-gray wing tips; greenish legs; two-tone bill; more gray smudging in second year.

Voice Piglike squawks.

Similar Species Immature Little Blue Heron has two-tone bill (dark tip, pale base), pale legs, and usually some gray smudging on white plumage; Snowy Egret has black bill, black legs, and yellow feet; Cattle Egret has short, thick yellow bill and yellowish legs that barely extend beyond tail in flight; the Great Egret has yellow bill and black legs; rare white phase of Great Blue is much larger and has yellow bill and yellow legs (not dark). The white phase of the Reddish Egret has a dark or two-tone bill (dark tip, pinkish base) and dark legs.

Habitat Mainly freshwater marshes, lakes, ponds.

Abundance and Distribution Common to uncommon resident* in Florida and elsewhere in the region along the lower coastal plain, withdrawing somewhat from inland areas in winter; uncommon to rare summer resident (Apr.–Sept.) in the Upper coastal plain, scarce or absent in winter.

Where to Find Okefenokee National Wildlife Refuge, Georgia; Eufaula National Wildlife Refuge, Alabama; Hugh Taylor Birch State Park, Florida; Bogue Chitto National Wildlife Refuge, Mississippi.

Range Breeds along Coastal Plain of eastern United States from Maine to Texas south through lowlands to Peru and southern Brazil, West Indies; winters from southern United States south through breeding range.

69. Tricolored Heron

Egretta tricolor
(L-26 W-36)

Slate blue body; red eye; greenish lores; rusty chin; white central stripe down neck streaked with dark blue; maroon on breast;

white belly and thighs; buffy plumes on back (breeding). **Immature** Rusty and slate above, whitish below.

Voice Crowlike "krraww," repeated.

Similar Species Similar pattern to the much larger Great Blue Heron but note white (not chestnut) thighs, and lack of black on head.

Habitat Bays, estuaries, lakes, ponds.

Abundance and Distribution Common to uncommon resident* in Florida and along the lower coastal plain in the rest of the Southeast, withdrawing somewhat from inland areas in winter; occasional wanderer inland (Aug.–Oct.).

Where to Find Fort Pulaski National Monument, Georgia; Dauphin Island, Alabama; Gulf Islands National Seashore, Florida/Mississippi.

Range Breeds in the Coastal Plain of the eastern United States from Maine to Texas, south through coastal lowlands to Peru and northern Brazil, West Indies; winters from Gulf states south through breeding range.

70. Reddish Egret
Egretta rufescens
(L-29 W-39)

A medium-sized heron; slate blue body; pinkish beige head, neck, and breast with shaggy plumes; two-tone bill, pink at base and black at tip; bluish lores; dark legs; nonbreeding plumage is duller with shorter plumes. **White phase** Entirely white with two-tone bill; dark legs. **Immature (both phases)** Bill entirely dark.

Habits Peculiar feeding behavior involving arching of wings over head ("canopy") and various runs and lurches in somewhat tipsy fashion.

Voice "Krraaah."

Similar Species Immature Little Blue Heron has two-tone bill (dark tip, pale base), pale legs, and usually some gray smudging on white plumage; Snowy Egret has black bill, black legs, and yellow feet; Cattle Egret has short, thick yellow bill and yellowish legs that barely extend beyond tail in flight; the Great Egret has yellow bill and black legs; rare white phase of Great Blue is much larger and has yellow bill and yellow legs (not dark). The white phase of the Reddish Egret has a dark or two-tone bill (dark tip, pinkish base) and dark legs.

Habitat Shallow tidal pools.

Abundance and Distribution Common to uncommon resident* along the coast in Central and South Florida and the Keys; rare to casual wanderer inland and northward in Florida and along the immediate coast in the rest of the Southeast from May–Oct.

Where to Find Everglades National Park, Florida; J. N. "Ding" Darling National Wildlife Refuge, Florida; Wassaw National Wildlife Refuge, Georgia.

Range Breeds locally along coast in Florida and the Gulf states, both coasts of Mexico and Greater Antilles; winters through breeding range to Lesser Antilles and coastal Venezuela.

Herons, Egrets, Bitterns

SUMMER
MIGRATION
WINTER
PERMANENT

71. Cattle Egret
Bubulcus ibis
(L-20 W-36)

A small, entirely white heron; yellow-orange bill and legs; buff coloration and plumes on crest, breast and back (breeding). **Immature** Like adult but lacks buff coloration, and legs are dark.

Similar Species The stubby Cattle Egret has short, thick yellow bill and yellowish legs that barely extend beyond tail in flight; immature Little Blue Heron has two-tone bill (dark tip, pale base), pale legs, and usually some gray smudging on white plumage; Snowy Egret has black bill, black legs, and yellow feet.

Habitat The Cattle Egret is not an aquatic species, although it occasionally nests on bay islands. It prefers grasslands where it feeds on insects, mainly grasshoppers.

Abundance and Distribution Common summer resident* (Apr.–Sept.) in Florida and elsewhere in the southeast along the coastal plain; common to uncommon winter resident (Oct.–Mar.) in Central and South Florida and the Keys, increasingly scarce northward during this season.

Where to Find Stephen C. Foster State Park, Georgia; Choctaw National Wildlife Refuge, Alabama; Dahomey National Wildlife Refuge, Mississippi; Lower Suwannee National Wildlife Refuge, Florida.

Range Formerly strictly an Old World species, the Cattle Egret appeared in South America in the late 1800s and has expanded steadily northward, reaching Florida in the early 1940s. Current distribution includes most temperate and tropical regions of the world. Northern populations are migratory.

72. Green Heron
Butorides virescens
(L-19 W-28)

A small, dark heron; olive back; black cap; chestnut neck; white throat with chestnut striping; yellow eye and yellow lores; white malar stripe; grayish belly; greenish legs; bill dark above, yellowish below. **Immature** Heavily streaked below.

Habits Forages in a very slow, deliberate manner.

Voice A loud "kyoook."

Similar Species Least Bittern is buffy, not dark, and has two-tone wings; Green Heron wings are uniformly dark in flight.

Habitat Streams, rivers, lakes, marshes.

Abundance and Distribution Common to uncommon permanent resident* in peninsular Florida; common to uncommon summer resident* (Mar.–Oct.), casual or absent in winter, elsewhere in the region.

Where to Find Fort Pulaski National Monument, Georgia; Eufaula National Wildlife Refuge, Alabama; Chassahowitzka National Wildlife Refuge, Florida; Fort Caroline National Memorial/ Timucuan Ecological and Historic Preserve, Florida; Vicksburg National Military Park, Mississippi.

Range Breeds from southern Canada south to northern Argentina (including Green-backed Heron form, *B. striatus*); West Indies; winters from southern United States southward through breeding range.

73. Black-crowned Night-Heron
Nycticorax nycticorax
(L-26 W-45)

A rather squat heron; black on back and crown with long, trailing white plumes (breeding); gray wings; pale gray breast and belly; white forehead, cheek and chin; red eye; dark beak; pale legs. **Immature** Dark brown above, heavily streaked with white; whitish below streaked with brown; red eye; bluish lores; pale legs.

Habits Mostly nocturnal.

Voice "Kwark."

Similar Species Immature Yellow-crowned Night-Heron has longer legs that extend well beyond end of tail in flight;

blackcrown's toes barely reach beyond end of tail; also the blackcrown is streaked on back, not spotted as in yellowcrown.

Habitat Bays, lakes, marshes.

Abundance and Distribution Common to uncommon resident* in most of Florida (rare in the Keys) and elsewhere in the Southeast along the lower coastal plain; uncommon to rare summer resident* (Apr.–Sept.) in the upper coastal plain, scarce or absent in winter.

Where to Find Stephen C. Foster State Park, Georgia; Meaher State Park, Alabama; J. N. "Ding" Darling National Wildlife Refuge, Florida; Bogue Chitto National Wildlife Refuge, Mississippi.

Range Breeds locally in temperate and tropical regions of the world; withdraws from seasonally cold portions of breeding range in winter.

74. Yellow-crowned Night-Heron
Nyctanassa violacea
(L-24 W-42)

Gray body, streaked with black above and on wings; black head with white cheek patch and creamy crown and plumes (breeding); red eye; dark bill; pale legs. **Immature** Dark brown above, finely spotted with white; whitish below streaked with brown; dark bill; yellow legs; red eye

Voice "Aaak."

Similar Species Immature Yellow-crowned Night-Heron has longer legs that extend well beyond end of tail in flight; blackcrown's toes barely reach beyond end of tail; also the blackcrown is streaked on back, not spotted as in yellowcrown.

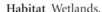

Habitat Wetlands.

Abundance and Distribution Common to uncommon summer resident* (Apr.–Oct.) in Florida and along the coastal plain elsewhere; uncommon to rare summer resident* inland; uncommon to rare in winter except in Central and South Florida and the Keys where present throughout the year as a permanent resident.

Where to Find Okefenokee National Wildlife Refuge, Georgia; Meaher State Park, Alabama; Hobe Sound National Wildlife Refuge, Florida; Yazoo National Wildlife Refuge, Mississippi.

Range From the southeastern United States south in coastal regions to Peru and southern Brazil, West Indies; winters from coastal Gulf states south through breeding range.

Ibises and Spoonbills
Family Threskiornithidae

Ibises are small to medium-sized, heronlike birds with long, decurved bills.

75. White Ibis
Eudocimus albus
(L-25 W-39)

Entirely white with long, pink, decurved bill; pink facial skin; yellow eye; pink legs. **Immature** Brown above; white below; neck and head mottled brown and whitish; pinkish bill and legs.

Voice Various "aaaah"s and "aaaww"s.

Similar Species Immature White Ibis has pinkish bill and legs; immature Glossy Ibis has dark bill and legs; immature White Ibis has white neck and underparts; immature Glossy Ibis is entirely dark with some streaking on the head and neck.

Habitat Bays, rivers, estuaries.

Abundance and Distribution Common to uncommon summer resident* (Apr.–Sept.) in Florida and elsewhere along the coastal plain; uncommon to rare winter resident (Oct.–Mar.) in the lower coastal plain, increasingly scarce inland during this season.

Where to Find George L. Smith State Park, Georgia; Choctaw National Wildlife Refuge, Alabama; J. N. "Ding" Darling National Wildlife Refuge, Florida; Noxubee National Wildlife Refuge, Mississippi.

Range Coastal southeastern United States south to French Guiana and Peru, West Indies; withdraws from northern portions in winter.

76. Glossy Ibis
Plegadis falcinellus
(L-22 W-36)

Body entirely dark purplish brown with green sheen on wings and back; bare dark skin on face, edged with bluish skin (breeding); dark bill; dark legs; brown eyes. **Immature** Brownish throughout with white streaking on head and neck; dark bill and legs.

Similar Species Immature Glossy Ibis is entirely dark with some streaking on the head and neck; immature White Ibis has pinkish bill and legs; immature Glossy Ibis has dark bill and legs; immature White Ibis has white neck and underparts.

Habitat Bays, marshes, lakes, ponds.

Abundance and Distribution Common to uncommon resident* in coastal Georgia and peninsular Florida, rare to casual in the Keys; casual or absent elsewhere in the region along the lower coastal plain.

Where to Find Merritt Island National Wildlife Refuge, Florida; Harris Neck National Wildlife Refuge, Georgia; Kaliga Park, Florida.

Range Breeds along coast of eastern United States from Maine to Louisiana south through West Indies to northern Venezuela and in Old World temperate and tropical regions; withdraws from colder portions of breeding range in winter.

77. Roseate Spoonbill
Platalea ajaja
(L-30 W-51)

A medium-sized, heron-bodied bird with long, spatulate bill; pink body and legs; white neck and breast; dark nape; bald crown of greenish skin; bright red shoulder patch. **Immature** Whitish body with pinkish wings.

Habits Forages by swishing bill back and forth through water, capturing invertebrates.

Voice "Rraaaak-ak-ak-ak," etc.

Habitat Bays, estuaries, lakes, ponds.

Abundance and Distribution Common to uncommon permanent resident* in Central and South Florida; uncommon to rare or casual northward, principally during post-breeding movements (May–Oct.); uncommon summer resident* (Apr.–Sept.) in the Keys, scarcer in winter.

Where to Find Everglades National Park, Florida; Merritt Island National Wildlife Refuge, Florida; J. N. "Ding" Darling National Wildlife Refuge, Florida.

Range Coastal areas of the Gulf states south through coastal regions to northern Argentina and the West Indies; partially withdraws from the northern portions of the breeding range in winter.

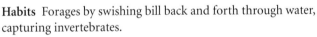

Ibises, Spoonbills

Figure 20. Merritt Island National Wildlife Refuge's Cruickshank Trail, named in honor of the great Florida ornithologist and conservationist, is a good place to see a wide variety of birdlife including skimmers, spoonbills, herons, egrets, and rails.

Storks
Family Ciconiidae

Tall, long-legged, heavy-billed, long-necked wading birds.

78. Wood Stork
Mycteria americana
(L-41 W-66)

ENDANGERED. A large white-bodied bird with long, heavy bill, down-turned toward the tip; black primaries and secondaries; naked, black-skinned head and neck; pale legs with pinkish feet. **Immature** Patterned like adult but with grayish feathering on neck and head; yellowish bill.

Habitat Lakes, coastal marshes, bays.

SUMMER
MIGRATION
WINTER
PERMANENT

Abundance and Distribution Common to uncommon resident* in most of peninsular Florida, somewhat scarcer in summer (Jun.–Sept.) when many birds migrate northward after breeding; rare to casual in the Keys. Uncommon to rare summer resident in northwestern peninsular Florida and the Panhandle, growing increasingly scarce westward along the Gulf coast; common to rare summer resident* along the lower coastal plain in extreme North Florida and Georgia, with breeding populations in the Okefenokee Swamp, and Lewis Island along the Altamaha drainage; scarce to absent in these areas in winter.

Where to Find Okefenokee National Wildlife Refuge, Georgia;

Corkscrew Swamp Sanctuary, Immokalee, Florida; Everglades National Park, Florida; Choctaw National Wildlife Refuge, Alabama.

Range From Georgia, Florida and the Gulf states south in coastal regions to central Argentina; West Indies.

New World Vultures
Family Cathartidae

Large, dark, diurnal scavengers with long, hooked bills and featherless heads, forage mostly from the air for carrion.

79. Black Vulture
Coragyps atratus
(L-26 W-57)

Entirely black with naked black-skinned head; primaries silvery from below.

Habits Black Vultures do not normally soar except during migration; they alternate flapping and gliding, usually at low levels.

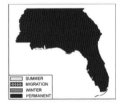

Similar Species Turkey Vultures soar, seldom flapping, and normally hold their wings at an angle while Black Vultures hold their wings horizontally during glides; Black Vultures have silvery primaries while Turkey Vultures have silvery primaries and secondaries.

Habitat Mainly open areas.

Abundance and Distribution Common to uncommon resident* nearly throughout, although casual or absent in the lower (western) Keys.

Where to Find Eufaula National Wildlife Refuge, Alabama; Dahomey National Wildlife Refuge, Mississippi; Okefenokee National Wildlife Refuge, Georgia; Arbuckle Creek Road, Lorida, Florida.

Range Breeds from eastern (New Jersey) and southwestern (Arizona) United States south to central Argentina; winters from central and southern United States south through breeding range.

80. Turkey Vulture
Cathartes aura
(L-26 W-69)

Dark brown with naked, red-skinned head; relatively long tail; silvery flight feathers (outlining black wing lining). **Immature** Black head.

Habits Soars for long periods with wings held at an angle above horizontal.

Similar Species Turkey Vultures soar, seldom flapping, and normally hold their wings at an angle while Black Vultures hold their wings horizontally during glides; Black Vultures have silvery primaries while Turkey Vultures have silvery primaries and secondaries.

Habitat Nearly ubiquitous except in extensive agricultural areas.

Abundance and Distribution Common resident* throughout.

Where to Find Piedmont National Wildlife Refuge, Georgia; Oak Mountain State Park, Alabama; Blackwater River State Park, Florida; Noxubee National Wildlife Refuge, Mississippi.

Range Breeds from southern Canada south to southern South America, Bahamas and Cuba; winters from central and southern United States south through breeding range.

Flamingos
Order Phoenicopteriformes
Family Phoenicopteridae

Colorful, storklike birds with long sinuous necks and large bent bills.

81. Greater Flamingo
Phoenicopterus ruber
(L-45 W-63)

A large, long-legged, long-necked, pink bird with heavy, right-angled bill; black primaries and secondaries; legs pink; bill pink tipped with black. **Immature** Similar to adult but paler.

Habits Swishes bill through water to strain invertebrate prey.

Habitat Coastal marshes.

Abundance and Distribution Rare and local resident in the Everglades, especially Florida Bay, the vast coastal wetland

bordered by the mainland on the north and Key Largo on the south.

Where to Find Everglades National Park, Florida (in particular, Snake Bight Bay near the Flamingo Visitor Center).

Range Resident locally in tropical and subtropical areas of the world; mainly in the Caribbean region of the New World.

Kites, Hawks, Ospreys, and Eagles
Order Falconiformes
Family Accipitridae

A diverse assemblage of diurnal raptors, all of the accipiters have strongly hooked bills and powerful talons. Clark and Wheeler (1987) and Dunne and Sutton (1989) provide identification guides for advanced students of this difficult group.

82. Osprey
Pandion haliaetus
(L-23 W-63)

Dark brown above; white below, often with dark streaking (females); white crown with ragged crest from back of head; broad dark line extending behind yellow eye; white chin and cheek; extended wings are white finely barred with brown with prominent dark patches at wrist.

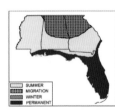

Habits Feeds mainly on fish snatched from water surface.

Voice A shrill "kew," repeated.

Habitat Estuaries, lakes, rivers, bays.

Abundance and Distribution Common to rare transient (Aug.–Oct., Mar.–Apr.) throughout; uncommon to rare summer resident* (Mar.–Oct.) in the upper coastal plain with some remaining through the winter; common resident* in peninsular Florida, the Keys, and along the immediate coast in the Florida Panhandle, Mississippi, Alabama, and Georgia.

Where to Find Stephen C. Foster State Park, Georgia; Lake George, Ocala National Forest, Florida; Weeks Bay National Estuarine Research Reserve, Alabama; Gulf Islands National Seashore, Mississippi.

Range Breeds in boreal, temperate, and some tropical localities of Old and New World, particularly along coasts; winters mainly in tropical and subtropical zones.

83. Swallow-tailed Kite
Elanoides forficatus
(L-23 W-48)

White body and head; black back, wings, and long, deeply forked tail; in flight note swallow tail and white wing linings outlined by black flight feathers.

Habits Primarily insectivorous.

Voice A high-pitched, squeaky "whee ki-we ki-we ki-we," etc.

Habitat Riparian forest, woodlands, marshy grasslands.

Abundance and Distribution Uncommon to rare summer resident* (Mar.–Aug.) along the lower coastal plain and throughout peninsular Florida (more numerous in Central and South Florida); rare to casual transient (Mar., Aug.) elsewhere in the region.

Where to Find DePuts Management Area, Florida; Crooked River State Park, Georgia; Okefenokee National Wildlife Refuge, Georgia; Choctaw National Wildlife Refuge, Alabama.

Range Formerly bred across the eastern United States, now United States populations are rare and local in Texas, Louisiana, Mississippi, South Carolina, and Georgia, with good numbers remaining only in Florida; breeds from the southeastern United States south to Argentina; winters mainly in South America.

84. White-tailed Kite
Elanus leucurus
(L-16 W-42)

Gray above; white below; red eyes and yellow legs; black shoulders; in flight note white tail and silvery wings with black wrist mark. **Immature** Rusty wash on back, head, and breast.

Habits Often hovers while foraging.

Voice A shrill "kee kee kee," etc.

Habitat Prairie, savanna, thorn forest.

Abundance and Distribution Rare and local resident* in Central and South Florida; scattered records elsewhere along the coastal plain; has bred in southwestern Mississippi.

Where to Find Arbuckle Creek Road, Lorida, Florida; Everglades National Park, Florida.

Range Resident from Oregon, California, Oklahoma, Louisiana, and Florida south to central Argentina.

85. Snail Kite

Rostrhamus sociabilis
(L-17 W-39)

Entirely dark brown with white rump and base of tail; red lores and cere; red eyes; red-orange legs; long, hooked bill. **Female and Immature** Dark brown and rusty above; variably streaked buff and brown below with buffy throat and eyebrow.

Habits Feeds mainly on *Pomacea* snails.

Voice A low, nasal, froglike "ah-ah-ah-ah-ah-ah-ah-ah."

Habitat Fresh water wetlands.

Abundance and Distribution Uncommon to rare and extremely local resident* of Central and South Florida.

Where to Find Miccosukee Indian Restaurant, Florida; Kaliga Park, Florida; Clewiston, Florida; Everglades National Park, Florida.

Range Resident in Florida and Cuba, and from southern Mexico south to central Argentina.

86. Mississippi Kite

Ictinia mississippiensis
(L-15 W-35)

Dark gray above; pale gray below with black primaries and tail; red eye; orange-yellow legs; gray cere; in flight note pointed wings, uniform gray underparts, and dark, slightly forked tail. **Immature** Streaked rusty below; barred tail; red or yellow eye.

Habitat Riparian and oak woodlands; deciduous forest and swamps; savanna.

Abundance and Distribution Uncommon summer resident* (Apr.–Sept.) along the coastal plain of Mississippi, Alabama, Georgia, the Panhandle, and North Florida; rare transient (Apr., Sept.) in Central and South Florida where there are a few winter reports as well.

Where to Find St. Catherine Creek National Wildlife Refuge, Mississippi; Altamaha River/Atkinson Tract, Georgia; Blackwater River State Park, Florida; Natchez Trace Parkway, Mississippi (Mile 122, Cypress Swamp); Choctaw National Wildlife Refuge, Alabama.

Range Breeds in the southern United States; winters south to central South America.

Figure 21. Everglades National Park is huge, with five major visitor centers and hundreds of miles of roads and hiking trails, plus various boat tours to the vast number of sites within the park that are accessible only by water. Nevertheless, finding the right place to locate your particular bird of interest is not so hard. Pick up a park map and Everglades National Park Bird Checklist/Habitat Guide at the nearest visitor center, and ask a ranger for specific instructions. Then go hunting for the everglades avian attractions that intrigue you the most—like Mangrove Cuckoo, Antillean Nighthawk, Smooth-billed Ani, Snail Kite, and White-crowned Pigeon.

87. Bald Eagle
Haliaeetus leucocephalus
(L-35 W-84)

Huge size; dark brown body; white head and tail; yellow beak and legs. **Immature** Entirely brown with whitish wing linings and base of tail. Adult plumage is attained in 4–5 years over which time the head and tail become whiter, and remainder of body uniformly dark.

Habits Feeds primarily on fish.

Voice A descending "keee chip-chip-chip-chip."

Similar Species Immature Golden Eagle has well-defined white (not whitish) base of tail and white wing patches at base of primaries. Also, Golden Eagles show brownish feathering to the feet while Bald Eagles have bare, yellow legs.

Habitat Lakes, rivers, estuaries.

Abundance and Distribution Uncommon resident* in most of Florida; uncommon to rare winter resident (Sept.–Mar.) and rare to casual summer resident* (Apr.–Sept.) along the coastal plain of

Georgia, Alabama, Mississippi, and the western Florida Panhandle; rare transient, winter visitor, and summer visitor elsewhere in the region.

Where to Find Panther Swamp National Wildlife Refuge, Mississippi; Savannah National Wildlife Refuge, Georgia; Lake Guntersville State Park, Alabama; Cedar Keys National Wildlife Refuge, Florida.

Range Breeds across Canada and northern United States, south along coasts to Florida, California, and Texas; winters throughout breeding range from southern Canada southward, particularly along the coasts and at larger inland lakes.

88. Northern Harrier

Circus cyaneus
(L-19 W-42)

A slim, long-tailed, long-winged hawk; gray above; pale below with dark spots; white rump; yellow eye and cere; long, yellow legs. **Adult Female** Streaked dark brown and tan above; whitish below heavily streaked with brown; yellow eyes; pale yellowish cere; yellow legs; barred tail; white rump. **Immature** Like female but buffy below.

Habits Flies low over open areas, usually within a few feet of the ground, alternately flapping and gliding; wings at an angle during glides; often hovers just above the ground.

Voice A rapid, descending "cheek-cheek-cheek-cheek-cheek."

Similar Species Similar haunts and habits as Short-eared Owl, but white rump is distinctive.

Habitat Marshes, grasslands, estuaries, agricultural areas.

Abundance and Distribution Common to uncommon transient and winter resident (Sept.–May) throughout the Southeast. A few remain through the summer; has bred*.

Where to Find Fort Pulaski National Monument, Georgia; Oak Mountain State Park, Alabama; St. Andrews State Recreation Area, Florida; Hillside National Wildlife Refuge, Mississippi.

Range Breeds across boreal and temperate regions of Northern Hemisphere; winters in temperate and tropical zones.

89. Sharp-shinned Hawk

Accipiter striatus

(L-12 W-24)

Slate gray above; barred rusty and white below; gray crown with rusty face; red eye; yellow cere; barred tail; long, yellow legs; as in other accipiters, the female is much larger than the male. **Immature** Brown above; streaked brown and white on head, breast, and belly.

Habits All three accipiters (sharpshin, Cooper's, and goshawk) are distinguished from other hawks by their relatively short, broad wings and long tails, and by their behavior in flight, which is characterized by a series of rapid wingbeats followed by a short, flat-winged glide. They seldom soar except during migration. All three species are forest bird hunters.

Voice A rapid, high-pitched "kew-ki-ki-ki-ki-ki-ki," etc.

Similar Species The calls of the three similar species of accipiters are different; sharpshin has a squared tail (slightly rounded in the larger Cooper's Hawk); immature sharpshin tail has narrow and indistinct terminal white band (immature Cooper's terminal white tail band is broader and more distinct); head does not extend much beyond bend of wing in gliding sharpshin (head extends well beyond bend of wing in gliding Cooper's); immature sharpshin has heavy streaking on breast (immature Cooper's has finer streaking). The immature Merlin is also similar to the immature sharpshin, but has dark eyes (not red) and dark tail with thin, light bands (not broad light bands as in sharpshin).

Habitat Forests.

Abundance and Distribution Uncommon transient and winter resident (Sept.–Apr.) throughout the Southeast; has bred* in the mountains of north Georgia.

Where to Find Moccasin Creek State Park, Georgia; Cheaha State Park, Alabama; Noxubee National Wildlife Refuge, Mississippi; St. Joseph Peninsula State Park, Florida.

Range Breeds from subarctic Alaska and Canada to northern Argentina (except prairie regions and most of southern United States), also in Greater Antilles; winters from northern coastal regions and southern Canada south through breeding range.

90. Cooper's Hawk
Accipiter cooperii
(L-18 W-32)

Slate gray above; barred rusty and white below; gray crown with rusty face; red eye; yellow cere; barred tail; long, yellow legs. **Immature** Brown above; streaked brown and white on head, breast, and belly.

Habits All three accipiters (sharpshin, Cooper's and goshawk) are distinguished from other hawks by their relatively short, broad wings and long tails, and by their behavior in flight, which is characterized by a series of rapid wingbeats followed by a short, flat-winged glide. They seldom soar except during migration. All three species are forest bird hunters.

Voice A wheezy "peeew," repeated.

Similar Species The calls of the three similar species of accipiters are different; Cooper's has a rounded tail (square in the smaller sharpshin); immature Cooper's terminal white tail band is broad and distinct; immature sharpshin tail has narrow and indistinct terminal white band; head does not extend much beyond bend of wing in gliding sharpshin (head extends well beyond bend of wing in gliding Cooper's); immature Cooper's has relatively fine streaking on breast (immature sharpshin has heavier streaking).

Habitat Forests.

Abundance and Distribution Common transient (Sept.–Oct., Apr.), uncommon winter resident (Nov.–Mar.), and uncommon to rare summer resident* (May–Aug.) in Georgia, Alabama, and Mississippi; Uncommon to rare resident* in North and Central Florida; uncommon to rare transient and winter resident in South Florida and the Keys.

Where to Find Wassaw National Wildlife Refuge, Georgia; Eufaula National Wildlife Refuge, Alabama; St. Catherine Creek National Wildlife Refuge, Mississippi; Tall Timbers Research Station, Florida.

Range Breeds from southern Canada to northern Mexico; winters from northern United States to Honduras.

SUMMER
MIGRATION
WINTER
PERMANENT

91. Red-shouldered Hawk
Buteo lineatus
(L-19 W-39)

Mottled dark brown and white above with rusty shoulders; barred rusty and white below; tail dark with 3 or 4 narrow, whitish bars; brown eye; pale yellowish cere; yellow legs; in flight note brown

and white barring on flight feathers, pale white patch at base of primaries ("window"), and rusty wing linings. **Immature** Brown mottled with white above; buff streaked with brown on breast, barred on belly; rusty shoulders.

Habits Red-shouldered Hawks are relatively tame, often allowing close approach.

Voice A strident "ki-cheek ki-cheek ki-cheek keeew."

Similar Species Voice is distinctive. Immature is similar to other immature buteos but usually shows rusty shoulders; it is the only species in the region with a crescent-shaped wing "window" visible in flight; tail appears to be dark with light bars. The Red-tailed Hawk immature has unstreaked upper breast, and tail appears light with narrow, dark bars. Immature Rough-legged Hawk shows dark belly and light tail with dark, subterminal band. The immature Red-shouldered Hawk is also similar to the immature Broad-winged Hawk. Immature redshoulder often has reddish tinge on shoulders. Also, the redshoulder tail appears to be dark with light bands, while the broadwing appears to be white with dark bands.

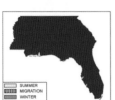

Habitat Riparian forest, woodlands, swamps.

Abundance and Distribution Common to uncommon resident* nearly throughout the Southeast except the Lower Keys, where rare to casual mainly as a spring transient.

Where to Find Chewalla Lake, Holly Springs National Forest, Mississippi; Ocmulgee National Monument, Georgia; Cheaha State Park, Alabama; Jonathan Dickinson State Park, Florida.

Range Breeds from southeastern Canada and the eastern United States south to central Mexico, also California; winters from central United States south through breeding range.

Kites, Hawks, Ospreys, Eagles

92. Broad-winged Hawk
Buteo platypterus
(L-16 W-35)

Dark brown above; barred rusty and white below; dark tail with 2 white bands equal in width to dark bands; brown eye; yellowish cere; yellow legs; in flight note whitish flight feathers with black tips; buffy wing linings. **Immature** Brown above; streaked brown and white below; tail narrowly barred with brown and white.

SUMMER
MIGRATION
WINTER
PERMANENT

Voice A high-pitched "ki-cheeeee," occasionally imitated by Blue Jays.

Similar Species The immature Red-shouldered Hawk is very similar to the immature Broad-winged Hawk. Immature redshoulder often has reddish tinge on shoulders. Also, the redshoulder tail appears to be dark with light bands, while the broadwing appears to be white with dark bands. Additionally, the soaring broadwing lacks the pale, crescent-shaped "wing window" near the outer tips of the primaries characteristic of the redshoulder.

Habitat Deciduous forests, but seen in migration kettles over any habitat.

Abundance and Distribution Common transient and summer resident* (Mar.–Oct.) in the highlands of Georgia and Alabama; common to uncommon transient (Sept.–Oct., Mar.–May) throughout the Southeast except peninsular Florida where rare; uncommon to rare summer resident* (May–Aug.) in the coastal plain of Georgia, Alabama, and Mississippi, the Panhandle, and North Florida; rare winter resident (Nov.–Mar.) in Central and South Florida and the Keys.

Where to Find Cloudland Canyon State Park, Georgia; DeSoto State Park, Alabama; Chewalla Lake, Holly Springs National Forest, Mississippi; Florida Caverns State Park, Florida.

Range Breeds across southern Canada from Alberta eastward and the eastern half of the United States south to Texas and Florida; winters from southern Mexico south to Brazil; resident in West Indies.

93. Short-tailed Hawk
Buteo brachyurus
(L-15 W-35)

Dark brown above; white below; dark brown head with white at base of beak; yellow cere and legs; chestnut patch on side of breast; finely barred tail with broad, dark subterminal band. **Dark Phase** Dark brown throughout; whitish forehead; in flight—wing linings are dark, flight feathers are light, barred with dark brown; tail as in light phase. **Immature, Light Phase** Mottled brown above; buffy white below with sparse brown streaking; tail finely barred. **Immature, Dark Phase** Dark brown mottled with buff above and below; finely barred tail.

Habitat Savanna, open woodlands.

Abundance and Distribution Uncommon to rare resident* in

SUMMER
MIGRATION
WINTER
PERMANENT

South Florida; rare summer resident* (Mar.–Sept.) in North and Central Florida; uncommon to rare winter resident (Oct.–Mar.), rare to casual in summer, in the Keys.

Where to Find Avon Park Bombing Range, Florida; Everglades National Park, Florida; Florida Keys National Wildlife Refuges, Florida.

Range Resident in South Florida and from northern Mexico to northern Argentina.

94. Swainson's Hawk
Buteo swainsoni
(L-20 W-50)

Brown above; reddish brown breast; buffy belly with sparse brown streaking on flanks; whitish chin and cere; yellowish legs; in flight note dark flight feathers, whitish wing linings; barred tail with broad, dark subterminal band. **Dark Phase** Entirely dark brown; tail as in light phase, usually paler toward base. **Immature, Light Phase** Dark above; mottled white and brown below; often with white forehead and dark patches on breast.

Habits Soars with wings slightly angled above the horizontal.

Voice A shrill, descending "keeeeeeee."

Habitat Prairies, savanna, thorn forest, desert scrub.

Abundance and Distribution Rare to casual winter resident (Oct.–Mar.) in South Florida and the Keys.

Where to Find Everglades National Park, Florida; Florida Keys National Wildlife Refuges, Florida.

Range Breeds in the deserts and Great Plains of western North America from Alaska and Canada south to northwestern Mexico; winters in southern South America.

95. Red-tailed Hawk
Buteo jamaicensis
(L-22 W-53)

A large hawk, extremely variable in plumage; most common adult plumage is mottled brown and white above; white below with dark streaks and speckling across belly; rusty tail (appears whitish from below); in flight, dark forewing lining contrasts with generally light underwing. **Immature** Mottled brown and white above; streaked

brown and white below; brown tail finely barred with grayish white. **Light Phase (Krider's)** Much paler; pale orange tale. **Dark Phase (Harlan's)** Dark throughout with some white speckling; dark tail, whitish at base, darker at tip with rusty wash.

Voice A hoarse, drawn-out screech: "ke-aaaaaaaah."

Similar Species Rusty tail is distinctive for adults. Immature is similar to other immature buteos but usually shows unstreaked upper breast and light-colored tail with several dark bars; immature redshoulder has streaked breast, rusty shoulders, crescent-shaped wing "window" in flight, and tail appears to be dark with light bars. **Immature** Rough-legged Hawk shows dark belly and light tail with dark, subterminal band.

Habitat Open areas, woodlands.

Abundance and Distribution Common to uncommon resident* nearly throughout the Southeast; rare winter resident (Oct.–Apr.) in the Florida Keys.

Where to Find Piedmont National Wildlife Refuge, Georgia; Little River Canyon National Preserve, Alabama; Chassahowitzka National Wildlife Refuge, Florida; Vicksburg National Military Park, Mississippi.

Range Breeds from subarctic of Alaska and Canada to Panama; winters northern United States south through breeding range; resident in West Indies.

96. Golden Eagle
Aquila chrysaetos
(L-34 W-71)

Huge; dark brown with golden wash on top and back of head and shaggy neck; legs feathered to feet; appears entirely dark in flight. **Immature** Dark brown with white patch at base of primaries and basal half of tail white.

Voice A rapid series of nasal chips.

Similar Species Immature Golden Eagle has well-defined white (not whitish as in Bald Eagle) base of tail and white wing patches at base of primaries; also has golden sheen to nape of neck.

Habitat Open areas.

Abundance and Distribution Rare winter visitor (Oct.–Mar.) in Georgia, Alabama, Mississippi, and the Florida Panhandle; casual elsewhere in Florida.

Where to Find Savannah National Wildlife Refuge, Georgia; Tallahatchie National Wildlife Refuge, Mississippi; Eufaula National Wildlife Refuge, Alabama.

Range Breeds primarily in open and mountainous regions of boreal and temperate zones in Northern Hemisphere; winters in central and southern portions of breeding range.

Falcons and Caracaras
Family Falconidae

With the exception of the caracara, the falcons are sleek birds with pointed wings and long, square tails.

97. Crested Caracara
Caracara cheriway
(L-23 W-50)

Black body; black, crested crown; white face and neck; white breast barred with black; red cere and eyering; bluish bill; long, yellow legs; in flight note white patches on basal half of primaries and white (actually finely barred) tail with dark terminal band. **Immature** Buffy neck and breast.

Habits Often feeds on carrion along the road.

Voice A low croak.

Similar Species The whitish neck, breast, primaries, and tail with black bar are distinctive.

Habitat Thorn forest, savanna, prairie, arid scrub.

Abundance and Distribution Uncommon to rare and local resident* in Central Florida; scattered records elsewhere in the region.

SUMMER
MIGRATION
WINTER
PERMANENT

Where to Find Lake Kissimmee State Park, Florida; Driggers Road, Lake Placid, Florida; Three Lakes Wildlife Management Area, Lake Marian Highlands, Florida.

Range From the southwestern United States to southern Argentina; also South Florida and Cuba.

98. American Kestrel
Falco sparverius
(L-10 W-22)

A small falcon; gray crown; black and white facial pattern; orange buff back and underparts spotted with brown; blue-gray wings; orange tail with black subterminal bar edged in white. **Female** Rusty back and wings barred with brown.

Habits Perches or hovers a few feet off the ground while foraging; often seen on telephone wires along the road.

Voice A rapid, high-pitched "kle-kle-kle-kle-kle," etc.

Similar Species The Merlin shows a distinctly dark tail barred with white; lacks the facial pattern of the kestrel.

Habitat Open areas.

Abundance and Distribution Common winter resident (Sept.–Apr.) and rare summer resident* throughout the southeast, except highlands where absent as a breeder; uncommon to rare summer resident* (May–Aug.) in the Panhandle and the northern half of the Florida Peninsula.

Where to Find Seminole State Park, Georgia; Fort Toulouse, Alabama; St. Andrews State Recreation Area, Florida; Natchez Trace Parkway, Mississippi.

Range Breeds nearly throughout Western Hemisphere from subarctic Alaska and Canada to southern Argentina, West Indies; winters from north temperate regions south through breeding range.

99. Merlin
Falco columbarius
(L-11 W-25)

A small falcon; slate above, buffy below with dark brown spots and streaks; white throat; brown eyes, yellow cere and legs; black tail, white at base, with two white bars and white terminal edging. **Female** Dark brown above.

Habits A bird hunter; sallies from low perches, using surprise and speed to capture prey.

Voice "Kwe kwe kwe kwe kwe," etc.

Similar Species Merlin shows a distinctly dark tail barred with white; lacks facial pattern of kestrel.

Falcons, Caracaras

Habitat Open woodlands, hedgerows, second growth; often hunts small birds in trees or shrubs bordering water in winter.

Abundance and Distribution Uncommon to rare transient (Oct.–Nov., Mar.–Apr.; more numerous in fall) and winter resident (Nov.–Mar.) throughout the Southeast; most numerous along the coast.

Where to Find Sapelo Island National Estuarine Research Reserve, Georgia; J. N. "Ding" Darling National Wildlife Refuge, Florida; Blakely Island, Alabama; Dahomey National Wildlife Refuge, Mississippi.

Range Breeds across boreal and north temperate regions of Old and New World; winters in south temperate and tropical zones.

100. Peregrine Falcon
Falco peregrinus
(L-18 W-40)

THREATENED. A large falcon; dark gray above; white below with spotting and barring on belly and thighs; black crown and cheek with white neck patch; brown eye; yellow eyering, cere, and legs; in flight note large size, long pointed wings, long tail, whitish underparts finely barred and spotted; black and white facial pattern. **Immature** Dark brown above; buffy below spotted and streaked with brown; has facial pattern of adult.

SUMMER
MIGRATION
WINTER
PERMANENT

Habits Forages by flying with swift, powerful wingbeats, well up in the air, then stooping on prey.

Voice A rapid "kee kee kee kee."

Habitat Open areas, usually near water.

Abundance and Distribution Common fall transient (Sept.–Oct.) in the Keys; uncommon to rare transient (Sept.–Oct., Mar.–Apr.) elsewhere along the coast throughout the Southeast; rare to casual winter resident (Oct.–Mar.) in Florida and other Gulf coastal areas; casual in summer.

Where to Find Blackbeard Island National Wildlife Refuge, Georgia; Everglades National Park, Florida; Meaher State Park, Alabama; Gulf Islands National Seashore, Mississippi.

Range Breeds (at least formerly) in boreal and temperate regions of the Northern Hemisphere; winters mainly in the tropics.

Rails, Coots, and Gallinules
Order Gruiformes
Family Rallidae

Except for the ubiquitous, ducklike coot, the rallids are secretive marsh birds, heard more often than seen. They have cone-shaped or long, narrow bills, short, rounded wings, short tails, and long toes for support in walking on floating vegetation.

101. Yellow Rail
Coturnicops noveboracensis
(L-7 W-13)

A small (cowbird-sized) rail; dark brown with tawny stripes above; dark brown crown; broad tawny eyebrow; dark brown mask; whitish chin; tawny underparts barred with black on the flanks; short, yellowish bill and pale legs; in flight (a rarely observed event) shows white secondaries.

Habits Extremely secretive.

Voice "Tik tik tik-tik-tik tik tik tik-tik-tik," etc., like hitting two stones together.

Habitat Wet prairies, marshes.

Abundance and Distribution Rare to casual transient and winter resident (Sept.–May) nearly throughout the Southeast in marshes along the immediate coast; inland on the Florida Peninsula.

Where to Find Gulf State Park, Alabama; Cumberland Island National Seashore, Georgia; Avon Park Bombing Range, Florida; Mississippi Sandhill Crane National Wildilfe Refuge, Mississippi.

Range Breeds in east and central Canada and northeastern and north-central United States; winters along the southern Atlantic and Gulf coasts of United States; resident in central Mexico.

Figure 22. The Mississippi Sandhill Crane National Wildlife Refuge, near Biloxi on the Mississippi Gulf coast, was created to protect an endangered breeding population of these birds, but many other species can be found there as well.

102. Black Rail
Laterallus jamaicensis
(L-6 W-10)

A tiny (sparrow-sized) rail; dark grayish black with chestnut nape and black and white barring on flanks; short, black bill.

Habits Secretive.

Voice "Tic-ee-toonk."

SUMMER
MIGRATION
WINTER
PERMANENT

Habitat Wet prairies, marshes.

Abundance and Distribution Rare transient (Oct., Apr.–May) along the immediate coast throughout the Southeast; rare to casual summer resident* (May–Sept.) along the Georgia, Mississippi, Alabama, Florida Panhandle, and North Florida coasts; rare to casual resident* in Central and South Florida and the Keys.

Where to Find Everglades National Park, Florida; Wassaw National Wildlife Refuge, Georgia; Dauphin Island, Alabama; Gulf Islands National Seashore, Mississippi.

Range Breeds locally in California, Kansas, and along the east coast from New York to Texas, also West Indies, Central and South America; winters along Gulf coast and in tropical breeding range.

103. Clapper Rail
Rallus longirostris
(L-13 W-20)

A large rail; streaked brown and tan above; buffy below with gray and white barring on flanks; head and neck buffy with dark crown; long, pinkish or yellowish bill; pale greenish legs.

Voice "Chik chik chik chik chik," etc., like hitting a rock with a metal rod.

Similar Species King Rail inhabits fresh water (occasionally brackish) marshes—not salt marshes, and is rustier overall, darker barred on flanks, has black lores. However, plumage in both species is variable, and they are known to interbreed.

Habitat Salt and brackish marshes.

Abundance and Distribution Common resident* in salt and brackish marsh throughout the Southeast; casual inland in peninsular Florida.

Where to Find Crooked River State Park, Georgia; Gulf State Park, Alabama; Fort Caroline National Memorial/Timucuan Ecological and Historic Preserve; Gulf Islands National Seashore, Mississippi.

Range Resident along coast from Connecticut to Belize, California to southern Mexico; West Indies and much of coastal South America to southeastern Brazil and Peru.

104. King Rail
Rallus elegans
(L-15 W-22)

A large rail; streaked brown and rusty above; tawny below with black and white barring on flanks; head and neck tawny with dark crown and darkish stripe through eye; long bill with dark upper and pinkish or yellowish lower mandible; pale, reddish legs.

Voice A series of low grunts: "ih ih ih ih ih," etc.

Similar Species King Rail inhabits fresh water (occasionally brackish) marshes—not salt marshes, and is rustier overall, darker barred on flanks, has black lores. However, plumage in both species is variable, and they are known to interbreed.

Habitat Freshwater marshes.

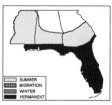

Abundance and Distribution Uncommon to rare resident* in fresh water marshes along the coastal plain of Georgia, Alabama,

Mississippi, and Florida; most withdraw in winter (Oct.–Mar.) from inland areas; casual transient in the Florida Keys.

Where to Find Shepard State Park, Mississippi; Savannah National Wildlife Refuge, Georgia; Gulf State Park, Alabama; Lake Woodruff National Wildlife Refuge, Florida.

Range Breeds across the eastern half of the United States south to central Mexico; winters along the coast from Georgia to Texas and south to southern Mexico; resident in Cuba.

105. Virginia Rail
Rallus limicola
(L-10 W-14)

Similar to the King Rail but about half the size; streaked brown and rusty above; tawny below with black and white barring on flanks; gray head with rusty crown; white throat; long reddish bill; pale legs.

Voice "Kik kik kik ki-deek ki-deek ki-deek," etc.

Similar Species The smaller Virginia Rail has gray face (tawny in larger King Rail) and tawny throat (white in King Rail).

SUMMER
MIGRATION
WINTER
PERMANENT

Habitat Freshwater and brackish marshes.

Abundance and Distribution Uncommon to rare winter resident (Sept.–May) in marshes mainly along the coastal plain in Georgia, Alabama, Mississippi, the Panhandle, North, and Central Florida; uncommon to rare transient (Sept.–Oct., Mar.–Apr.) through the piedmont and highlands; scarcer in South Florida and absent from the Keys; casual in summer*.

Where to Find Bon Secour National Wildlife Refuge, Alabama; Gulf Islands National Seashore, Mississippi; Arrowhead Public Fishing Area, Georgia; St. Andrews State Recreation Area, Florida.

Range Breeds locally from southern Canada to southern South America; winters along coast and in subtropical and tropical portions of breeding range.

106. Sora
Porzana carolina
(L-9 W-14)

A medium-sized rail; streaked brown and rusty above; grayish below with gray and white barring on flanks; gray head with rusty crown; black at base of bill; black throat and upper breast; short, yellow bill;

Figure 23. "... with a step I stand on the firm-packed sand, free, by a world of marsh that borders a world of seas ..." So wrote Sidney Lanier in "The Marshes of Glynn," a tribute to the woodlands, marshes, and beaches of Glynn County, Georgia, written in 1879. As this photo of the mouth of the South Brunswick River shows, the marshes are still there, and they still serve as an excellent place to hunt for common but elusive species like Clapper, Virginia, and Sora rails, as well as rarities like Yellow and Black rails.

SUMMER
MIGRATION
WINTER
PERMANENT

greenish legs. **Female** Amount of black on throat and breast reduced. **Immature** Browner overall, lacks black on throat and breast.

Voice "Ku-week," also a long descending series of whistles.

Similar Species Same size and habitat preferences as Virginia Rail but note short, yellowish, cone-shaped bill in Sora (reddish and long in Virginia Rail).

Habitat Fresh and brackish water marshes.

Abundance and Distribution Common to uncommon transient (Sept.–Oct., Apr.–May) throughout the Southeast; common to rare winter resident (Nov.–Apr.) in Florida and along the coast in Alabama, Mississippi, and Georgia.

Where to Find Weeks Bay National Estuarine Research Reserve, Alabama; Fort Caroline National Memorial/Timucuan Ecological and Historic Preserve, Florida; South Brunswick River, Georgia; Yazoo National Wildlife Refuge, Mississippi.

Range Breeds from central Canada to southern United States; winters along coast and from southern United States to northern South America and West Indies.

107. Purple Gallinule
Porphyrio martinica
(L-13 W-23)

A large rail with short, cone-shaped bill and extremely long toes; iridescent green back; purple head and underparts; blue frontal shield of naked skin on forehead; red bill with yellow tip; yellow legs. **Immature** Buffy overall, darker on back.

Habits The extremely long toes enable this rail to walk on floating vegetation without sinking.

Voice A chickenlike "cuk cuk cuk cuk cuk-kik cuk-kik," etc.

Similar Species Clapper and King rails have long, pointed (not short, cone-shaped) bills; immature Common Moorhen is grayish rather than brownish, and shows white edging along folded wing.

Habitat Freshwater marshes.

Abundance and Distribution Uncommon to rare summer resident* (Mar.–Oct.) in the Panhandle and North Florida and along the coastal plain in Georgia, Mississippi, and Alabama; scarce or absent in these areas in winter; uncommon to rare resident* in Central and South Florida.

Where to Find Fort Pulaski National Monument, Georgia; Jaycee Park, Lake Okeechobee, Florida; Tallahatchie National Wildlife Refuge, Mississippi; Gulf State Park, Alabama.

Range Breeds from the eastern United States south to northern Argentina, West Indies; winters from southern Gulf states south through the breeding range.

108. Common Moorhen
Gallinula chloropus
(L-14 W-23)

A large rail with short, cone-shaped bill and extremely long toes; entirely sooty gray with white edging along wing and white undertail coverts; red frontal shield of naked skin on forehead; red bill with yellow tip; greenish legs. **Winter** Similar to Summer but with olive or dull reddish brown bill, frontal shield, and legs.

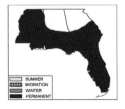

Habits The extremely long toes enable this rail to walk on floating vegetation without sinking; swims more than most other rails.

Voice Low croaks and whiny, high-pitched squeaks.

Similar Species Winter and juvenile Common Moorhen show white edging along folded wing, which American Coot lacks.

Habitat Fresh water marshes.

Abundance and Distribution Common to uncommon resident* along the coastal plain of Georgia, Mississippi, Alabama, and the Panhandle; mainly a summer resident* in the interior; common resident* throughout peninsular Florida, although scarcer in the Keys.

Where to Find Harris Neck National Wildlife Refuge, Georgia; St. Andrews State Recreation Area, Florida; Gulf Islands National Seashore, Mississippi; Eufaula National Wildlife Refuge, Alabama.

Range Breeds locally in temperate and tropical regions of the world; winters mainly in subtropical and tropical zones.

109. American Coot
Fulica americana
(L-16 W-26)

A large, black rail, more ducklike than rail-like in appearance and behavior; white bill with dark tip; red eye; greenish legs and lobed toes. **Immature** Paler; pale gray bill.

Habits Swims in open water, tipping and diving for food instead of skulking through reeds like most rails; pumps head forward while swimming.

Voice Various croaks and catlike mews.

Similar Species Juvenile coot lacks white wing edging of Common Moorhen.

Habitat Ponds, lakes, marshes, bays.

Abundance and Distribution Common to uncommon winter resident (Sept.–May) throughout the Southeast; uncommon to rare summer resident (May–Sept., has bred*) in Florida and elsewhere in the region along the coastal plain.

Where to Find Pearl River Waterfowl Refuge, Mississippi; Seminole State Park, Georgia; Wheeler National Wildlife Refuge, Alabama; Canaveral National Seashore, Florida.

Range Breeds from central Canada to Nicaragua and West Indies; winters along coast and from central United States to northern Colombia, West Indies.

Limpkins
Family Aramidae

The family has only one species as a member, the Limpkin; a dark, long-legged marsh bird, night-heron-like in appearance.

110. Limpkin
Aramus guarauna
(L-27 W-42)

Dark brown body with broad white streaking on back, wings, and breast; finely streaked on neck; head a pale brown; red eye; bill long, slightly down-turned, orange at base, dark at tip; dark legs.

Habits The name derives from its odd, limping, awkward, jerky gait during which the tail is pumped upward at each step; mainly crepuscular and nocturnal.

Voice A loud, ringing, gooselike honking: "kow," also "keee-ooow."

Similar Species Immature night-herons have short, heavy bills; immature ibises have much longer, down-curved bills.

Habitat Marshes, swamps, lagoons, mangroves.

Abundance and Distribution Uncommon to rare resident* throughout peninsular Florida except extreme North Florida where casual; rare to casual in the Panhandle except extreme west where casual or absent.

Where to Find Kaliga Park, Florida; Wakulla Springs State Park, Florida; Altamaha River/Atkinson Tract, Georgia; Jaycee Park, Lake Okeechobee, Florida.

Range Florida; southern Mexico to northern Argentina; Greater Antilles.

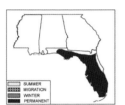

SUMMER
MIGRATION
WINTER
PERMANENT

Cranes
Family Gruidae

Long-legged, long-necked birds of marsh and grasslands. Unlike herons, cranes fly with legs and neck extended. Unlike ducks and geese, they often glide in flight.

111. Sandhill Crane

Grus canadensis
(L-42 W-74)

A tall, long-necked, long-legged, gray-bodied bird with bustle-like tail; black legs; red crown. **Immature** Rusty tinge to gray body; lacks red crown.

Habits Normally in family groups of two adults and one or two young.

Voice A loud croaking bugle: "crrrrahh."

Similar Species The larger Whooping Crane is white (tinged with rust in immature), not gray as in Sandhill Crane.

SUMMER
MIGRATION
WINTER
PERMANENT

Habitat Prairie, savanna, grasslands, pasture, croplands, estuaries, lakes, ponds.

Abundance and Distribution Uncommon to rare transient (Nov.–Dec., Feb.–Mar.) across most of Georgia and eastern Alabama; uncommon resident* at the Mississippi Sandhill Crane National Wildlife Refuge in Mississippi, the Okefenokee Swamp region of southern Georgia, and in most of peninsular Florida; uncommon to rare winter resident (Nov.–Apr.) in the Panhandle and extreme North Florida; casual in the Keys.

Where to Find Mississippi Sandhill Crane National Wildlife Refuge, Mississippi; Kaliga Park, Florida; Okefenokee National Wildlife Refuge, Georgia; Paynes Prairie State Preserve, Florida.

Range Formerly bred over much of North America; now breeds in Alaska and northern Canada, south locally in the northwestern and north-central United States, Mississippi (endangered population), and Florida; winters from the southern United States to southern Mexico.

112. Whooping Crane

Grus americana
(L-51 W-87)

ENDANGERED. A very tall, long-necked, long-legged, white-bodied bird; black legs; red, black, and white facial pattern. **Immature** Rusty tinge to white body, especially on neck; lacks facial pattern of adult.

Habits Normally in family groups of one or two adults and one or two immatures.

Voice A loud, gooselike honk.

Similar Species The larger Whooping Crane is white (tinged with rust in immature), not gray as in Sandhill Crane

Habitat Estuaries, prairie marshes, savanna, grassland, pasture, cropland.

Abundance and Distribution Introduced in Three Lakes Wildlife Management Area, Kissimmee Prairie, Osceola County, Florida, in 1993.

Where to Find Three Lakes Wildlife Management Area, Florida.

Range The historic range extended from the Arctic coast south to central Mexico, and from Utah east to New Jersey, into South Carolina, Georgia, and Florida. Current nesting range of the self-sustaining natural wild population is restricted to Wood Buffalo National Park in Canada; current wintering ground of this population is restricted to the Texas Gulf Coast at Aransas National Wildlife Refuge and vicinity. In 2004, this population was estimated at 213 individuals.

Plovers
Order Charadriiformes
Family Charadriidae

Plovers are rather compact shorebirds with relatively long legs, short necks, and short, thick bills.

113. Black-bellied Plover
Pluvialis squatarola
(L-12 W-25)

A Killdeer-sized plover; checked black and white on back; white crown, nape, and shoulder; black face, throat, and breast; white belly and undertail coverts. **Winter** Heavy black bill contrasts with whitish at base of bill; pale eyebrow; crown and back brownish mottled with white; breast is mottled with brown; belly white; black legs.

Voice A gull-like "keee keee kee-a-wee keee," etc.

Similar Species The Black-bellied Plover has black "armpits" (axillaries—visible only in flight), which golden-plover species lack.

Habitat Beaches, bays, mudflats, estuaries.

Abundance and Distribution Common to rare transient (Sept.–Oct., Apr.–May) throughout the coastal plain; common winter

resident (Aug.–May), mainly along the coast; uncommon to rare in summer (Jun.–Jul.) (non-breeding) along the coast.

Where to Find Tybee Island Beach, Georgia; Canaveral National Seashore, Florida; Bon Secour National Wildlife Refuge, Alabama; Buccaneer State Park, Mississippi.

Range Breeds in the high Arctic of Old and New World; winters along temperate and tropical coasts of the world.

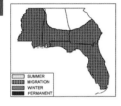

114. American Golden-Plover
Pluvialis dominica
(L-11 W-23)

A Killdeer-sized plover; checked black, white, and gold on back and crown; white "headband" running from forehead, over eye and down side of neck; black face and underparts. **Winter** Heavy black bill contrasts with white at base of bill; pale eyebrow; crown and back brown and white often flecked with gold; underparts white, speckled with brown on breast; gray legs.

Voice A whistled "kew-wee."

Similar Species The American Golden-Plover lacks the black axillaries which show clearly on the Black-bellied Plover in flight.

Habitat Intertidal mudflats; beaches.

Abundance and Distribution Rare transient (Aug.–Nov., Mar.–Apr.) throughout Florida and along the coastal plain of Georgia,

Figure 24. St. Marks Lighthouse at the eponymous North Florida refuge serves as a picturesque backdrop to rich wetland habitats. Common Goldeneye, Hooded and Red-breasted mergansers, Bufflehead, and Greater Scaup are among the many anatine winter visitors.

Mississippi, and Alabama; rare to casual winter visitor (Dec.–Feb.) throughout Florida.

Where to Find Harris Neck National Wildlife Refuge, Georgia; Eufaula National Wildlife Refuge, Alabama; St. Marks National Wildlife Refuge, Florida; Gulf Islands National Seashore, Mississippi.

Range Breeds in high Arctic of New World; winters in South America.

115. Snowy Plover
Charadrius alexandrinus
(L-7 W-14)

A small plover; grayish brown crown, back, and wings; white forehead, face, collar, and underparts; broad, dark line behind eye; partial dark band across breast, broken in the middle; black bill; black legs.

Immature Similar to adult but paler with dark gray legs.

Voice A low, whistled "pew-weet."

Similar Species The other small, pale plover (Piping) has a white rump, visible in flight (brown in Snowy Plover); adult Piping has dull orange legs, even in winter (Snowy's are black).

Habitat Mudflats, estuaries, bays.

Abundance and Distribution Uncommon to rare and declining resident* along the Gulf Coast of Florida (mainly the Panhandle), Alabama, and Mississippi.

Where to Find Bon Secour National Wildlife Refuge, Alabama; Gulf Islands National Seashore, Mississippi; St. George Island State Park, Florida.

Range Breeds locally in temperate and tropical regions of the world; winters mainly in subtropical and tropical areas.

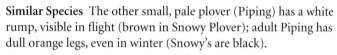

116. Wilson's Plover
Charadrius wilsonia
(L-8 W-16)

A smallish plover with a heavy, black bill; brown back and head; white forehead; black lores; white chin and collar; black band across throat; white underparts; pinkish legs. **Female and Immature** Brown breast band.

Voice "Peet peet peet," etc.

Similar Species The smaller, short-billed Semipalmated Plover has orange (not pinkish) legs.

Habitat Bays, mudflats.

Abundance and Distribution Uncommon to rare summer resident* (Apr.–Oct.) along the immediate coast in Georgia, Alabama, Mississippi, and the Panhandle; uncommon to rare resident* along the coast elsewhere in Florida.

Where to Find Hobe Sound National Wildlife Refuge, Florida; Cumberland Island National Seashore, Georgia; Bon Secour National Wildlife Refuge, Alabama; Shepard State Park, Mississippi.

Range Breeds along both coasts from northwestern Mexico in the west and Virginia in the east south to northern South America; West Indies; winters mainly in tropical portions of breeding range.

117. Semipalmated Plover
Charadrius semipalmatus
(L-7 W-15)

A small plover; brown back and head; white forehead; white postorbital stripe; orange eyering; orange bill, black at tip; black lores; white chin and collar; black band across throat; white underparts; orange or yellow legs. **Winter** Brown breast band; dull, dark bill (may show some orange at base). **Immature** Similar to adult but eyering yellow, bill black at tip, brown at base, legs brown anteriorly, yellow posteriorly.

Voice A whistled "tew-wee."

Similar Species The other small plovers occurring here are paler and have incomplete breast bands. The Wilson's Plover is larger, heavy billed, and has flesh-colored legs (orange legs in adult Semipalmated Plover, grayish in juvenile).

Habitat Estuarine mudflats, salt flats, beaches, bayshores.

Abundance and Distribution Common to rare transient (Aug.–Oct., Apr.–May) throughout the coastal plain; common winter resident (Aug.–May), mainly along the coast; rare in summer (Jun.–Jul., nonbreeding) along the coast.

Where to Find Wassaw National Wildlife Refuge, Georgia; J. N. "Ding" Darling National Wildlife Refuge, Florida; Dauphin Island, Alabama; US 90 between Gulfport and Biloxi, Mississippi.

Range Breeds in high Arctic of North America; winters mainly along temperate and tropical coasts from Georgia and California to southern South America, West Indies.

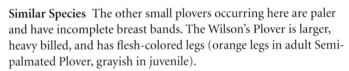

118. Piping Plover
Charadrius melodus
(L-7 W-15)

THREATENED. A small plover; grayish brown crown, back and wings; white forehead with distinct black band across forecrown; white chin, throat collar, and underparts; partial or complete black band across breast; orange bill tipped with black; orange legs; white rump. **Winter** Lacks black breast and crown bands; dark bill.

Voice "Peep," repeated.

Similar Species Semipalmated is dark brown on back (not pale) and has a complete breast band, even in winter.

Habitat Beaches.

Abundance and Distribution Uncommon to rare winter resident (Sept.–May), mainly along the immediate coast, throughout the Southeast; rare to casual in summer (May–Aug., nonbreeding).

Where to Find Blackbeard Island National Wildlife Refuge, Georgia; Hobe Sound National Wildlife Refuge, Florida; Bon Secour National Wildlife Refuge, Alabama; West Ship Island, Mississippi; Honeymoon Island State Park, Florida.

Range Breeds locally in southeastern and south-central Canada, northeastern and north-central United States; winters along the coast from South Carolina to Veracruz, also in West Indies.

Plovers

119. Killdeer
Charadrius vociferus
(L-10 W-20)

A medium-sized plover; brown back and head; orange rump; white forehead; white postorbital stripe; orange eyering; dark bill; black lores; white chin and collar; two black bands across throat and upper breast; white underparts; pale legs.

Habits Feigns broken wing when young or nest are approached.

Voice "Kill de-er," also various peeps.

Similar Species The Killdeer is the only plover in this region with two black bars across the breast; others have one or none.

Habitat Open areas.

Abundance and Distribution Common to uncommon resident* throughout the Southeast.

Where to Find Chassahowitzka National Wildlife Refuge,

Florida; Blakely Island, Alabama; Rum Creek Wildlife Management Area, Georgia; Wall Doxey State Park, Mississippi.

Range Breeds from subarctic Canada and Alaska south to central Mexico, Greater Antilles, western South America; winters along coast from Washington and Massachusetts, and inland from southern United States, south to northern and western South America, West Indies.

Oystercatchers
Family Haematopodidae

Stout, gull-like birds; black or black and white with a long, brilliant orange bill.

120. American Oystercatcher
Haematopus palliatus
(L-19 W-35)

Gull-sized bird; black hood; long, bright orange bill; red eyering; brown back; white breast and belly; pinkish legs; broad white bars on secondaries and white base of tail show in flight. **Immature** Brown head; dull orange bill.

Habits Feeds on oysters and other mussels by prying open the shells .

Voice A strident "weeep."

Habitat Beaches, bays.

Abundance and Distribution Uncommon to rare resident* along the immediate Atlantic coast in Georgia, North and Central Florida, and the Central Florida Gulf coast north to the Panhandle, also coastal Alabama, and Mississippi; locally uncommon to casual in South Florida and the Keys.

Where to Find Cumberland Island National Seashore, Georgia; Bon Secour National Wildlife Refuge, Alabama; Upper Tampa Bay Regional Park, Florida.

Range Breeds locally along coast from northwestern Mexico and Massachusetts south to southern South America, West Indies.

Avocets and Stilts

Family Recurvirostridae

A small family of medium-sized, long-legged, long-billed, long-necked shorebirds.

121. Black-necked Stilt
Himantopus mexicanus
(L-14 W-27)

Spindly shorebird with long neck, needle-like bill, and long legs; black head, nape, and back; white at base of bill, throat, and underparts; white patch behind eye; pink legs. **Female** Similar to male but paler. **Immature** Brown rather than black.

Voice A rapid, buzzy "keer-keer-keer," etc.

Habitat Mudflats, marshes, estuaries, ponds.

Abundance and Distribution Common to rare summer resident* (Apr.–Sept.) in Florida and along the immediate coast in Georgia, Alabama, and Mississippi; rare and local winter resident (Oct.–Apr.) in Central and South Florida.

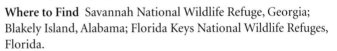

Where to Find Savannah National Wildlife Refuge, Georgia; Blakely Island, Alabama; Florida Keys National Wildlife Refuges, Florida.

Range Breeds locally in western United States and along coast in east from Massachusetts south locally along coasts of Middle and South America to northern Argentina, West Indies; winters from North Carolina south through breeding range.

122. American Avocet
Recurvirostra americana
(L-18 W-32)

Long-legged, long-necked shorebird with long, upturned bill; black and white back and wings; white belly; rusty orange head; whitish at base of bill; gray legs. **Winter** Head and neck mostly whitish with little rusty tinge.

Habits Forages by swinging submerged bill from side to side as it walks along.

Voice "Kleet kleet kleet," etc.

Habitat Estuaries, ponds, lakes, mudflats, flooded pastures, bays.

SUMMER
MIGRATION
WINTER
PERMANENT

Abundance and Distribution Uncommon to rare transient and winter resident (Sept.–Apr.) and rare and local summer resident (May–Aug., nonbreeding) in Central and South Florida and the Keys; uncommon to rare transient (Aug.–Nov., Feb.–Apr.) and rare winter resident (Dec.–Jan.) in the Panhandle and North Florida and along the immediate coast in Mississippi, Alabama, and Georgia.

Where to Find McKay Bay Nature Park, Florida; Blakely Island, Alabama; Noxubee National Wildlife Refuge, Mississippi; Jekyll Island, Georgia.

Range Breeds western and central Canada south through western United States to northern Mexico; winters southern United States to southern Mexico.

Sandpipers
Family Scolopacidae

Scolopacids constitute a diverse assemblage of shorebirds. Breeding plumage for sandpipers is worn for only a short time, mostly on Arctic breeding grounds. As a result it is the winter plumage that is most often critical for identification of shorebirds in the Southeast. Many second-year birds and other nonbreeders remain on the wintering ground or migration route through the summer.

123. Greater Yellowlegs
Tringa melanoleuca
(L-14 W-25)

Mottled grayish brown above; head, breast, and flanks white heavily streaked with grayish brown; white belly and rump; long, yellow legs; bill long, often slightly upturned and darker at tip than at base. **Winter** Paler overall; streaking on breast and head is reduced.

Voice Call: rapid sequence of three descending notes, "tew tew tew."

Similar Species The Greater Yellowlegs is noticeably larger than the Lesser Yellowlegs; the descending 3-note call of the Greater is quite different from the Lesser's "pew" call, which is generally given as a single note or series of notes on the same

pitch; Greater's bill is longer, thicker, slightly upturned and dusky (rather than dark) for basal third of lower mandible.

Habitat Mudflats, estuaries, marshes, prairies, flooded agricultural fields.

Abundance and Distribution Common to uncommon transient (Aug.–Oct., Mar.–Apr.), uncommon to rare winter resident (Nov.–Feb.), and rare to casual summer resident (May–Jul.) nearly throughout the Southeast except in the highlands where casual or absent.

Where to Find Harris Neck National Wildlife Refuge, Georgia; Eufaula National Wildlife Refuge, Alabama; Hobe Sound National Wildlife Refuge, Florida; Arkabutla Lake, Mississippi.

Range Breeds in northern Canada and Alaska; winters coastal United States south to southern South America, West Indies.

124. Lesser Yellowlegs
Tringa flavipes
(L-11 W-20)

Mottled grayish brown above; head, breast and flanks white heavily streaked with grayish brown; white belly and rump; yellow legs. **Winter** Paler overall; streaking on breast and head is reduced.

Voice Single "pew" alarm note, repeated.

Similar Species The Lesser Yellowlegs is significantly smaller than the Greater Yellowlegs; the "pew" call of the Lesser is quite different from the Greater's 3-note, descending sequence; Lesser's bill is shorter, thinner, straight, and dark to the base (rather than yellowish or dusky for the basal third of lower mandible).

Habitat Mudflats, pond borders, flooded prairies, swales, estuaries.

Abundance and Distribution Common to uncommon transient (Aug.–Oct., Mar.–Apr.), uncommon to rare winter resident (Nov.–Feb.) and rare to casual summer resident (May–Jul.) nearly throughout the Southeast except in the highlands where casual or absent.

Where to Find Chassahowitzka National Wildlife Refuge, Florida; Blakely Island, Alabama; Arkabutla Lake, Mississippi; Grand Bay Wildlife Management Area, Georgia.

Range Breeds northern Canada and Alaska; winters from Atlantic (South Carolina) and Pacific (southern California) coasts of United States south to southern South America, West Indies.

Sandpipers

125. Solitary Sandpiper
Tringa solitaria
(L-9 W-17)

Dark gray back and wings with white spotting; heavily streaked with grayish brown on head and breast; white eyering; long, greenish legs; tail dark in center, barred white on outer portions. **Winter** Streaking on head and breast reduced or faint.

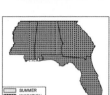

Habits Often bobs while foraging.

Voice Call: a high-pitched "tseet-eet."

Similar Species Spotted Sandpiper is found in similar habitats; however it bobs almost continuously, shows white on wings in flight (no white on wings in Solitary), has a pale eyebrow (Solitary has eyering), shorter legs, and no white spotting on folded wings; tail barring is much more prominent in the Solitary. Stilt Sandpiper and yellowlegs show white rump in flight (dark in Solitary).

Habitat Ponds, rivers, lakes.

Abundance and Distribution Uncommon to rare transient (Jul.–Oct., Mar.–May) throughout the Southeast; rare to casual winter resident (Nov.–Feb.) in South Florida and the Keys.

Where to Find Rum Creek Wildlife Management Area, Georgia; St. Marks National Wildlife Refuge, Florida; John W. Kyle State Park, Mississippi; Eufaula National Wildlife Refuge, Alabama.

Range Breeds across Arctic and boreal North America; winters from southern Atlantic (Georgia, Florida) and Gulf coasts of United States south to southern South America, West Indies.

126. Willet
Catoptrophorus semipalmatus
(L-15 W-27)

Large, heavy-bodied, long-billed shorebird; mottled grayish brown above and below; whitish belly; broad white stripe on wing is conspicuous in flight. **Winter** Gray above, whitish below.

Voice Shrill "will will-it," repeated.

Similar Species Large size, white wing stripes, and flight call separate this from other shorebirds.

Habitat Estuaries, beaches, coastal ponds, marshes, mudflats.

Abundance and Distribution Common resident* along the immediate coast throughout the Southeast; rare to casual transient

Figure 25. Grand Bay Wildlife Management Area near Valdosta in southwest Georgia is great for Summer Tanager, Pine Warbler, Yellow-throated Warbler, King Rail, American and Least bitterns and a host of other southern floodplain species.

(Jun., Aug.–Sept.) and winter visitor (Oct.–Apr.) in interior Florida Peninsula.

Where to Find Dauphin Island, Alabama; Hobe Sound National Wildlife Refuge, Florida; Buccaneer State Park, Mississippi; Tybee Island Beach, Georgia.

Range Breeds southwestern and south-central Canada and northwestern and north-central United States, along Atlantic and Gulf coasts (Nova Scotia to Texas), West Indies; winters coastal North America (California and Virginia) south to northern half of South America, West Indies.

127. Spotted Sandpiper
Actitis macularius
(L-8 W-13)

Grayish brown above, white with dark spots below; white eyebrow; bill pinkish with dark tip; legs pinkish. **Winter** Lacks spots; white below extending toward back at shoulder; grayish smear on side of breast; legs yellowish.

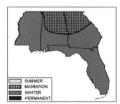

Habits Teeters almost continually while foraging; flight peculiar, with stiff-winged bursts and brief glides.

Voice "Peet weet."

Similar Species The Solitary Sandpiper is found in similar habitats; however, it pauses between bobs, shows no white on wings in flight (white on wings in Spotted), has eyering and no pale eyebrow (Spotted has no eyering and a pale eyebrow), longer legs, and white spotting on folded wings (absent in Spotted); tail barring is much less prominent in the Spotted than the Solitary.

Habitat Streams, ponds, rivers, lakes, beaches.

Abundance and Distribution Uncommon to rare transient and winter resident (Jul.–May) and rare to casual summer resident (Jun.) nearly throughout the Southeast, although scarcer in the highlands; has bred* in Mississippi and at piedmont sites.

Where to Find Cumberland Island National Seashore, Georgia; Gulf Islands National Seashore, Florida; Bon Secour National Wildlife Refuge, Alabama; Arkabutla Lake, Mississippi.

Range Breeds throughout temperate and boreal North America; winters from the southern United States south to northern Argentina, West Indies.

128. Upland Sandpiper
Bartramia longicauda
(L-12 W-22)

The shape of this bird is unique: large, heavy body, long legs, long neck, small head, and short bill. Plumage is light brown with dark brown streaks on back and wings; buff head, neck, and breast mottled with brown; large brown eye.

Voice Call: "kip-ip," repeated.

Similar Species The Buff-breasted Sandpiper is found in similar habitats; however, it has clear, unstreaked, buffy underparts contrasting with white wing linings in flight.

Habitat Prairie, pastures, plowed fields.

Abundance and Distribution Uncommon to rare transient (Aug.–Sept., Apr.) throughout the Southeast.

Where to Find Rum Creek Wildlife Management Area, Georgia; Lake Apopka Restoration Area, Florida; Wall Doxey State Park, Mississippi; Pinto Pass Nature Observatory, Battleship Park, Alabama.

Range Breeds across northeast and north-central United States and in Great Plains of Canada; winters South America.

129. Whimbrel
Numenius phaeopus
(L-18 W-33)

Mottled gray and brown above; grayish below with dark flecks; crown striped with dark brown and gray.

Sandpipers

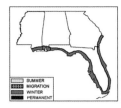

Voice Call: "kee kee kee kee."

Similar Species Long-billed Curlew is larger, buffy, has a very long, decurved bill, and is not striped prominently on crown.

Habitat Tall grasslands, estuaries, oyster reefs.

Abundance and Distribution Uncommon to rare transient (Sept.–Oct., Apr.–May) and winter resident (Nov.–Mar.) along the immediate coast throughout the Southeast.

Where to Find Cumberland Island National Seashore, Georgia; John W. Kyle State Park, Mississippi; Sanibel Island, Florida.

Range Breeds in high Arctic of Old and New World; winters in subtropical and tropical regions.

130. Long-billed Curlew
Numenius americanus
(L-23 W-38)

A large, heavy-bodied bird with very long, decurved bill; mottled brown and buff above; uniformly buffy below; rusty wing linings visible in flight.

Voice Call: a strident "per-leee," repeated.

Similar Species Long-billed Curlew is larger than the Whimbrel, buffy, has a very long, decurved bill, and is not striped prominently on crown (as is the Whimbrel).

Habitat Grasslands, pastures, lawns, golf courses.

Abundance and Distribution Rare winter resident (Aug.–Apr.) in Central and South Florida (mainly Gulfside) along the immediate coast, and the Keys; casual in Alabama, Mississippi, and elsewhere in Florida.

Where to Find Sanibel Island, Florida; Everglades National Park, Florida.

Range Breeds in prairie regions of western United States and southwestern Canada; winters from central California and southern portions of California, Arizona, Texas, and Louisiana south through southern Mexico.

131. Marbled Godwit
Limosa fedoa
(L-18 W-31)

Mottled buff and dark brown above; buffy below barred with brown; long, upturned bill pink at base, dark at tip; rusty wing linings. **Winter** Ventral barring faint or lacking.

Sandpipers

Voice Call: "koo-wik" repeated.

Similar Species The Marbled Godwit is mottled buff and brown at all seasons (not gray and white as in the Hudsonian Godwit, a casual visitor in the Southeast); Marbled Godwit rump is mottled buff (not white as in Hudsonian), and underwing is cinnamon (not dark gray as in Hudsonian).

Habitat Bay shores, mudflats, estuaries, flooded grasslands.

Abundance and Distribution Uncommon to rare winter resident (Sept.–Apr.) along the immediate coast in Alabama, Mississippi, Georgia, the Panhandle, and North Florida; common to uncommon resident (nonbreeding) along the coast in Central and South Florida (mainly Gulfside); rare to casual visitor to the Keys.

Where to Find Blackbeard Island, Georgia; Pinto Pass Nature Observatory, Battleship Park, Alabama; Gulf Islands National Seashore, Mississippi; Lanark Reef, Florida.

Range Breeds northern Great Plains of Canada and extreme northern United States; winters coastal United States from California and South Carolina south to northern South America.

132. Ruddy Turnstone
Arenaria interpres
(L-10 W-19)

A plump bird with slightly upturned bill; rufous above, white below with black breast; black and white facial pattern; two white stripes on wings; white band across tail; orange legs. **Winter** Grayish above; white below with varying amounts of black on breast and face.

Voice Calls: a single, whistled "tew," also a low chatter.

Habitat Beaches, mudflats.

Abundance and Distribution Common winter resident (Aug.–May) and uncommon to rare summer resident (Jun.–Jul.) along the immediate coast throughout the Southeast.

Where to Find Harris Neck National Wildlife Refuge, Georgia; Hobe Sound National Wildlife Refuge, Florida; Bon Secour National Wildlife Refuge, Alabama; Gulf Islands National Seashore, Mississippi.

Range Breeds in high Arctic of Old and New World; winters in south temperate and tropical regions.

133. Red Knot
Calidris canutus
(L-11 W-21)

A plump bird, mottled brown and russet above and on crown; rusty below. **Winter** Pale gray above; grayish breast; whitish belly; white eyebrow; white, finely barred rump.

Voice Call: a hoarse "kew kew."

Similar Species Dowitchers are white up the back; Sanderling is smaller and lacks white rump; other peeps of similar plumage are sparrow sized.

Habitat Beaches, bay shorelines, mudflats.

Abundance and Distribution Common to uncommon transient (Sept.–Oct., Apr.–May), uncommon to rare winter resident (Nov.–Mar.), and rare to casual summer resident (Jun.–Jul., nonbreeding) along the coast throughout the Southeast; rare to casual transient (Apr.–Jun., Sept.–Nov.) in inland Florida.

Where to Find Sanibel Island, Florida; Tybee Island Beach, Georgia; Gulf State Park, Alabama.

Range Breeds in Old and New World high Arctic; winters in temperate and tropical coastal regions.

134. Sanderling
Calidris alba
(L-8 W-16)

A chunky, feisty peep of the beaches; dappled brown, white, and black on back and crown; rusty flecked with white on face and breast; short black legs and bill; lacks hind toe (hallux); white wing stripe. **Winter** As in Breeding but mottled gray and white above; white below; white eyebrow; grayish shoulder patch extends to side of breast.

Habits Spends considerable time in chases and fights with other Sanderlings.

Voice Call: "kwit."

Similar Species Other winter peeps are more or less streaked with grayish on throat and breast (throat and breast are white on winter Sanderling); also Sanderling has palest back.

Habitat Beaches.

Abundance and Distribution Common to uncommon resident (nonbreeding) along the immediate coast throughout the South-

Figure 26. Located just minutes away from the insane helter skelter of I-95, Harris Neck National Wildlife Refuge on the Georgia coast is a serenely different world—one of magnificent, moss-draped oaks and tidal creeks frequented by American Oystercatchers, Black-necked Stilts (summer), and American Avocets (transients).

east, somewhat scarcer in summer (May–Jul.); rare to casual transient (Mar.–May, Jul.–Oct.) in inland Florida.

Where to Find Gulf Islands National Seashore, Florida; Buccaneer State Park, Mississippi; Bon Secour National Wildlife Refuge, Alabama; Harris Neck National Wildlife Refuge, Georgia.

Range Breeds in high Arctic of Old and New World; winters on temperate and tropical beaches.

135. Semipalmated Sandpiper
Calidris pusilla
(L-6 W-12)

Dark brown, russet, and white above; finely streaked brown and white on head and breast; pale eyebrow with some rusty on crown and cheek; white belly; partial webbing between toes (hence "semipalmated"). **Winter** Grayish above with grayish wash on head and breast; white belly.

Voice Call: "chit" or "chek."

Similar Species Winter-plumaged Western Sandpiper is essentially identical to winter Semipalmated. They can be separated by voice ("chek" in Semipalmated, "zheet" in Western). The bill of the Western averages longer than that of Semipalmated, and in longer-billed birds there is a noticeable droop at the tip. However, there is considerable overlap in this and all other characters used to separate the winter-plumaged birds in the field, except voice (Phillips 1975).

Habitat Mudflats, ponds, lakes.

Abundance and Distribution Common transient (Aug.–Oct., Apr.–May) nearly throughout the Southeast, although less numerous inland in Georgia, Mississippi, and Alabama.

Where to Find Hobe Sound National Wildlife Refuge, Florida; Tybee Island Beach, Georgia; Bon Secour National Wildlife Refuge, Alabama; Noxubee National Wildlife Refuge, Mississippi.

Range Breeds in high Arctic of North America; winters along both coasts of Middle and South America to Paraguay (east) and northern Chile (west), West Indies.

136. Western Sandpiper
Calidris mauri
(L-6 W-12)

Dark brown, russet, and white above; finely streaked brown and white on head and breast; pale eyebrow; partial webbing on toes; similar to Semipalmated Sandpiper but whiter on back, and with distinct rusty cheek and supraorbital patches. **Winter** Grayish above with grayish wash on head and breast; white belly.

Voice Call: "zheet."

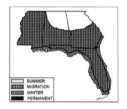

SUMMER
MIGRATION
WINTER
PERMANENT

Similar Species Winter-plumaged Western Sandpiper is essentially identical to winter Semipalmated. They can be separated by voice ("chek" in Semipalmated, "zheet" in Western). The bill of the Western averages longer than that of Semipalmated, and in longer-billed birds there is a noticeable droop at the tip. However, there is considerable overlap in this and all other characters used to separate the winter-plumaged birds in the field, except voice (Phillips 1975).

Habitat Beaches, mudflats, ponds, lakes, estuaries, swales.

Abundance and Distribution Common to uncommon transient and winter resident (Aug.–Mar.), uncommon to rare in summer (Apr.–Jul.) nearly throughout the Southeast, although less numerous inland in Georgia, Alabama, and Mississippi.

Where to Find Rum Creek Wildlife Management Area, Georgia; Eufaula National Wildlife Refuge, Alabama; Gulf Islands National Seashore, Mississippi; St. Andrews State Recreation Area, Florida.

Range Breeds in high Arctic of northern Alaska and northeastern Siberia; winters along both coasts of United States from California and North Carolina south to northern South America, West Indies.

137. Least Sandpiper
Calidris minutilla
(L-6 W-12)

Dark brown and buff on back and wings; head and breast streaked with brown and white; relatively short, thin bill; white belly; yellowish legs (sometimes brown with caked mud). **Winter** Brownish gray above; buffy wash on breast.

Voice Call: "preep."

Similar Species Yellowish legs are distinctive (other small peeps have dark legs), as is call note.

Habitat Ponds, lakes, swales, mudflats.

Abundance and Distribution Common transient (Aug.–Sept., Apr.–May) throughout the Southeast; common to uncommon winter resident (Oct.–Mar.) and uncommon to rare in summer (Jun.–Jul.) in Florida and along the coast in Georgia, Alabama, and Mississippi.

Where to Find Bon Secour National Wildlife Refuge, Alabama; Hobe Sound National Wildlife Refuge, Florida; Arkabutla Lake, Mississippi; Grand Bay Wildlife Management Area, Georgia.

Range Breeds across northern North America; winters from coastal (Oregon, North Carolina) and southern United States south to northern half of South America, West Indies.

138. White-rumped Sandpiper
Calidris fuscicollis
(L-8 W-15)

Dark and tan on back and wings; finely streaked brown and white on head, breast, and flanks; white rump; dark legs; wings extend beyond tail. **Winter** As in breeding but gray above, white below with gray wash on breast and white eyebrow.

Voice Call: "teet."

Similar Species The rarer Curlew Sandpiper is also white rumped but has long, decurved bill.

Habitat Swales, mudflats, lakes, ponds.

Abundance and Distribution Uncommon to rare spring transient (Apr.–May) throughout the Southeast; rare to casual in fall (Jul.–Nov.) in Florida.

Where to Find Fort Caroline National Memorial/Timucuan Ecological and Historic Preserve, Florida ; Eufaula National

Figure 27. Fort Caroline and the Timucuan Ecological and Historic Preserve are located just east of Jacksonville, Florida, preserving a wide array of coastal habitats including hammocks and tidal marshes. French explorers first landed at the site in 1562, and were greeted by friendly Timucuan who, like many hosts, found their guests to be interesting visitors but difficult neighbors.

Wildlife Refuge, Alabama; Rum Creek Wildlife Management Area, Georgia; John W. Kyle State Park, Mississippi; Fort De Soto County Park, Florida.

Range Breeds in high Arctic of North America; winters in South America east of the Andes.

139. Baird's Sandpiper
Calidris bairdii
(L-8 W-15)

A medium-sized sandpiper, dark brown and buff on back and wings; buffy head and breast flecked with brown; wings extend beyond tail.

Voice Call: "chureep."

Similar Species Brownish (rather than grayish) winter plumage makes this bird look like a large Least Sandpiper. Long wings, black bill and legs, and dark rump separate it from the Least and other peeps.

Habitat Ponds, lakes, swales.

Abundance and Distribution Rare to casual transient (Aug.–Oct., Apr.–May), more numerous in fall along the coast.

Where to Find Okaloosa County Holding Ponds, Fort Walton Beach, Florida.

Range Breeds in high Arctic of North America and northeastern Siberia; winters in western and southern South America.

140. Pectoral Sandpiper
Calidris melanotos
(L-9 W-17)

Dark brown, tan, and white on back and wings; head and breast whitish, densely flecked with brown; belly white, the dividing line between mottled brown breast and white belly distinct; dark bill; yellow legs.

Voice Call: "prip."

Similar Species No other sandpiper shows sharp contrast of breast and belly markings.

Habitat Wet prairies, ponds, lakes, swales, agricultural fields.

Abundance and Distribution Common to rare transient (Aug.–Sept., Mar.–May) throughout the Southeast.

Where to Find Arrowhead Public Fishing Area, Georgia; Lake Apopka Restoration Area, Florida; Eufaula National Wildlife Refuge, Alabama; Yazoo National Wildlife Refuge, Mississippi.

Range Breeds in the high Arctic of northern North America; winters in southern half of South America.

141. Purple Sandpiper
Calidris maritima
(L-9 W-15)

Dark brown back and wings; head finely streaked with brown and white; belly white; breast and flanks whitish spotted with brown; bill yellow orange at base, dark at tip; yellow-orange legs; white eyering. **Winter** Back marked with gray and buff; head and breast slate gray with gray streaking on flanks.

Voice Call: "we-it."

Habitat Rocky shores and jetties.

Abundance and Distribution Rare winter resident (Oct.–Mar.), mainly along the Atlantic Coast of Georgia, the Panhandle, North and Central Florida; scarcer in South Florida.

Where to Find Tybee Island Beach, Georgia; Huguenot Memorial City Park, Florida.

Range Breeds in Arctic of northeastern North America, Greenland, Iceland, northern Scandinavia, and Siberia; winters along Atlantic Coast of North America; also shores of North and Baltic seas in Old World.

142. Dunlin
Calidris alpina
(L-9 W-16)

Rusty and dark brown on back and wings; white streaked with black on neck and breast; crown streaked with russet and black; large black smudge on belly; long bill droops at tip. **Winter** As in breeding but with dark gray back; head and breast pale gray with some streaking; white eyebrow; white belly.

Voice Call: a hoarse "zheet."

Similar Species Dark gray back and long, drooping bill distinguish the winter Dunlin from other gray-breasted peeps.

Habitat Ponds, lakes, beaches, mudflats.

Abundance and Distribution Common to uncommon transient and winter resident (Oct.–May) in Florida and along the coastal plain in Mississippi, Alabama, and Georgia.

Where to Find Bon Secour National Wildlife Refuge, Alabama; Hobe Sound National Wildlife Refuge, Florida; Gulf Islands National Seashore, Mississippi; Rum Creek Wildlife Management Area, Georgia.

Range Breeds in Arctic of Old and New World; winters in temperate and northern tropical regions.

143. Stilt Sandpiper
Calidris himantopus
(L-9 W-17)

A trim, long-necked, long-legged sandpiper, dark brown and buff on back and wings; crown streaked with dark brown and white; white eyebrow; chestnut pre- and postorbital stripe; white streaked with brown on neck; white barred with brown on breast and belly; long, yellow-green legs; white rump; long, straight bill (twice length of head). **Winter** Gray and white mottling on back; gray head with prominent eyebrow; gray throat and breast; whitish belly with gray flecks.

Habits Often feeds with rapid up-and-down motion in breast-deep water.

Voice Call: a low "whurp."

Similar Species Winter Lesser Yellowlegs has barred (not gray) tail; winter dowitchers have longer bill (3 times length of head), flanks with dark bars or spots, and show white on lower back in flight.

Habitat Mudflats, flooded pastures, lakes, ponds.

Abundance and Distribution Common to rare transient (Jul.–Oct., Apr.–May) in Florida and along the coastal plain in Mississippi, Alabama, and Georgia, scarcer in the piedmont; uncommon to rare winter resident (Nov.–Mar.) in Central and South Florida.

Where to Find Blakely Island, Alabama; Lake Apopka Restoration Area, Florida; Savannah National Wildlife Refuge, Georgia.

Range Breeds in Arctic of north-central Canada; winters in central South America.

144. Buff-breasted Sandpiper
Tryngites subruficollis
(L-8 W-17)

Dark brown feathering edged in buff or whitish on back; buffy head and underparts, spotted with brown on breast; streaked crown; large, dark eye; pale legs; wing linings appear white in flight.

Habits Often seen in small flocks that twist and turn erratically in flight over freshly plowed fields.

Voice Call: a low trill.

Similar Species The Buff-breasted Sandpiper and Upland Sandpiper are found in similar habitats; however, the buffbreast has unstreaked, buffy underparts contrasting with white wing linings in flight. The Upland Sandpiper has streaked underparts and buffy, streaked wing linings.

Habitat Grassland, stubble fields, overgrazed pastures.

Abundance and Distribution Rare transient (Jul.–Oct., Mar.–May), more numerous in fall (Sept.) throughout the Southeast.

Where to Find Savannah National Wildlife Refuge, Georgia; Lake Purdy, Alabama; Arkabutla Lake, Mississippi; Lake Apopka Restoration Area, Florida.

Range Breeds in Arctic of northern Alaska and northwestern Canada; winters in Paraguay, Uruguay, and northern Argentina.

145. Short-billed Dowitcher
Limnodromus griseus
(L-11 W-19)

A rather squat, long-billed sandpiper (bill is 3 times length of head); mottled black, white, and buff on back, wings, and crown; cinnamon buff on neck and underparts barred and spotted with

dark brown; belly white; white line above eye with dark line through eye; white tail barred with black; white on rump extending in a wedge up back; bill dark; legs greenish. **Winter** Grayish crown, nape, and back; white line above eye and dark line through eye; grayish neck and breast fading to whitish on belly; flanks and undertail coverts spotted and barred with dark brown. **Juvenile** Patterned like adult but paler brown above and on head, and with buffy neck and breast.

Habits Often feeds with rapid up-and-down motion, breast-deep in water, usually in small flocks.

Voice Call: "tu tu" or "tu tu tu" repeated.

Similar Species Short-billed has a two or three note whistle, "tu tu tu" while the Long-billed has a thin "eek."

Habitat Mudflats, flooded pastures, ponds, lakes, estuaries.

Abundance and Distribution Common to uncommon transient and winter resident (Aug.–May), mainly along the coast, throughout the Southeast.

Where to Find Hobe Sound National Wildlife Refuge, Florida; Gulf Islands National Seashore, Mississippi; Weeks Bay National Estuarine Research Reserve, Alabama; Wassaw Island National Wildlife Refuge, Georgia.

Range Breeds across central Canada and southern Alaska; winters coastal United States (California, South Carolina) south to northern South America, West Indies.

146. Long-billed Dowitcher
Limnodromus scolopaceus
(L-11 W-19)

A squat, long-billed sandpiper (bill is 3 times length of head); mottled black, white, and buff on back, wings, and crown; cinnamon buff on neck and underparts barred and spotted with dark brown; belly white; white line above eye with dark line through eye; white tail barred with black; white on rump extending in a wedge up back; bill dark; legs greenish. **Winter** Grayish crown, nape, and back; white line above eye and dark line through eye; grayish neck and breast fading to whitish on belly; flanks and undertail coverts spotted and barred with dark brown. **Juvenile** Patterned like adult in winter.

Voice Call: a thin "eek," often repeated.

Figure 28. Pine Beach Trail at Alabama's Bon Secour National Wildlife Refuge truly does provide "safe harbor" from the scurry of coastal tourism. An hour's walk takes you through a variety of seaside habitats including oak, pine, and palmetto woodlands, marshes, and ponds. In addition to Gopher Tortoises and endangered Alabama Beach Mice (you will probably need help from a screech-owl to find these), the trail is a good place to see Anhingas, Great Egrets, Snowy Egrets, Little Blue Herons, and Green Herons.

Similar Species The Long-billed Dowitcher has a thin "eek" call while the Short-billed has a two or three note whistle, "tu tu tu."

Habitat Mudflats, flooded pastures.

Abundance and Distribution Locally uncommon to rare transient and winter resident (Sept.–Apr.) along the Georgia coastal plain, peninsular Florida, and coastal Alabama; rare to casual transient and winter resident (Sept.–Apr.) elsewhere in the region.

Where to Find Wassaw National Wildlife Refuge, Georgia; Bon Secour National Wildlife Refuge, Alabama; Driggers Road, Florida.

Range Breeds in coastal Alaska, northwestern Canada, and northeastern Siberia; winters southern United States to Guatemala.

147. Wilson's Snipe
Gallinago delicata
(L-11 W-17)

Dark brown back with white stripes; crown striped with dark brown and gray; neck and breast streaked grayish brown and white; whitish belly; tan rump; tail banded with rust and black; very long bill (3 times length of head).

Habits Normally solitary, retiring, and wary; gives an explosive "zhrrt" when flushed and flies in erratic swoops and dips.

Voice Song: given on wing from high in the air, "cheek cheek cheek cheek" etc., plus a winnowing sound (made by air passing through the tail feathers).

Habitat Marshes, bogs, flooded pastures, wet ditches.

Abundance and Distribution Common to uncommon winter resident (Oct.–Apr.) nearly throughout the Southeast, somewhat scarcer in the highlands.

Where to Find Laura S. Walker State Park, Georgia; Lagoon Park, Montgomery, Alabama; Yazoo National Wildlife Refuge, Mississippi; St. Andrews State Recreation Area, Florida.

Range Breeds in north temperate and boreal regions of the New World; winters in south temperate and tropical regions.

148. American Woodcock
Scolopax minor
(L-11 W-17)

A fat, short-legged, long-billed bird with no apparent neck and hardly any tail; dark and grayish brown above; gray-brown neck and breast becoming rusty on belly and flanks; dark brown crown with thin, transverse gray stripes; large, brown eye; overall impression of flushed bird is cinnamon buff because of underparts and wing linings.

Habits Nocturnal and diurnal; feeds, sings, and displays mornings, evenings, and at night.

Voice A buzzy, nasal "peent," also a flight song composed of a long trill followed by various "chik," "cheek," and "cherk" sounds made by air passing through the bird's feathers as it descends; wings make a whistling sound when bird is flushed.

Habitat Moist woodlands, swamp borders.

Abundance and Distribution Uncommon to rare resident* in the piedmont and upper coastal plain of Georgia, Mississippi, and Alabama; uncommon to rare winter resident of the Panhandle and North Florida, casual in summer (has bred*); rare to casual resident* in Central and South Florida and absent from the Keys.

Where to Find Okefenokee National Wildlife Refuge, Georgia; DeSoto State Park, Alabama; Noxubee National Wildlife Refuge, Mississippi.

Range Breeds across the eastern half of the United States and southeastern Canada; winters from the southern half of the breeding range into south Texas and South Florida.

Sandpipers

149. Wilson's Phalarope
Phalaropus tricolor
(L-9 W-17)

Female A trim, thin-billed, long-necked bird; chestnut and gray on the back; gray crown and nape; black extending from eye down side of neck; white chin; chestnut throat; white breast and belly. **Male** Similar but paler. **Winter** Grayish brown above, white below; gray head with white eyebrow; white chin; rusty throat.

Habits Unlike other shorebirds, phalaropes often swim, whirling in tight circles, while foraging.

Voice Call: a nasal "wak," repeated.

Similar Species Other phalaropes have white foreheads and black and white facial pattern in winter.

Habitat Ponds, lakes, mudflats, flooded pastures.

Abundance and Distribution Rare transient, mainly in fall (Aug.–Sept.).

Where to Find Savannah National Wildlife Refuge, Georgia; Lake Apopka Restoration Area, Florida.

Range Breeds in western United States, southwestern Canada, and in Great Lakes region; winters western and southern South America.

150. Red-necked Phalarope
Phalaropus lobatus
(L-8 W-14)

Female Black with rusty striping on back and flanks; white below; neck and nape orange; head black; chin white. **Male** Similar in pattern but paler. **Winter** Black back with white striping; white below; white forehead; gray-black crown; white eyebrow; black postorbital (behind the eye) stripe.

Habits Unlike other shorebirds, phalaropes often swim, whirling in tight circles, while foraging.

Voice Call: a hoarse "chik" or "ker-chik."

Similar Species Winter Red Phalarope has a pearl gray, unstreaked back; Red-necked is almost black on back, striped with white.

Habitat Mainly pelagic in winter, but also found occasionally at marshes, ponds, or lakes.

Abundance and Distribution Rare transient (Sept.–Oct., Mar.–Apr.), mainly offshore in the Atlantic.

Where to Find Pelagic birding trips.

Range Breeds in Arctic regions of the Old and New World; winters at sea in southern Pacific and Indian oceans.

151. Red Phalarope
Phalaropus fulicarius
(L-9 W-17)

Female Black back striped with buff; neck and underparts rusty orange; black cap; white cheek; relatively short heavy bill is yellow at base, black at tip. **Male** Similar in pattern but paler. **Winter** Uniform pearl gray on back; white below; white forehead and front half of crown; gray rear half of crown and nape line; dark postorbital stripe; bill blackish.

Habits Unlike other shorebirds, phalaropes often swim, whirling in tight circles, while foraging.

Similar Species Winter Red Phalarope has a pearl gray, unstreaked back; Red-necked is almost black on back, striped with white.

Habitat Mainly pelagic in winter, but also found occasionally on beaches and mudflats.

Abundance and Distribution Rare transient and winter visitor, mainly offshore in the Atlantic (Sept.-May).

Where to Find Pelagic birding trips.

Range Breeds in Old and New World Arctic; winters in southern Pacific and Atlantic oceans.

Jaegers and Skuas, Gulls, Terns, and Skimmers
Family Laridae

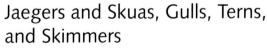

The Laridae are subdivided into four distinct groupings: (1) jaegers and skuas, (2) gulls, (3) terns, and (4) skimmers.

The jaegers and skuas are dark, heavy-bodied, Herring Gull–sized birds with hooked, predatory beaks and protruding central tail feathers. The wings are long, pointed, and sharply angled at the wrist. Usually three to four years are spent in subadult and immature plumages before full adult plumage, with the characteristic central tail feathers, is achieved. Until that time, the central tail feathers are only slightly or moderately protruding.

These are the hawks of the oceans. They feed on stolen fish and the eggs and young of other seabirds. Characteristic behavior is chasing gulls and terns in attempts to rob them of captured fish. They are pelagic except during the breeding season. The most probable locality for locating a jaeger is along the immediate coast and offshore islands, or at sea.

Gulls are variable in size; most are various patterns of gray and white as adults although several species are black headed. Like jaegers, they have several intermediate plumages between hatching and attainment of full adult plumage at two to four years of age. Only a few of these plumages are described here: adult breeding plumage, winter plumage (where applicable), and a "typical" immature plumage.

Terns are thin-billed, trim-bodied seabirds. Most species forage by plummeting into the water from a height of 10 to 30 feet to catch fish.

The skimmers are long-winged birds with long bills shaped like a straight razor and with the lower mandible protruding beyond the upper. They feed by flying above the water with the lower mandible dipped just below the surface to capture fish.

Identification to species of the immatures for some groups within the Laridae can be difficult or impossible in the field. Harrison (1983) and Grant (1982) provide detailed descriptions and keys for advanced students of these birds.

152. Pomarine Jaeger
Stercorarius pomarinus
(L-22 W-48)

Protruding central tail feathers are twisted; dark brown above; white collar tinged with yellow; whitish below with dark breast band and undertail coverts.
Dark Phase Completely dark brown with white at base of primaries; cheeks tinged with yellow; dark cap. **Immature** Barred brown or brown and white below.

Similar Species The Pomarine Jaeger has twisted tail feathers; Parasitic Jaeger has pointed tail feathers; Long-tailed Jaeger has very long central tail feathers (half of body length).

Habitat Pelagic, beaches.

Abundance and Distribution Uncommon to rare transient and rare to casual winter visitor, mainly offshore in the Atlantic

SUMMER
MIGRATION
WINTER
PERMANENT

(Sept.–Apr.); large flocks sometimes seen off the Florida Atlantic coast in fall.

Where to Find Pelagic birding trips.

Range Breeds in Old and New World Arctic; winters in temperate and tropical oceans.

153. Parasitic Jaeger
Stercorarius parasiticus
(L-19 W-42)

Dark brown above; white collar and white below with faint brown breast band; pointed, protruding central tail feathers; wings dark but whitish at base of primaries. **Dark Phase** Completely dark brown. **Immature** Dark brown above; barred reddish brown or brown and white below.

Similar Species Parasitic Jaeger has pointed tail feathers; the Pomarine Jaeger has twisted tail feathers; Long-tailed Jaeger has very long central tail feathers (half of body length).

Habitat Pelagic; beaches.

Abundance and Distribution Uncommon to rare transient and rare to casual winter visitor, mainly offshore in the Atlantic (Oct.–Apr.); large flocks sometimes seen off the Florida Atlantic coast in fall.

Where to Find Pelagic birding trips.

Range Breeds in Old and New World Arctic; winters in temperate and tropical oceans.

154. Laughing Gull
Larus atricilla
(L-17 W-40)

Black head; gray back and wings with black wingtips; white collar, underparts, and tail; scarlet bill and black legs; partial white eyering. **Winter** As in breeding but head whitish with dark gray ear patch; black bill. **Immature** Brownish above and on breast; white belly and tail with black terminal bar.

Voice A raucous, derisive "kaah kah-kah-kah-kah kaah kaah," also a single "keeyah."

Similar Species Laughing Gull has black wingtips and whitish head with dark ear patches in winter; Franklin's Gull shows white tips on black primaries and a darkish hood in winter.

Habitat Beaches, bays, lakes, agricultural areas.

Abundance and Distribution Common resident* mainly along the immediate coast throughout the region; common to rare inland in winter (Nov.–Apr.) in Florida.

Where to Find Crooked River State Park, Georgia; Weeks Bay National Estuarine Research Reserve, Alabama; Biscayne National Park, Florida; Gulf Marine State Park, Mississippi.

Range Breeds along both coasts in North America from New Brunswick on the east and northern Mexico on the west, south to northern South America, West Indies; winters along coasts from southern United States to central South America.

155. Franklin's Gull
Larus pipixcan
(L-15 W-36)

Black head; gray back and wings; white bar bordering black wingtips spotted terminally with white; white collar, underparts, and tail; underparts variously tinged with rose; scarlet bill and legs; partial white eyering. **Winter** As in breeding but head with a partial, dark hood; black bill. **Immature** Similar to winter adult but with black terminal tail band.

Voice "Ayah."

Similar Species Franklin's Gull shows white tips on black primaries and a darkish hood in winter. Laughing Gull has black wingtips and whitish head with dark ear patches in winter.

Habitat Pastures, flooded fields, bays.

Abundance and Distribution Rare visitor to the Florida mainland, principally at garbage dumps (where they still exist) with other gulls in winter (Nov.–Dec.).

Where to Find Honeymoon Island State Park, Florida; Reddington Beach, Florida.

Range Breeds north-central United States and south-central Canada; winters along Pacific coast of Middle and South America.

156. Bonaparte's Gull
Larus philadelphia
(L-14 W-32)

A small gull; black head; gray back; wings gray with white outer primaries tipped in black; white collar, underparts, and tail; black bill; red legs. **Winter**

White head with black ear patch. **Immature** Like winter adult but with black tail band and brown stripe running diagonally across gray wing; flesh-colored legs; black bill.

Voice A high-pitched, screechy "aaaanhh."

Similar Species Two other black-headed gull species occur regularly in the region: the Laughing Gull and Franklin's Gull. Both are much larger than the Bonaparte's Gull. Also, Bonaparte's Gull has red or flesh-colored legs and feet (not dark as in Laughing and Franklin's). Also, Bonaparte's has white outer primaries tipped with black (Laughing has black outer primaries and Franklin's has black outer primaries tipped with white).

Habitat Marine, bays, estuaries, lakes.

Abundance and Distribution Common to rare winter visitor (Dec.–Mar.), mainly along the coast.

Where to Find Merritt Island National Wildlife Refuge, Florida; St. Andrews State Recreation Area, Florida; Cumberland Island National Seashore, Georgia; Gulf Islands National Seashore, Mississippi.

Range Breeds across north-central and northwestern North America in Canada and Alaska; winters south along both coasts, from Washington on the west and Nova Scotia on the east, to central Mexico; also the Great Lakes, Bahamas, and Greater Antilles.

157. Ring-billed Gull
Larus delawarensis
(L-16 W-48)

White body; gray back; gray wings with black outer primaries tipped with white; bill orange yellow with black, subterminal ring; legs pale yellow. **Immature** Like adult but mottled with brown or gray; bill pale with black tip; whitish tail with black terminal band.

Voice A strident "ayah."

Similar Species Immature Herring Gulls are much larger; tail is mostly dark in Herring Gull, lacking a subterminal band as in immature Ring-billed Gull, and lacks white terminal band.

Habitat Lakes, bays, beaches, estuaries.

Abundance and Distribution Common transient and winter resident (Oct.–Apr.) throughout the region; uncommon to rare summer resident (May–Sept., nonbreeding) in Florida and, mainly along the coast, elsewhere in the Southeast.

Where to Find Lake Sidney Lanier, Georgia; Lake Guntersville State Park, Alabama; Lakepoint Resort State Park, Alabama; John

W. Kyle State Park, Mississippi; Lake Woodruff National Wildlife Refuge, Florida.

Range Breeds in the Great Plains region and scattered areas elsewhere in the northern United States and southern Canada; winters across most of United States except northern plains and mountains south to Panama.

158. Herring Gull
Larus argentatus
(L-24 W-57)

White body; gray back; gray wings with black outer primaries tipped with white; bill yellow with red spot on lower mandible; feet pinkish; yellow eye. **Winter** Head and breast smudged with brown. **Immature** Mottled dark brown in first winter; bill black; feet pinkish; tail dark; in second and third winter, grayish above, whitish below variously mottled with brown; tail with broad, dark, terminal band; bill pinkish with black tip; legs pinkish.

Voice The familiar, rusty gate squawking "Qeeyah kwa kwa kwa kwa" of all Hollywood shows that include an ocean scene.

Similar Species Adult Thayer's Gull (casual in the Southeast) can be distinguished (with difficulty) from Herring Gull, with which

Figure 29. Sapelo Island, Georgia, is home to a variety of beach-nesting shorebirds, including American Oystercatcher, Wilson's Plover, Least Tern, and Willet.

it used to be considered conspecific, by dark eye, darker pink legs, and outer primary black at base—white at tip (entirely black in adult Herring Gull).

Habitat Beaches, bays, marine, lakes, rivers.

Abundance and Distribution Uncommon transient and winter resident (Oct.–Apr.) throughout the region, scarcer inland; uncommon to rare summer resident (May–Sept., nonbreeding), mainly along the coast.

Where to Find Weeks Bay National Estuarine Research Reserve, Alabama; Gulf Islands National Seashore, Mississippi; Sapelo National Estuarine Research Reserve, Georgia; St. Andrews State Recreation Area, Florida.

Range Breeds in boreal and north temperate regions of both Old and New World; winters along coasts of far north southward into temperate and north tropical regions.

159. Lesser Black-backed Gull
Larus fuscus
(L-21 W-45)

White body; dark gray back and wings; outer primaries black sparsely tipped with white, appearing an almost uniform gray below; bill yellow with red spot on lower mandible; eyes and legs yellow. **Winter** Head and breast streaked with brown. **First Winter** White heavily marked with brown; bill black; feet pale pinkish. **Second Winter** Body white marked with brown; back and wings dark gray marked with brown; bill pinkish with black tip; legs pale yellow or pink .

SUMMER
MIGRATION
WINTER
PERMANENT

Similar Species First winter birds very similar to first winter Herring Gull but have paler rump; older birds are darker on the back and have yellow legs (pinkish in Great Black-backed Gull).

Habitat Beaches, marine.

Abundance and Distribution Uncommon to casual winter visitor (Dec.–Apr.), mainly along the Atlantic coast and at garbage dumps (where they still exist, as in Broward Co., Florida), rare to casual inland in the Florida Peninsula.

Range Breeds in Iceland and coastal northern Europe; winters along coasts of Europe and eastern North America.

160. Glaucous Gull
Larus hyperboreus
(L-27 W-60)

A very large gull; white body; pale gray back; yellow eyering and eye; wings pale gray with outer primaries broadly tipped with white above, mostly white from below; bill yellow with red spot on lower mandible; feet pinkish; wingtips barely extend beyond tail in sitting bird. **Winter** Head and breast smudged with brown. **First Winter** Mostly white or with light brown markings; bill pinkish with black tip; legs pinkish; tail white marked with brown. **Second and Third Winter** Back grayish; bill yellowish with dark tip.

Voice "Usually silent, occasionally utters hoarse, deep, Herring Gull-like scream." (Harrison 1983:347).

Similar Species The Glaucous Gull is a large, heavy-bodied gull with yellow eyering and eye, and white primaries.

Habitat Coastal regions.

Abundance and Distribution Rare to casual winter visitor (Dec.–May), mainly to the Florida northeast coast.

Where to Find Huguenot Memorial City Park, Jacksonville, Florida.

Range Breeds in circumpolar regions of Old and New World; winters coastal regions of northern Eurasia and North America.

161. Great Black-backed Gull
Larus marinus
(L-30 W-66)

A large gull; white body; black back; yellow eye; wings appear black above with white trailing edge, outer primaries tipped with white; bill very large, yellow with red spot on lower mandible; legs pinkish. **First Winter** White checked with brown above, paler below; rump paler; bill black; legs pale pink. **Second and Third Winter** Body white streaked with brown; black mottled with brown on back and wings; bill pinkish or yellowish with black tip; legs pale pinkish.

Voice Hoarse, low squawks and chuckles.

Habitat Seacoasts and large lakes.

Abundance and Distribution Uncommon to rare winter resident (Aug.–May), mainly along the Atlantic coast of Georgia, North and Central Florida; rare in South Florida and along the Gulf coast.

Where to Find Cumberland Island National Seashore, Georgia; Huguenot Memorial City Park, Jacksonville, Florida.

Range Breeds in coastal northeastern North America and northeastern Eurasia; winters in breeding range and south to the southeastern United States and southern Europe.

162. Black-legged Kittiwake
Rissa tridactyla
(L-17 W-36)

A small gull; white body; gray back; white, slightly forked tail; dark eye; wings gray above, white below tipped with black; bill yellow; legs dark. **Winter** Nape and back of crown gray with dark ear patch.

First Winter White marked with black "half-collar" on nape; gray back; dark diagonal stripe on upper wing; black ear patch; tail white with black terminal band; bill and legs black.

Voice "Kitt-ee-waak."

Similar Species Immature Bonaparte's Gull lacks dark half-collar at base of neck.

Habitat Pelagic, coasts.

Abundance and Distribution Uncommon to rare and irregular winter visitor (Nov.–Mar.), mainly offshore in the Atlantic.

Where to Find Pelagic birding trips.

Range Breeds circumpolar in Old and New World; winters in northern and temperate seas of the Northern Hemisphere.

163. Gull-billed Tern
Sterna nilotica
(L-15 W-36)

A medium-sized tern with a heavy, black bill; black cap and nape; white face, neck, and underparts; gray back and wings; tail with shallow fork; black legs. **Winter** Crown white finely streaked with black.

Habits This bird does not dive like most terns. It swoops and sails over marshland for insects.

Voice A harsh, nasal "kee-yek" or "ka-wup."

Similar Species Heavy, black, gull-like bill and shallow tail fork are distinctive.

Jaegers, Skuas, Gulls, Terns, Skimmers

Habitat Marshes, wet fields, grasslands, bays.

Abundance and Distribution Uncommon to rare summer resident* (May–Aug.) in Florida and along the immediate coast in Georgia, Alabama, and Mississippi; rare winter visitor (Sept.–Apr.) in extreme South Florida.

Where to Find Bon Secour National Wildlife Refuge, Alabama; Harris Neck National Wildlife Refuge, Georgia; Vilano Beach Boat Ramp, St. Augustine, Florida.

Range Breeds locally in temperate and tropical regions of the world; winters in subtropics and tropics.

164. Caspian Tern
Sterna caspia
(L-21 W-52)

A large tern with large, heavy, blood orange bill; black cap and nape; white face, neck, and underparts; gray back and wings; tail moderately forked; black legs. **Winter** Black cap streaked with white.

Voice A low squawk, "aaaak," repeated.

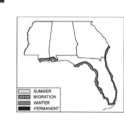

Similar Species Caspian Tern primaries appear dark from below, Royal Tern primaries appear whitish; Royal has white forehead (not black flecked with white) most of the year; Royal's call is a screechy "kee-eer," not a squawk like the Caspian. Also, the bill of the Caspian Tern is generally a bright, reddish orange while that of the Royal Tern is a paler orange.

Habitat Beaches, bays, marine, estuaries, lakes.

Abundance and Distribution Uncommon to rare and local winter resident (Aug.–May) mainly along coasts throughout the region; rare summer resident* (Jun.–Jul.); rare to casual or absent from the Florida Panhandle.

Where to Find Cumberland Island National Seashore, Georgia; Pine Island County Park, Florida; Fairhope Park, Alabama; Gulf Islands National Seashore, Mississippi.

Range Breeds locally inland and along the coast in temperate, tropical and boreal areas of the world; winters in south temperate and tropical regions.

165. Royal Tern
Sterna maxima
(L-20 W-45)

A large tern with yellow or yellow-orange bill; black cap with short, ragged crest; black nape; white face, neck, and underparts; gray back and wings; tail forked; black legs. **Winter** White forehead and crown; black nape.

Voice A screechy "keee-eer."

Similar Species Royal Tern primaries appear whitish from below, Caspian Tern primaries appear dark; Royal has white forehead (not black flecked with white as in the Caspian Tern) most of the year; Royal's call is a screechy "kee-eer," not a squawk like the Caspian. Also, the bill of the Caspian Tern is generally a bright, reddish orange while that of the Royal Tern is a paler orange.

Habitat Beaches, bays.

Abundance and Distribution Common to uncommon resident*, mainly along the coast; scarcer in summer in Florida; uncommon to casual and local inland in Florida in winter (Nov.–Apr.).

Where to Find Bon Secour National Wildlife Refuge, Alabama; Chassahowitzka National Wildlife Refuge, Florida; Tybee Island Beach, Georgia; Gulf Marine State Park, Mississippi.

Range Breeds locally in temperate and tropical regions of Western Hemisphere and west Africa; winters in warmer portions of breeding range.

166. Sandwich Tern
Sterna sandvicensis
(L-15 W-34)

A trim, medium-sized tern with long, pointed black bill, tipped with yellow; black cap and short, ragged crest; black nape; white face, neck, and underparts; gray back and wings; tail deeply forked; black legs. **Winter** White forehead; crown white, finely streaked with black; black nape.

Voice "Keerr-rik."

Similar Species The combination of slim, yellow-tipped, black bill and black legs is distinctive.

Habitat Marine, bays, often associated with Royal Tern.

Abundance and Distribution Common to rare resident* in coastal, peninsular Florida; uncommon to rare transient and summer resident* (Apr.–Oct.), most numerous in fall (Aug.–Sept.), in coastal Georgia, Alabama, Mississippi, and Florida Panhandle; small numbers winter inland in Polk Co., Florida, each year.

Where to Find Dauphin Island, Alabama; Hobe Sound National Wildlife Refuge, Florida; J. N. "Ding" Darling National Wildlife Refuge, Florida; Blackbeard National Wildlife Refuge, Georgia; Gulf Islands National Seashore, Mississippi.

Range Breeds locally along Atlantic, Gulf, and Caribbean coasts of North and South America from Virginia to Argentina, West Indies; winters through subtropical and tropical portions of breeding range and on the Pacific coast of Middle and South America from southern Mexico to Peru.

167. Roseate Tern
Sterna dougallii
(L-16 W-28)

A medium-sized tern; black bill reddish at base; black cap and nape; white face, neck; underparts white tinged with pink; gray back and wings; black outer primaries; tail very long, white, and deeply forked, extends well beyond folded wings in sitting bird; red legs. **Winter** White forehead and crown; back of crown and nape black; bill black. **First Breeding** Like adult but with white forehead.

Habits Flies with distinctive rapid, shallow wingbeats.

Voice "Chewee," mellow (for a tern).

Similar Species Roseate has completely white tail; Common Tern has gray outer edgings and white inner edgings; Forster's Tern has white outer edgings and gray inner edgings; Common Tern tail does not extend beyond the folded wings of sitting bird as it does in the Roseate; also the Roseate Tern "chewee" call is distinctive ("kee-arr" in Forster's, "keeeyaak" or "keyew" in Common).

Habitat Beaches, marine, bays.

Abundance and Distribution Common (at breeding colonies) to rare summer resident* (Apr.–Sept.) in the Lower Florida Keys and at Dry Tortugas; rare to casual transient (Mar.–Jun., Sept.–Oct.) offshore, especially in the Atlantic.

Where to Find Dry Tortugas National Park, Florida; Lower Florida Keys National Wildlife Refuges, Florida.

Range Breeds locally along coasts of temperate and tropical regions of the world (in United States from Maine to North Carolina and Florida); winters mainly in tropical portions of breeding range.

168. Common Tern

Sterna hirundo
(L-14 W-31)

SUMMER
MIGRATION
WINTER
PERMANENT

A medium-sized tern; red bill, black at tip; black cap and nape; white face, neck, and underparts; gray back and wings; entire outer primary, tips, and basal portions of other primaries are black (gray from below); forked tail with gray outer edgings, white inner edgings; red legs. **Winter** White forehead and crown; back of crown and nape black; bill black; sitting bird shows a dark bar at the shoulder (actually upper wing coverts). **First Breeding** Similar to adult winter.

Voice A harsh "keeeyaak," also "keyew keyew keyew."

Similar Species Winter Arctic Tern has white (not dark) basal portions of primaries from below. Roseate has completely white tail; Common Tern has gray outer edgings and white inner edgings; Forster's Tern has white outer edgings and gray inner edgings; Common Tern tail does not extend beyond the folded wings of sitting bird as it does in the Roseate; also the Roseate Tern "chewee" call is distinctive ("kee-arr" in Forster's, "keeeyaak" or "keyew" in Common).

Habitat Beaches, bays, marshes, lakes, rivers.

Abundance and Distribution Common to rare transient (Aug.–Oct., Apr.–May), principally offshore or along the immediate coast; has bred*; large flocks are reported from both coasts of Florida in fall and spring.

Where to Find Dauphin Island, Alabama; Hobe Sound National Wildlife Refuge, Florida; Savannah National Wildlife Refuge, Georgia; Gulf Islands National Seashore, Mississippi.

Range Breeds locally in boreal and temperate regions of Old and New World (mostly Canada, northeastern United States, and West Indies); winters in south temperate and tropical regions.

169. Forster's Tern

Sterna forsteri
(L-15 W-31)

A medium-sized tern; orange or yellow bill with black tip; black cap and nape; white face and underparts; gray back and wings; forked tail, white on outer edgings, gray on inner; orange legs. **Winter** White head with blackish ear patch; bill black.

Voice "Chew-ik."

Similar Species Winter Common and Arctic terns have back of

Jaegers, Skuas, Gulls, Terns, Skimmers

crown and nape black (crown and nape are usually white in Forster's Tern).

Habitat Marshes, bays, beaches, marine.

Abundance and Distribution Common to uncommon transient and winter resident (Sept.–Apr.) in Florida and along the coast in Georgia, Alabama, and Mississippi; some nonbreeders remain through the summer (May–Aug.).

Where to Find Dauphin Island, Alabama; J. N. "Ding" Darling National Wildlife Refuge, Florida; St. Simons Island, Georgia; Gulf Islands National Seashore, Mississippi.

Range Breeds locally across the northern United States, south-central and southwestern Canada, and Atlantic and Gulf coasts; winters coastally from southern United States to Guatemala; also Greater Antilles.

170. Least Tern
Sterna antillarum
(L-9 W-20)

ENDANGERED. A small tern; yellow bill with black tip; black cap and nape with white forehead; white face and underparts; gray back and wings; tail deeply forked; yellow legs. **Winter** White head with blackish postorbital stripe and nape; bill brown; legs dull yellow.

Voice A high-pitched "ki-teek ki-teek ki-teek," etc.

Similar Species Least Tern has black nape, not white as in winter Forster's Tern; also Forster's Tern is much larger.

Habitat Bays, beaches, rivers, lakes, ponds.

Abundance and Distribution Common to uncommon summer resident* (Apr.–Sept.), mainly along the immediate coast, although locally common inland in Florida at breeding colonies on gravel rooftops and runways.

Where to Find Cumberland Island National Seashore, Georgia; Dauphin Island, Alabama; St. Andrews State Recreation Area, Florida; Gulf Islands National Seashore, Mississippi.

Range Breeds along both coasts from central California (west) and Maine (east) south to southern Mexico; endangered inland population breeds along rivers of Mississippi drainage; West Indies; winters along coast of northern South America.

171. Bridled Tern

Sterna anaethetus
(L-15 W-30)

Dark gray above, white below; black cap with white forehead and eyebrow; white collar; black bill and feet; deeply forked, brown tail edged in white. **Immature** Similar in pattern to adult, but paler above with grayish brown cap.

Similar Species Sooty Tern lacks collar, and white stripe extends to, but not behind, eye (extends behind eye in Bridled Tern).

Habitat Marine, bays, beaches.

Abundance and Distribution Uncommon to rare summer visitor (Apr.–Sept.) offshore; has bred* in the Keys.

Where to Find Pelagic bird trips.

Range Breeds locally on islands in tropical seas (including West Indies).

172. Sooty Tern

Sterna fuscata
(L-17 W-32)

Black above, white below; black cap with white forehead; black bill and feet; tail deeply forked, black with white edging. **Immature** Dark brown throughout with white spotting.

Habits Does not dive for fish as other terns do. It plucks fish from surface.

Jaegers, Skuas, Gulls, Terns, Skimmers

Figure 30. Service at Fort Jefferson on the Dry Tortugas must have seemed a lot like a prison sentence to nineteenth-century soldiers. There's not much there except the fort, the sun, the beach, and the sea. For twenty-first-century birders, though, it is a delightful day's outing from Key West by boat or seaplane to see some of the rarest birds on the continent, such as Masked and Brown boobies, White-tailed Tropicbirds, and Brown Noddys.

Voice A creaky "waky wak."

Similar Species Sooty Tern lacks collar, and white stripe extends to, but not behind, eye (extends behind eye in Bridled Tern).

Habitat Marine, bays, beaches.

Abundance and Distribution Common resident* in the Dry Tortugas and rare summer resident in the Lower Keys (Apr.–Aug.); otherwise, an uncommon to rare summer visitor (May–Sept.) offshore.

Where to Find Dry Tortugas National Park, Florida.

Range Breeds locally on tropical and subtropical coasts and islands throughout the world.

173. Black Tern
Chlidonias niger
(L-10 W-24)

A small tern; dark gray throughout except white undertail coverts; slightly forked tail. **Winter** Dark gray above, white below with dark smudge at shoulder; white forehead; white crown streaked with gray; gray nape; white collar.

Voice A high-pitched, repeated "kik kik kik."

Habits Note swallowlike flight in pursuit of insects.

Habitat Marshes, bays, estuaries, lakes, ponds.

Abundance and Distribution Common to rare transient (Jul.–Oct., Apr.–May) throughout, mainly along the coast; more numerous in fall (Aug.–Sept.) in Georgia and Florida and in spring in Alabama and Mississippi.

Where to Find Harris Neck National Wildlife Refuge, Georgia; Gulf State Park, Alabama; Everglades National Park, Florida; Gulf Islands National Seashore, Mississippi.

Range Breeds in temperate and boreal regions of Northern Hemisphere; winters in tropics.

174. Brown Noddy
Anous stolidus
(L-16 W-32)

Brown except for grayish forehead and crown. **Immature** Almost entirely brown, somewhat paler on forehead.

Habits Picks fish from surface rather than diving for them.

Voice A squawk: "karrr-rrak."

Similar Species Black Noddy has a darker body than the Brown Noddy contrasted with a whiter cap, limited mostly to the forehead, and a relatively thin bill.

Habitat Marine, beaches.

Abundance and Distribution Common resident* in the Dry Tortugas, Florida; otherwise an uncommon to rare summer visitor (Jun.–Oct.) offshore.

Where to Find Dry Tortugas National Park, Florida.

Range Resident of southern temperate and tropical seas.

175. Black Noddy
Anous minutus
(L-14 W-30)

Entirely black except for whitish forehead. **Immature** Like adult, but crown is less distinct.

Habits Picks fish from surface rather than diving for them.

Similar Species Black Noddy has a darker body than the Brown Noddy contrasted with a whiter cap, limited mostly to the forehead, and a relatively thin bill.

Habitat Marine, beaches.

Abundance and Distribution Rare to casual summer resident (Apr.–Aug.) in the Dry Tortugas, Florida.

Where to Find Dry Tortugas National Park, Florida.

Range Resident of tropical seas.

176. Black Skimmer
Rynchops niger
(L-18 W-45)

Black above; white below; long, straight razor-shaped bill, red with black tip; lower mandible is longer than the upper. **Immature** Like adult but mottled brown and white above.

Habits Flies over the water with the lower mandible dipped below the surface to capture fish.

Voice A mellow "kip," "kee-yip," or "kee-kee-yup."

Habitat Beaches, bays, estuaries.

Abundance and Distribution Common resident* along the immediate coast throughout the region and locally inland in Florida.

Where to Find Blackbeard Island National Wildlife Refuge, Georgia; Biscayne National Park, Florida; Dauphin Island, Alabama; US 90 between Gulfport and Biloxi, Mississippi; St. Andrews State Recreation Area, Florida.

Range Breeds from southern California (west) and New York (east) south to southern South America along coasts and on major river systems; winters in south temperate and tropical portions of breeding range, West Indies.

Doves and Pigeons
Order Columbiformes
Family Columbidae

The columbids are small to medium-sized, chunky birds with relatively small heads. Larger species are generally referred to as pigeons while smaller ones are doves. They feed on fruits and seeds, and produce "crop milk" (specialized cells sloughed from the esophagus) to feed their young. Clutch size is normally two throughout the group.

177. Rock Pigeon
Columba livia
(L-13 W-23)

The Rock Pigeon or domestic pigeon is highly variable in color, including various mixtures of brown, white, gray, and dark blue; the "average" bird shows gray above and below with head and neck iridescent purplish green; white rump; dark terminal band on tail.

Voice A series of low "coo"s.

Habitat Cities, towns, agricultural areas.

Abundance and Distribution Common resident* throughout the region.

Where to Find Atlanta, Georgia; Birmingham, Alabama; Miami, Florida; Jackson, Mississippi.

Range Resident of Eurasia and North Africa; introduced into the Western Hemisphere where resident nearly throughout at farms, towns, and cities.

SUMMER
MIGRATION
WINTER
PERMANENT

178. White-crowned Pigeon
Patagioenas leucocephala
(L-14 W-24)

A large, dark-bodied pigeon with white crown patch and iridescent nape (in good light); red feet. **Female** Gray crown patch. **Immature** Dingy, brownish white crown patch.

Habits Often travels in flocks to feeding areas.

Voice "Cooo-ca-rooo" or "cooo-ca-rooo-cooo."

Habitat Nests in mangroves on offshore islands; feeds on fruits in hardwood hammocks.

Abundance and Distribution Uncommon summer resident* (Apr.–Sept.) in South Florida and the Keys; uncommon to rare in winter (Oct.–Mar.).

Where to Find Castellow Hammock Preserve, Florida; Everglades National Park, Florida; Florida Keys National Wildlife Refuges, Florida.

Range Breeds from extreme south Florida and the Florida Keys south through the Bahamas, Greater Antilles, Lesser Antilles south to Antigua, the Caymans through the western Caribbean to the western Caribbean coastal areas (Yucatan south to Panama); winters mainly in southern portion of breeding range; nonbreeders north occasionally as far as Ft. Pierce, Florida.

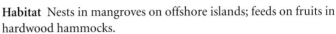

179. Ringed Turtle-Dove
Streptopelia risoria
(L-12 W-20)

Brownish buff above; pale buff below; bluish gray at bend of wing; black half-collar on the back of the neck; whitish primaries; white tips on the outer rectrices from above, entire bottom half of tail appears white from below; orange feet; eyes red.

Voice "COO-cooo cooo."

Similar Species The breast of the Eurasian Collared-Dove is purplish rather than pale buff as in the Ringed Turtle-Dove, and the primaries are dark instead of pale. Also the Ringed Turtle-Dove usually accents the first syllable of the song while the Eurasian Collared-Dove usually accents the second.

Habitat Residential areas.

Abundance and Distribution Introduced and apparently established locally in Pinellas Co., Florida.

Where to Find Downtown St. Petersburg (Jct of 29th St. and Dartmouth Ave.), Florida.

Range The Ringed Turtle-Dove is a domesticated species. Previously, it was thought to have been derived from the Eurasian Collared-Dove but taxonomic work indicates that the African Collared-Dove (*Streptopelia roseogrisea*) was the ancestral form (A.O.U. 1998).

180. Eurasian Collared-Dove
Streptopelia decaocto
(L-12 W-20)

Dusty brown body; black half-collar across back of neck; dark brown primaries; square tail with outer rectrices brownish at the base and whitish at the tip; orange feet; red eye.

Voice "Coo-COOO cooo."

Similar Species The breast of the Eurasian Collared-Dove is purplish rather than pale buff as in the Ringed Turtle-Dove, and the primaries are dark instead of pale. Also the Ringed Turtle-Dove usually accents the first syllable of the song while the Eurasian Collared-Dove usually accents the second.

Habitat Pines, wetlands, mangroves, residential areas.

Abundance and Distribution Common but local resident* in most residential areas of peninsular Florida, coastal Georgia, and the Keys; evidently populations are continuing to expand northward and westward in the Southeast.

Where to Find Cedar Keys National Wildlife Refuge, Florida; Key West, Florida; J. N. "Ding" Darling National Wildlife Refuge, Florida.

Figure 31. The harbor at Key West is a good site for Eurasian Collared-Doves though really almost any Florida residential area will do. This locality, however, has the added attraction of having the world's highest density of raunchy "T" shirt shops and bars selling strange alcoholic concoctions.

Range Throughout Europe, the Middle East, and western Asia (east to Myanmar). Introduced into Japan and the Bahamas. Populations derived from birds introduced into the Bahamas have spread to elsewhere in the West Indies, Florida, and other scattered localities in the southeastern United States.

181. White-winged Dove
Zenaida asiatica
(L-12 W-20)

Grayish brown above, grayish below; gray wings with broad white band on secondaries (visible as a broad white stripe along front edge of folded wing); light blue skin around red-orange eye; black whisker; red legs; broad white corners on square tail.

Voice A hoarse "caroo-co-coo" (who cooks for you) or "carroo coo-ooo coo-wik coo-ooo coo-wik."

SUMMER
MIGRATION
WINTER
PERMANENT

Habitat Pine forest, wetlands, residential areas, agricultural areas.

Abundance and Distribution Rare winter resident (Oct.–May) in Florida, mainly along the coast of the Panhandle and upper Gulf coast of the Peninsula; uncommon to rare resident* in the Miami area and Central Florida north to Orange and Volusia counties (expanding from introduced populations); uncommon to rare winter visitor in South Florida and the Keys.

Where to Find Castellow Hammock Preserve, Florida; Everglades National Park, Florida; Florida Keys National Wildlife Refuges, Florida; Dry Tortugas National Park, Florida (spring).

Range Breeds from the southwestern United States south through Middle and western South America to Chile; also in South Florida, the Bahamas, and Greater Antilles; winters from northern Mexico south through the breeding range.

182. Mourning Dove
Zenaida macroura
(L-12 W-18)

Tan above, orange buff below; brownish wings spotted with dark brown; tail long, pointed, and edged in white; gray cap; black whisker; purplish bronze iridescence on side of neck; blue eyering; brown eye and bill; pink feet.

Voice A low, hoarse "hoo-wooo hooo ho hooo."

Similar Species The long, pointed tail separates this from other doves that occur in the region.

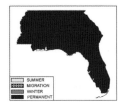

Habitat Woodlands, pastures, old fields, second growth, scrub, residential areas.

Abundance and Distribution Common resident* throughout the region.

Where to Find Fort Mountain State Park, Georgia; Vicksburg National Military Park, Mississippi; Bladon Springs State Park, Alabama; Tall Timbers Research Station, Florida.

Range Breeds from southern Canada south through United States to highlands of central Mexico, Costa Rica, Panama, Bahamas, Greater Antilles; winters in south temperate and tropical portions of breeding range.

183. Common Ground-Dove
Columbina passerina
(L-7 W-11)

A very small dove; grayish brown above with dark brown spotting on wing; gray tinged with pink below with scaly brown markings on breast; gray pileum; red eye; pink bill; flesh-colored legs; rusty wing patches show in flight; black outer tail feathers with white edgings. **Female** Like male but grayish below (not pinkish), and gray crown is less distinct.

Habits Thrusts head forward while walking.

Voice "Hoo-wih," repeated.

Habitat Sandy or grassy shrublands.

Abundance and Distribution Locally common to rare resident* in Florida and along the coast in Georgia, Alabama, and Mississippi; uncommon to rare or absent inland.

Where to Find Okefenokee National Wildlife Refuge, Georgia; Hobe Sound National Wildlife Refuge, Florida; DuPuis Management Area, Florida; Conecuh National Forest, Alabama; Gulf Islands National Seashore, Mississippi.

Range Southern United States south to northern half of South America, West Indies.

Parrots and Parakeets
Order Psittaciformes
Family Psittacidae

Parrots are brightly colored (often shades of green), noisy birds with large, hooked bills. They usually travel in pairs within flocks. The status of parrots in Florida is not clear. In recent years there have been increasing numbers of sightings, including reports of Burrowing Parrots, Budgerigars, and many other species not native to the region that are presumably escapes. Therefore, most parrot sightings have been written off as escaped cage birds. However, it is now evident from the number of sightings, and nests as well, that several of these species are established as breeding populations. A study is needed to further clarify the status of the many members of this group that have been sighted but not yet confirmed as breeding populations.

184. Budgerigar
Melopsittacus undulatus
(L-7 W-13)

Unlike the familiar bright blues and yellows of the domesticated forms of this species, most wild budgies are green with yellow faces, barred black and greenish yellow on the back, with long blue-green tails. Their small size, brilliant colors, and distinctive snubbed bills are unmistakable.

Habits Budgies nest in tree cavities, and often travel in large flocks.

Voice Raucous, squeaky chattering.

Habitat Residential areas.

Abundance and Distribution Uncommon to rare and local resident* of the west-central Florida Gulf coast (populations shift in location from year to year).

Where to Find Sarasota, Florida; Freedom Lake Park, St. Petersburg, Florida.

Range Australia. Introduced into west-central Florida.

185. Monk Parakeet
Myiopsitta monachus
(L-12 W-21)

Green above; blue-green outer primaries and rectrices; grayish white forehead and face; grayish white breast with faint barring; yellowish band across belly; green undertail coverts; long, pointed tail. **Immature** Like adult but with greenish forehead.

Habits Builds large colonial nests of sticks and grasses placed on poles or trees; feeds in flocks—often on agricultural crops.

Voice A harsh, screeching "eeeh," repeated.

Habitat Open woodland, savanna, riparian forest, agricultural and residential areas.

Abundance and Distribution Common to rare and local resident* in residential areas of Central and South Florida, especially along the coast; scattered records elsewhere in the region.

Where to Find Tropical Audubon Society Office, Miami, Florida.

Range Central Bolivia, Paraguay, and southern Brazil south to central Argentina; now established in many parts of the eastern and southern United States.

186. Red-masked Parakeet
Aratinga erythrogenys
(L-13 W-22)

Green body with long, graduated, green tail; brilliant red face, underwing coverts, and bend of wing; flesh-colored bill and feet.

Habitat Wooded residential areas.

Abundance and Distribution Rare and local resident*, mainly in the Greater Miami area.

Where to Find Curtiss Parkway, Miami, Florida.

Range Western South America. Introduced in South Florida.

187. Black-hooded Parakeet
Nandayus nenday
(L-14 W-22)

Green body; black head and bill; red nape and thighs; flesh-colored feet; bluish cast on green breast; long, dark, graduated tail; dark primaries and secondaries contrast with green wing linings in flight.

Habitat Wooded residential areas.

Abundance and Distribution Uncommon to rare and local resident* in some Florida cities (e.g., Miami, Sarasota, St. Petersburg, and Ft. Lauderdale)

Where to Find Curtiss Parkway, Miami, Florida.

Range Southern South America. Introduced in Florida.

188. Yellow-chevroned Parakeet

Brotogeris chiriri
(L-9 W-16)

Green-bodied, relatively small parakeet with graduated tail and broad, yellow wing bar across primaries and secondaries; flesh-colored bill and feet.

Similar Species The White-winged Parakeet, formerly considered conspecific with the Yellow-chevroned Parakeet, is virtually identical in size, shape, and coloration except for a broad, white wing patch (outer secondaries and interior primaries), visible mainly in flight.

Habitat Residential parkland.

Abundance and Distribution Common to rare and local resident* in southeast Florida.

Where to Find Curtiss Parkway, Miami.

Range Southern Amazon basin to northern Argentina in South America. Introduced into southeast Florida.

189. White-winged Parakeet

Brotogeris versicolurus
(L-9 W-16)

Green-bodied, relatively small parakeet with graduated tail and broad, yellow wing bar across primaries and secondary coverts; white inner primaries and outer secondaries; flesh-colored bill and feet.

Similar Species The Yellow-chevroned Parakeet, formerly considered conspecific with the White-winged Parakeet, is virtually identical in size, shape, and coloration except it lacks the broad, white wing patch (outer secondaries and interior primaries), visible mainly in flight.

Habitat Residential parkland.

Abundance and Distribution Common to rare and local resident* in southeast Florida (Ft. Lauderdale, Miami).

Where to Find Curtiss Parkway, Miami.

Range Northern Amazon basin of South America. Introduced into Southeast Florida.

Parrots, Parakeets

SUMMER
MIGRATION
WINTER
PERMANENT

190. Red-crowned Parrot
Amazona viridigenalis
(L-12 W-20)

Green body; red crown and wing patch.

Habits Parrots are almost always seen in pairs, even in flocks in flight.

Voice Loud screams: "keek bereeek keek keek."

Habitat Riparian forest, open woodlands.

Abundance and Distribution Rare and local resident* in southeast Florida (Ft. Lauderdale, Miami).

Where to Find Downtown Ft. Lauderdale, Florida; Curtiss Parkway, Miami, Florida.

Range Gulf lowlands of northeastern Mexico. Introduced into South Florida.

Cuckoos and Anis
Order Cuculiformes
Family Cuculidae

Cuckoos are a family of trim, long-tailed birds found in both the Old and New worlds; several species lay their eggs in other birds' nests. Like parrots, woodpeckers, and some other avian groups, cuckoos perch with two toes forward and two toes backward (most birds have 3 toes forward and one toe backward).

191. Black-billed Cuckoo
Coccyzus erythropthalmus
(L-12 W-16)

A thin, streamlined bird with long, graduated tail; red eyering; black bill; brown above; white below; dark brown tail with white tips.

Habits Slow, deliberate, reptilian foraging movements.

Voice A mellow "coo-coo-coo," repeated.

Similar Species Yellow-billed and Mangrove cuckoos have a yellow eyering (red in blackbill); Yellow-billed Cuckoo has a partially yellow upper mandible (dark in blackbill and Mangrove Cuckoo), and entirely yellow lower mandible (dark in blackbill), prominent white tail spots (small spots in blackbill), and rusty wing patch visible in flight (lacking in both Mangrove and blackbill); also,

Mangrove Cuckoo has black mask, buffy underparts (not white as in blackbill and yellowbill).

Habitat Deciduous and mixed forest; also overgrown fields with shrubby second growth.

Abundance and Distribution Rare fall transient (Sept.–Oct.) throughout; rare to casual spring transient (May), mainly Panhandle.

Where to Find Little River Canyon National Preserve, Alabama; Okefenokee National Wildlife Refuge, Georgia.

Range Breeds in the northeastern quarter of the United States and southeastern Canada; winters in the northern half of South America.

192. Yellow-billed Cuckoo
Coccyzus americanus
(L-12 W-17)

A thin, streamlined bird with long, graduated tail; dark bill with partially yellow upper mandible, and completely yellow lower mandible and eyering; brown above; white below; dark brown tail with white tips; rusty wing patches visible in flight.

Habits Slow, deliberate, reptilian foraging movements.

Voice A metallic "ka-ka-ka-ka-ka-ka cow cow cow," also a low, hoarse "cow."

Similar Species Yellow-billed and Mangrove cuckoos have a yellow eyering (red in blackbill); Yellow-billed Cuckoo has a partially yellow upper mandible (dark in blackbill and Mangrove Cuckoo), and entirely yellow lower mandible (dark in blackbill), prominent white tail spots (small spots in blackbill), and rusty wing patch visible in flight (lacking in both Mangrove and blackbill); also, Mangrove Cuckoo has black mask, buffy underparts (not white as in blackbill and yellowbill).

Habitat Deciduous woodlands and second growth.

Abundance and Distribution Common to uncommon transient and summer resident* (Apr.-Oct.) throughout the region.

Where to Find Cloudland Canyon State Park, Georgia; Choctaw National Wildlife Refuge, Alabama; Bogue Chitto National Wildlife Refuge, Mississippi; Lower Suwannee National Wildlife Refuge, Florida.

Range Breeds from southeastern Canada and nearly throughout the United States into northern Mexico and West Indies; winters in north and central South America.

Cuckoos, Anis

193. Mangrove Cuckoo
Coccyzus minor
(L-12 W-17)

Grayish brown above; buffy below; black mask; dark, graduated tail with white tips.

Voice Similar to that of Yellow-billed Cuckoo but faster and lower pitched.

Similar Species Other cuckoos lack black mask and have white (not buffy) breast.

Habitat Mangrove swamps, coastal woodlands and scrub.

Abundance and Distribution Uncommon to rare summer resident* (Apr.–Sept.) along the Central and South Florida coast (mainly gulfside) and the Keys, rare to casual in winter.

Where to Find Everglades National Park, Florida; J. N. "Ding" Darling National Wildlife Refuge, Florida; Lower Florida Keys National Wildlife Refuges, Florida.

Range Breeds from South Florida, coastal Mexico and Central America to Panama; West Indies; winters in all except northern portions of breeding range and along Venezuelan coast.

Figure 32. Key West was once just a colorful outpost of Hemingway's "islands in the stream." A place where the water, "was dark blue when you looked out at it when there was no wind. But when you walked out into it there was just the green light of the water over that floury white sand and you could see the shadow of any big fish a long time before he could ever come in close to the beach" (Hemingway 1970). A place for beach-combing, tarpon fishing, and dreaming. Now it's a '60s-style, party weekend theme park for frustrated baby-boomers. Nevertheless, the breezes are still warm, the seas are still blue, and just a few minutes drive eastward at places like the Florida Keys National Wildlife Refuge on Big Pine Key, you can still find good reasons for braving 80 miles of 2-lane traffic on US 1. Mangroves and hammocks here are home to Great White Herons, Yellow-crowned Night-Herons, Roseate Spoonbills, Wood Storks, Reddish Egrets, and, of course, "cute little" Key Deer.

194. Smooth-billed Ani
Crotophaga ani
(L-14 W-16)

Black throughout; large, smooth, parrotlike bill; very long tail.

Habits Anis crawl around in shrubs in a ratlike fashion. They often associate in groups during much of the year, and sometimes nest communally.

Voice An ascending "kar-eek."

Similar Species Smooth-billed Ani bill has a raised central ridge; also the bill is smooth rather than grooved as in the Groove-billed Ani; calls are different.

Habitat Scrub, hedgerows, pastures.

Abundance and Distribution Uncommon to rare local resident* in South Florida and the Keys.

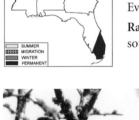

Where to Find Loxahatchee National Wildlife Refuge, Florida; Everglades National Park, Florida.

Range South Florida south through the West Indies and parts of southern Central America to southern South America.

195. Groove-billed Ani
Crotophaga sulcirostris
(L-14 W-16)

Black throughout; large, grooved, parrotlike bill; very long tail.

Habits Anis crawl around in shrubs in a ratlike fashion. They associate in groups throughout the year, and nest communally; often seen with cattle.

Voice "Chik bereek."

Similar Species Smooth-billed Ani bill has a raised central ridge; also the bill is smooth rather than grooved as in the Groove-billed Ani; calls are different.

Habitat Scrub, pastures, hedgerows.

Abundance and Distribution Rare winter resident (Oct.–Apr.) in the Florida Panhandle and coastal Mississippi; casual in peninsular Florida.

Where to Find Gulf Islands National Seashore, Florida; St. Vincent National Wildlife Refuge, Florida.

Range South Texas and northwestern Mexico south to northern Argentina and Chile.

Cuckoos, Anis

Barn Owls

Order Strigiformes
Family Tytonidae

Tytonid owls are a small, cosmopolitan family comprising 12 species, of which only one, the Barn Owl, occurs regularly in North America.

196. Barn Owl

Tyto alba
(L-16 W-45)

Tawny and gray above; white sparsely spotted with brown below; white, monkeylike face, and large, dark eyes; long legs.

Habits Almost strictly nocturnal.

Voice Eerie screeches and hisses.

Habitat Old fields, pasture, grasslands, farmland; roosts in barns, caves, abandoned mine shafts.

Abundance and Distribution Common to rare resident* in Florida and along the coastal plain in Georgia, Alabama, and Mississippi. Status of this species is poorly known because of its nocturnal habits, but numbers appear to increase in winter because of an influx of migrants from the north.

Where to Find Everglades National Park, Florida.

Range Resident in temperate and tropical regions nearly throughout the world.

Typical Owls

Family Strigidae

Strigid owls comprise a large family of fluffy-plumaged, mainly nocturnal raptors. Plumage coloration is mostly muted browns and grays; two toes forward and two backward when perched. Ear structures are asymmetrical for ranging distance to prey.

197. Eastern Screech-Owl

Megascops asio
(L-9 W-22)

Red Phase A small, long-eared, yellow-eyed owl with a pale bill;

rufous above; streaked with rust, brown, and white below; rusty facial disk with white eyebrows. **Gray Phase** Similar to red phase but gray rather than rusty. Brown birds intermediate between the two phases also occur.

Voice A quavering, descending whistle; also a low, quavering whistle on a single pitch.

Habitat Woodlands, residential areas.

Abundance and Distribution Common resident* throughout the Southeast, although rare or absent from the Lower Keys.

Where to Find Fort Mountain State Park, Georgia; Oak Mountain State Park, Alabama; Lower Suwannee National Wildlife Refuge, Florida; Clarkco State Park, Mississippi.

Range Resident from southeastern Canada and the eastern half of the United States to northeastern Mexico.

198. Great Horned Owl

Bubo virginianus
(L-22 W-52)

A large owl; mottled brown, gray, buff, and white above; grayish white below barred with brown; yellow eyes; rusty facial disk; white throat (not always visible); long ear tufts.

Habits Eats skunks as well as many other small to medium-sized vertebrates.

Voice A series of low hoots, "ho-hoo hooo hoo"; female's call is higher pitched than male's.

Similar Species The smaller Long-eared Owl (casual in the Southeast) is streaked rather than barred below and ear tufts are placed more centrally; other large owls lack long ear tufts.

Habitat Woodlands.

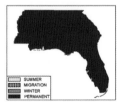

Abundance and Distribution Uncommon resident* nearly throughout the region, although absent from the Keys.

Where to Find DeSoto State Park, Alabama; Chewalla Lake, Holly Springs National Forest, Mississippi; Watson Mill Bridge State Park, Georgia; St. Marks National Wildlife Refuge, Florida.

Range New World except polar regions.

Typical Owls

199. Burrowing Owl
Athene cunicularia
(L-9 W-24)

A long-legged, terrestrial owl; brown spotted with white above; white collar, eyebrows, and forehead; white below with brown barring.

Habits Often associated with prairie dog towns in the western United States, this owl spends most of its time on the ground or perched on fence posts.

Voice A whistled "coo-hoo"; various other squeaks and whistles.

Similar Species The long legs and terrestrial habits are distinctive.

Habitat Prairies, pastures, agricultural areas.

Abundance and Distribution Uncommon and local resident* in most of peninuslar Florida, the Upper Florida Keys, and Okaloosa Co. in the Panhandle; also reported from the Gulf coast of Alabama, Mississippi, and the Panhandle.

Where to Find Everglades National Park, Florida; Arbuckle Creek Road, Lorida, Florida.

Range Breeds from southwestern Canada and the western United States south to central Mexico, Florida, and the West Indies; locally in South America.

Typical Owls

200. Barred Owl
Strix varia
(L-18 W-42)

A large, dark-eyed owl; brown mottled with white above; white barred with brown on throat and breast, streaked with brown on belly.

Voice "Haw haw haw ha-hoo-aw" (who cooks for you all).

Similar Species The Barred Owl has concentric rings of brown and white on the facial disk, a neck ruff of horizontal brown and white bars, and a breast and belly streaked with brown and white. This pattern and the lack of ear tufts are distinctive.

Habitat Deciduous and mixed forest.

Abundance and Distribution Common to uncommon resident* nearly throughout the region except for the Keys.

Where to Find Black Rock Mountain State Park, Georgia; Little River Canyon National Preserve, Alabama; St. Catherine Creek National Wildlife Refuge, Mississippi; Tall Timbers Research Station, Florida.

Range Resident from southern Canada and the eastern half of the United States; locally in northwestern United States and in the central plateau of Mexico.

201. Short-eared Owl
Asio flammeus
(L-15 W-42)

A medium-sized owl; brown streaked with buff above; buff streaked with brown below; round facial disk with short ear tufts and yellow eyes; buffy patch shows on upper wing in flight; black patch at wrist visible on wing lining.

Habits Crepuscular. Forages by coursing low over open areas—reminiscent of Northern Harrier.

Voice A sharp "chik-chik" and various squeaks.

Similar Species Tawny color and lack of ear tufts separate this from other owl species.

Habitat Grasslands, marshes, estuaries, agricultural fields.

Abundance and Distribution Rare to casual winter resident (Nov.–Mar.) in Florida and along the coastal plain in Georgia, Alabama, and Mississippi; uncommon to rare in spring (Mar.–May) in the Lower Keys and Dry Tortugas.

Where to Find Savannah National Wildlife Refuge, Georgia; St. Marks National Wildlife Refuge, Florida; Noxubee National Wildlife Refuge, Mississippi; Eufaula National Wildlife Refuge, Alabama.

Range Breeds in tundra, boreal, and north temperate areas of Northern Hemisphere, also in Hawaiian Islands; winters in southern portions of breeding range south to northern tropical regions.

Typical Owls

Goatsuckers, Nightjars, and Nighthawks

Order Caprimulgiformes
Family Caprimulgidae

Most of the caprimulgids have soft, fluffy plumage of browns, grays, and buff. Long, pointed wings and extremely large, bristle-lined mouth are also distinctive characters of the group. Usually crepuscular or nocturnal, they forage for insects in batlike fashion with characteristic swoops and dives.

202. Lesser Nighthawk
Chordeiles acutipennis
(L-9 W-22)

Mottled dark brown, gray and white above; whitish below with black bars; white throat; white band across primaries and tail; tail slightly forked. **Female** Buffy rather than white on throat, lacks white tail bar.

Habits Normally forages with a fluttering flight low over the ground.

Voice A quavering trill.

SUMMER
MIGRATION
WINTER
PERMANENT

Similar Species Common Nighthawk call is different (a sharp, nasal "bezzzt"); Common Nighthawk usually forages high above the ground; white on primary is closer to bend of wing in Common Nighthawk than in Lesser Nighthawk. In Florida, there are no winter specimen records for the Common Nighthawk, but there are several for the Lesser Nighthawk; thus winter nighthawks are likely to be this species (*fide* B. A. Anderson).

Habitat A variety of open and semi-open situations in both urban and rural environments.

Abundance and Distribution Rare to casual transient (Nov., Apr.–May) throughout Florida; rare to casual winter visitor (Dec.–Mar.) in South Florida.

Where to Find Loxahatchee National Wildlife Refuge, Florida; Eco Pond, Everglades National Park, Florida.

Range Breeds in the southwestern United States and northern Mexico south, through Central and South America to southern Brazil; winters from southern Mexico south, through the breeding range.

203. Common Nighthawk

Chordeiles minor
(L-9 W-23)

Mottled dark brown, gray, and white above; whitish below with black bars; white throat; white band across primaries and tail; tail slightly forked. **Female** Buffy rather than white on throat.

Habits Crepuscular. Normally forages high above the ground; has a dive display in which the bird plummets toward the ground, swerving up at the last moment and making a whirring sound with the wings.

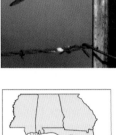

Voice "Bezzzt."

Similar Species In flight, the sleek dark form with the prominent white bar across the primaries is distinctive. Sitting, the bird is readily distinguished from other goatsuckers by the white throat and white bar visible even on the folded primaries.

Habitat A variety of open and semi-open situations in both urban and rural environments.

Abundance and Distribution Common to uncommon summer resident* (Apr.–Oct.) throughout the Southeast.

Where to Find Natchez State Park, Mississippi; Lower Suwannee National Wildlife Refuge, Florida; Tuskegee National Forest, Alabama; Chickamauga and Chattanooga National Military Park, Georgia.

Range Breeds locally from central and southern Canada south through the United States and Middle America to Panama; winters in South America.

204. Antillean Nighthawk

Chordeiles gundlachii
(L-8 W-20)

Mottled dark brown, gray, and white above; whitish below with black bars; white throat; white band across primaries and tail; tail slightly forked. **Female and Immature** Lack broad white tail band.

Voice "Pit pit pit."

Similar Species The Common Nighthawk is very similar in appearance to the Antillean Nighthawk, best distinguished by voice.

Habitat Coastal scrub.

Abundance and Distribution Uncommon to rare summer resident* (Apr.–Sept.) in the Florida Keys, especially the Lower Keys, and adjacent mainland.

Where to Find Florida Keys National Wildlife Refuges, Florida; Everglades National Park, Florida.

Range Breeds in extreme South Florida, the Florida Keys, Bahamas, and Greater Antilles; winters in South America.

205. Chuck-will's-widow
Caprimulgus carolinensis
(L-12 W-25)

A large nightjar; tawny, buff and dark brown above; chestnut and buff barred with dark brown below; white throat; long, rounded tail with white inner webbing on outer 3 feathers; rounded wings. **Female** Has buffy tips rather than white inner webbing on outer tail feathers.

Habits Nocturnal.

Voice "Chuck-wills-widow," also moaning growls.

Similar Species Lacks white wing patches of nighthawks; the smaller, darker Whip-poor-will has extensive white on tail in male, buff in female.

Habitat Open deciduous, mixed and pine woodlands.

Abundance and Distribution Common to uncommon summer resident* (Apr.–Sept.) nearly throughout the region, although scarce or absent from the highlands.

Where to Find Stephen C. Foster State Park, Georgia; Mississippi Sandhill Crane National Wildlife Refuge, Mississippi; Lake Woodruff National Wildlife Refuge, Florida; Oak Mountain State Park, Alabama.

Range Breeds across the eastern half of the United States, mainly in the southeast; permanent resident in parts of the West Indies; winters from eastern Mexico south through Central America to Colombia; also winters in South Florida and the West Indies.

206. Whip-poor-will
Caprimulgus vociferus
(L-10 W-19)

Dark brown mottled with buff above; grayish barred with dark brown below; dark throat and breast with white patch; rounded tail with white outer 3 feathers; rounded wings. **Female** Has buffy tips rather than white on outer tail feathers.

Habits Nocturnal.

Goatsuckers, Nightjars, Nighthawks

Voice A rapid, whistled "whip-poor-will" monotonously repeated.

Habitat Deciduous, mixed, and coniferous forest; also second growth forest and woodlots.

Abundance and Distribution Uncommon summer resident* (Apr.–Oct.) inland in Alabama, Mississippi, and Georgia; rare transient (Sept.–Oct., Apr.–May) along the coastal plain of Alabama, Mississippi, and Georgia; uncommon to rare transient and winter visitor (Sept.–Apr.) in most of Florida, although very scarce to absent in the Keys.

Where to Find Black Rock Mountain State Park, Georgia; Sipsey Wilderness, William B. Bankhead National Forest, Alabama; Tombigbee State Park, Mississippi; Biscayne National Park, Florida; Corkscrew Swamp Sanctuary, Florida.

Range Breeds across southeastern and south-central Canada and the eastern United States, also in the southwestern United States through the highlands of Mexico and Central America to Honduras; winters from northern Mexico to Panama, Cuba, also rarely along Gulf and Atlantic coasts of southeastern United States.

Swifts

Order Apodiformes
Family Apodidae

Swifts are small to medium-sized, stubby-tailed birds with long, pointed wings. In flight, an extremely rapid, shallow wingbeat is characteristic

Swifts

207. Chimney Swift
Chaetura pelagica
(L-5 W-12)

Dark throughout; stubby, square tail; long narrow wing.

Voice Rapid series of "chip"s.

Similar Species Cigar shape (stub tail), rapid wingbeat, and constant twittering during flight separate this bird from swallows.

Habitat Widely distributed over most habitat types wherever appropriate nesting and roosting sites are available (chimneys, cliffs, caves, crevices, hollow trees). Often seen over towns and cities where chimneys are available for roosting.

Abundance and Distribution Common summer resident* (Apr.–Sept.) throughout most of the Southeast, but an uncommon to rare transient in the Keys.

Where to Find Miami, Florida; Jackson, Mississippi; Birmingham, Alabama; Athens, Georgia.

Range Breeds throughout eastern North America; winters mainly in Peru.

Hummingbirds
Family Trochilidae

Hummingbirds are tiny, brilliantly colored birds that feed on nectar and insects. The only bird species in our region that can fly backwards.

208. Ruby-throated Hummingbird
Archilochus colubris
(L-4 W-4)

Green above; whitish below; red throat. **Female and Immature** Green above, whitish below; rounded green tail with whitish tips; immature male often shows red feathers on throat.

Voice Song: "chip chipit chip chipit chipit" etc.

Similar Species The rubythroat is the only hummingbird that breeds regularly in the eastern United States.

Habitat Woodlands, second growth, brushy pastures and fields; gardens.

Abundance and Distribution Common to uncommon summer resident* (Apr.–Sept.) in the Panhandle and North Florida, Georgia, Alabama, and Mississippi; uncommon to rare resident* in Central Florida; uncommon to rare transient and winter visitor (Sept.–Apr.) in South Florida and the Keys, casual in summer*.

Where to Find Moccasin Creek State Park, Georgia; Oak Mountain State Park, Alabama; Vicksburg National Military Park, Mississippi; Tall Timbers Research Station, Florida; Merritt Island National Wildlife Refuge, Florida.

Range Breeds in southern Canada and the eastern half of the United States; winters from southern Mexico to Costa Rica; also South Florida and Cuba.

Figure 33. Whether you choose to hike through the mixed hardwood forest or paddle the Sipsey Fork (a federal Wild and Scenic River), the Sipsey Wilderness of northwestern Alabama offers some of the state's most beautiful scenery and excellent birding. Ray Vaughan, in his book *Birder's Guide to Alabama and Mississippi*, says that spring warblers here are spectacular.

209. Black-chinned Hummingbird
Archilochus alexandri
(L-4 W-4)

Green above; whitish below; black throat. **Female and Immature** Green above, whitish below; rounded green tail with white tips; immature males often show black feathers on throat.

Voice Song: series of high-pitched "tsip" notes.

Similar Species Female blackchin is indistinguishable from female rubythroat in the field.

Habitat Residential gardens, coastal scrub.

Abundance and Distribution Rare to casual winter visitor (Oct.–Apr.) in southern Mississippi, southern Alabama, the Panhandle, and North Florida.

Where to Find Gulf Islands National Seashore, Florida.

Range Breeds in arid portions of southwestern Canada and the western United States south to northern Mexico; winters in central and southern Mexico.

210. Rufous Hummingbird
Selasphorus rufus
(L-4 W-4)

Rufous above; whitish below with rufous flanks and tail; orange-red gorget; green crown and wings; wings whistle in flight. **Female** Green above; white below with contrasting rufous flanks; throat often flecked with orange red; tail rufous at base with white tips.

Voice A high "zip" or a rasping "zee." (Edwards 1972:113).

Habitat Residential gardens.

SUMMER
MIGRATION
WINTER
PERMANENT

Abundance and Distribution Uncommon to casual winter visitor (Aug.–Mar.) to southern Mississippi, southern Alabama, the Panhandle and North Florida (Aug.–Mar.) and elsewhere along the Gulf coast.

Range Breeds in western Canada and the northwestern United States; winters from southern California, the Gulf coast, and south Texas south to southern Mexico.

Kingfishers
Order Coraciiformes
Family Alcedinidae

Kingfishers are stocky, vocal birds; predominantly slate blue or green with long, chisel-shaped bills and shaggy crests; generally found near water where they dive from a perch or from the air for fish.

211. Belted Kingfisher
Ceryle alcyon
(L-13 W-22)

Blue gray above with ragged crest; white collar, throat, and belly; blue-gray breast band. **Female** Like male but with chestnut band across belly in addition to blue-gray breast band.

Voice A loud rattle.

Habitat Rivers, lakes, ponds, bays.

Abundance and Distribution Common to uncommon resident* in Georgia, Alabama, Mississippi, the Panhandle, North, and Central Florida; more numerous in winter and less numerous in summer in the Panhandle and North

Florida and along the coastal plain of Georgia, Alabama, and Mississippi; uncommon winter resident (Sept.–Apr.) in Central and South Florida and the Keys.

Where to Find Tombigbee State Park, Mississippi; Reed Bingham State Park, Georgia; Lagoon Park, Montgomery, Alabama; St. Marks National Wildlife Refuge, Florida.

Range Breeds throughout most of temperate and boreal North America excluding arid Southwest; winters from southern portion of breeding range south through Mexico and Central America to northern South America; West Indies; Bermuda.

Woodpeckers
Order Piciformes
Family Picidae

A distinctive family of birds with plumages of mainly black and white. Long claws, stubby, strong feet, and stiff tail feathers enable woodpeckers to forage by clambering over tree trunks. The long, heavy, pointed bill is used for chiseling, probing, flicking, or hammering for arthropods. Most species fly in a distinct, undulating manner.

212. Red-headed Woodpecker
Melanerpes erythrocephalus
(L-10 W-18)

Black above, white below with scarlet head. **Immature** Head brownish.

Voice A loud "keeeer."

Habitat Open oak woodlands, riparian stands.

Abundance and Distribution Uncommon to rare resident* in the Panhandle, North, and Central Florida and the piedmont and coastal plain of Georgia, Alabama, and Mississippi, rare in the highlands; rare winter resident (Sept.–May) in South Florida, casual in the Keys.

Where to Find Tuskegee National Forest, Alabama; Cypress Swamp, Natchez Trace Parkway, Mississippi; Ocmulgee National Monument, Georgia; Wekiwa Springs State Park, Florida.

Range Eastern North America from the central plains and southern Canada to Texas and Florida.

213. Red-bellied Woodpecker
Melanerpes carolinus
(L-10 W-16)

Nape and crown red; barred black and white on back and tail; white rump; dirty white below with reddish tinge on belly. **Female** Crown whitish.

Voice A repeated "churr."

Similar Species Only the rare Red-cockaded among other woodpeckers found in the region has a back barred black and white, and it does not have the red cap and nape and white rump of the Red-bellied Woodpecker.

Habitat Riparian forests and mixed woodlands.

Abundance and Distribution Common resident* nearly throughout the region, although rare in the highlands.

Where to Find Sweetwater Creek State Conservation Park, Georgia; Tuskegee National Forest, Alabama; Mathews Brake National Wildlife Refuge, Mississippi; Lake Kissimmee State Park, Florida.

Range Eastern United States.

214. Yellow-bellied Sapsucker
Sphyrapicus varius
(L-8 W-15)

Black and white above; creamy yellow below with dark flecks on sides; breast black; throat, forehead, and crown red; black and white facial pattern. **Female** White throat. **Immature** Black wings with white patch, white rump, and checked black and white tail of adults; but barred brownish and cream on head, back, breast, and belly.

Voice A thin, nasal "cheerr."

Similar Species The yellow belly serves to distinguish this bird from the other woodpeckers in the region.

Habitat Deciduous and mixed forest.

Abundance and Distribution Common to rare winter resident (Oct.–Apr.) throughout the region; has bred* in the Georgia mountains.

Where to Find Lake Guntersville State Park, Alabama; Donivan Slough, Natchez Trace Parkway, Mississippi; Grand Bay Wildlife Management Area, Georgia; Lower Suwannee National Wildlife Refuge, Florida.

Range Breeds in temperate and boreal, wooded regions of Canada and the United States; winters from the southern United States south to Panama and the West Indies.

Woodpeckers

215. Downy Woodpecker
Picoides pubescens
(L-7 W-12)

Black and white above; white below; red cap on back portion of crown. **Female** Black cap.

Voice A sharp "peek"; a rapid, descending series of "pik"s.

Similar Species The white back separates this sparrow-sized woodpecker from all others except the thrush-sized Hairy Woodpecker, which is much larger (most races) and has lower, usually single, call note (although subspecies of both the Downy Woodpecker and the Hairy Woodpecker vary significantly in size).

Habitat Forests, second growth, and parklands.

Abundance and Distribution Common resident* nearly throughout the region; absent from the Keys.

Where to Find Cloudland Canyon State Park, Georgia; Bladon Springs State Park, Alabama; Wekiwa Springs State Park, Florida; Natchez State Park, Mississippi.

Range Temperate and boreal North America south to southern California, Arizona, New Mexico, and Texas.

216. Hairy Woodpecker
Picoides villosus
(L-9 W-15)

Black and white above; white below; red cap on back portion of crown. **Female** Black cap.

Voice A sharp "pick"; a descending series of "pick"s.

Similar Species The white back separates this thrush-sized woodpecker from all others except the sparrow-sized Downy Woodpecker, which is much smaller and has higher-pitched call note and rattle.

Habitat Coniferous, mixed, deciduous, and riparian woodlands.

Abundance and Distribution Uncommon to rare and local resident* nearly throughout the Southeast, although rare or absent from South Florida and the Keys.

Where to Find Cheaha State Park, Alabama; John W. Kyle State Park, Mississippi; Chickamauga and Chattanooga National Military Park, Georgia; Jay B. Starkey Wilderness Park, Florida.

Range Temperate and boreal North America south through the mountains of western Mexico and Central America to Panama. Bahamas.

Woodpeckers

217. Red-cockaded Woodpecker

Picoides borealis

(L-8 W-15)

ENDANGERED Barred black and white above; white below flecked with black along sides; white cheek bordered below by black stripe; red spot ("cockade") on back of head is generally not visible. **Female** No red spot.

Voice A "srip" call is given by family group members regularly as they forage.

Similar Species Only the Red-bellied Woodpecker among other woodpeckers found in the region has a back barred black and white, and it has a red cap and nape and white rump, which the Red-cockaded Woodpecker lacks.

Habitat Pine savanna—especially mature longleaf and loblolly pine stands, but also in slash, shortleaf, Virginia, and, probably, pitch pine.

Abundance and Distribution Uncommon and local resident* in the Panhandle, North and Central Florida and along the coastal

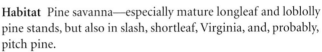

Figure 34. Okefenokee National Wildlife Refuge is a must stop for swamp aficionados. In addition to canebrake rattlesnakes, gators, and cottonmouths galore, there are good populations of Swallow-tailed Kites and Red-cockaded Woodpeckers.

Woodpeckers

plain of Georgia, Alabama, and Mississippi; rare and local resident* in South Florida (south to Monroe Co.).

Where to Find Noxubee National Wildlife Refuge, Mississippi; Oakmulgee District, Talladega National Forest, Alabama; Okefenokee National Wildlife Refuge, Georgia; Jonathan Dickinson State Park, Florida.

Range Southeastern United States.

218. Northern Flicker
Colaptes auratus
(L-12 W-20)

Barred brown and black above; tan with black spots below; black breast; white rump. Eastern forms have yellow underwings and tail linings, gray cap and nape with red occiput, tan face and throat with black mustache. **Female** Lacks mustache.

Voice A long series of "kek"s first rising, then falling; a "kleer" followed by several "wika"s.

Habitat Forests, parklands, orchards, woodlots, and residential areas; occasionally even nests in open areas—in banks or sawdust piles.

Abundance and Distribution Uncommon resident* nearly throughout the region, although casual or absent from the Keys; more numerous in winter.

Where to Find Lake Woodruff National Wildlife Refuge, Florida; Cheaha State Park, Alabama; Fort Yargo State Park, Georgia; St. Catherine Creek National Wildlife Refuge, Mississippi.

Range Nearly throughout temperate and boreal North America south in highlands of Mexico to Oaxaca. Leaves northern portion of breeding range in winter.

219. Pileated Woodpecker
Dryocopus pileatus
(L-17 W-27)

Black, crow-sized bird; black and white facial pattern; red mustache and crest; white wing lining. **Female** Black mustache.

Voice Loud "kuk kuk kuk kuk kuk kuk"—stops abruptly, does not trail off like flicker. The drum is a loud, sonorous rattle on a large log or stub, first increasing, then decreasing in pace—lasting 2–3 seconds.

Habitat Deciduous and mixed forest.

Woodpeckers

Abundance and Distribution Uncommon resident* nearly throughout the Southeast, although rare to absent from the Keys.

Where to Find Clear Springs Lake, Homochitto National Forest, Mississippi; Piedmont National Wildlife Refuge, Georgia; DeSoto State Park, Alabama; J. N. "Ding" Darling National Wildlife Refuge, Florida.

Range Much of temperate and boreal North America excluding Great Plains and Rocky Mountain regions.

Flycatchers and Kingbirds

Order Passeriformes
Family Tyrannidae

A large group of mostly tropical songbirds, robin sized or smaller. The flycatchers are characterized by erect posture, muted plumage coloration (olives, browns, and grays), a broad bill, hooked at the tip, and bristles around the mouth. Flycatchers are mostly insectivorous, often capturing their prey on the wing.

220. Olive-sided Flycatcher
Contopus cooperi
(L-8 W-13)

Olive above; white below with olive on sides of breast and belly; white tufts on lower back sometimes difficult to see.

Voice "Whit whew whew" (quick, three beers!).

Similar Species Eastern Wood-Pewee is smaller, has wing bars, and lacks dark olive along sides of breast and belly.

Habitat Breeds in hemlock and spruce-fir forests where it often perches on lone, tall, dead snags; found in a variety of forested habitats during migration.

Abundance and Distribution Rare to casual transient (Aug.–Sept., May) throughout the region, more numerous in fall.

Range Breeds in boreal forest across the northern tier of North America and through mountains in west south to Texas and northern Baja California; winters in mountains of South America from Colombia to Peru.

Flycatchers, Kingbirds

221. Eastern Wood-Pewee
Contopus virens
(L-6 W-10)

Dark olive above; greenish wash on breast; belly whitish; white wing bars.

Voice Song: plaintive "peeeaweee, peeeaweee, peeyer"; call: "peeyer."

Similar Species Pewees lack the eyering of *Empidonax* species, and show distinct wing bars, unlike phoebes.

Habitat Deciduous and mixed woodlands.

Abundance and Distribution Common to uncommon transient and summer resident* (Apr.–Oct.) in Georgia, Alabama, Mississippi, and the Florida Panhandle, uncommon to rare in North Florida; uncommon to rare transient (Aug.–Oct., Apr.–May) in Central and South Florida and the Keys.

Where to Find Oakmulgee District, Talladega National Forest, Alabama; Natchez State Park, Mississippi; Watson Mill Bridge State Park, Georgia; St. Marks National Wildlife Refuge, Florida.

Range Breeds in the eastern United States and southeastern Canada; winters in northern South America.

222. Yellow-bellied Flycatcher
Empidonax flaviventris
(L-5 W-8)

Greenish above; yellowish below; white wing bars and eyering; black legs.

Voice Song: a whistled "perweee"; call: a distinctive "squeeup." Both sexes sing and call during migration and on wintering ground.

Similar Species All *Empidonax* flycatchers are similar. The two yellowish species in this region are Yellow-bellied and Acadian. Calls are distinctive for each. Acadian has white throat, is not as yellow below, and has bluish legs. Yellow-bellied legs are black.

Habitat Breeds in highland bogs in hemlock and spruce-fir forests; on migration in a variety of forest and shrublands.

Abundance and Distribution Rare to casual transient (Aug.–Sept., May) throughout the region, more numerous in fall (Sept.).

Range Breeds northern United States and southern Canada west to British Columbia; winters from central Mexico south to Panama.

223. Acadian Flycatcher
Empidonax virescens
(L-6 W-9)

Green above; whitish below; yellow on flanks; white wing bars; whitish eyering; bluish legs.

Voice Song: a repeated "pit see"; call: a thin "peet."

Similar Species All *Empidonax* are similar. The two yellowish species in this region are Yellow-bellied and Acadian. Calls are distinctive for each. Acadian usually has white throat, is not as yellow below, and has bluish legs. Yellow-bellied legs are black.

Habitat Moist forest, riparian forest.

Abundance and Distribution Uncommon transient and summer resident* (Apr.–Sept.) nearly throughout Georgia, Alabama, Mississippi, the Panhandle, and North Florida, although scarcer in the highlands; uncommon to rare transient (Aug.–Oct., Apr.–May) in Central and South Florida and the Keys, more numerous in fall (Sept.).

Where to Find Cloudland Canyon State Park, Georgia; Sipsey Wilderness, William B. Bankhead National Forest, Alabama; Blackwater River State Park, Florida; Black Creek Trail, Mississippi.

Range Breeds across the eastern United States; winters from Nicaragua south through Central America to northern South America.

224. Alder Flycatcher
Empidonax alnorum
(L-6 W-9)

Brownish olive above, whitish below; greenish on flanks; white wing bars and eyering.

Voice Song: "fee-bee-o"; call: "pep."

Similar Species All of the whitish *Empidonax* are similar but distinguishable by song.

Habitat Swamp thickets, riparian forest.

Abundance and Distribution Rare transient (Aug.–Sept., Apr.–May) throughout the region, more numerous in fall (Sept.).

Range Breeds across the northern tier of the continent in Canada and Alaska and south through the Appalachians to North Carolina; winters in northern South America.

225. Willow Flycatcher

Empidonax traillii
(L-6 W-9)

Brownish olive above; whitish below turning to a creamy yellow on belly; greenish on flanks; white wing bars and eyering.

Voice Song: a buzzy, slurred "fitz-bew"; call: "wit."

Similar Species A combination of behavior, voice, habitat, and minute details of appearance are often needed to separate species of *Empidonax* flycatchers. The song of the Willow Flycatcher is distinctive, and it is the characteristic *Empidonax* species of willow bogs and swamps where it breeds. On migration, it is very difficult to separate from other members of the group.

Habitat Willow thickets, shrubby fields, riparian forest.

Abundance and Distribution Rare transient (Aug.–Sept., Apr.–May) throughout the region, more numerous in fall (Sept.); has bred* in the mountains of north Georgia.

Range Breeds through much of the northern and central United States; winters in northern South America.

226. Least Flycatcher

Empidonax minimus
(L-5 W-8)

Brownish above; white below; wing bars and eyering white.

Habits Bobs tail.

Voice Song: "che bec," given by both sexes during migration and on wintering grounds; call: a brief "wit."

Similar Species A combination of behavior, voice, habitat, and minute details of appearance are often needed to

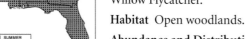

separate one species of *Empidonax* flycatcher from another. Tail bobbing habit of the Least can be used to separate it from the Willow Flycatcher.

Habitat Open woodlands.

Abundance and Distribution Rare transient (Aug.–Sept., Apr.–May) throughout the region, more numerous in fall (Sept.); rare winter visitor (Oct.–Mar.) in Central and South Florida; rare summer resident* (May–Aug.) in the mountains of north Georgia.

Where to Find Rabun Bald, Georgia.

Range Breeds in northern United States and southern and central Canada west to British Columbia, south in Appalachians to north Georgia; winters from central Mexico to Panama.

227. Eastern Phoebe
Sayornis phoebe
(L-7 W-11)

Dark brown above; whitish below. Dark cap often has crestlike appearance. Bobs tail. **Immature** White underparts tinged with yellow.

Voice "Febezzt feebezzt," repeated; call: a clear "tship."

Similar Species Eastern Wood-Pewee has distinct wing bars, which the phoebe lacks; *Empidonax* have wing bars and eyering.

Habitat Riparian forest; deciduous and mixed forest edge; various woodlands, parklands, and scrub during migration; good nest site localities seem to determine breeding habitat—cliffs, eaves, bridges.

Abundance and Distribution Common summer resident* (Mar.–Oct.) and uncommon to rare winter resident (Nov.–Feb.) in the highlands and piedmont of Georgia, Alabama, and Mississippi; common to uncommon winter resident (Oct.–Mar.) elsewhere in the Southeast except for the Florida Keys, where rare or absent.

Where to Find Chewalla Lake, Holly Springs National Forest, Mississippi; Moccasin Creek State Park, Georgia; Sipsey Wilderness, William B. Bankhead National Forest, Alabama; St. Vincent National Wildlife Refuge, Florida.

Range Breeds from eastern British Columbia across southern Canada south through eastern United States (except southern Coastal Plain); winters southeastern United States south through eastern Mexico to Oaxaca and Veracruz.

228. Vermilion Flycatcher
Pyrocephalus rubinus
(L-6 W-10)

Black above; scarlet below with scarlet cap. **Female** Brownish above with whitish throat and chest and orangish or yellowish belly, faintly streaked. **Immature Male** Like female, with increasing amounts of black above and red below in successive molts, achieving full male plumage in third winter.

Voice "Pit-a-see," repeated, often given in flight.

Habitat Scrub, thickets, shrubby areas; often near water (coastal wetlands, stream and pond borders).

Abundance and Distribution Rare to casual transient and winter resident (Oct.–Mar.) in most of Florida, although not reported from the Keys; mainly a fall transient in coastal Mississippi, Alabama, and the western Florida Panhandle.

Where to Find St. Marks National Wildlife Refuge, Florida.

Range From the southwestern United States south in the drier parts of Middle and South America to northern Argentina and Chile.

229. Ash-throated Flycatcher
Myiarchus cinerascens
(L-9 W-13)

Brown above; grayish white throat and breast; pale yellow belly.

Voice A harsh "zheep" or "zhrt" often preceded by a sharp "quip."

Similar Species The Ash-throated Flycatcher is much paler than either the Brown-crested or Great Crested flycatchers, and voice is completely different.

Habitat Open areas, scrub.

Abundance and Distribution Rare to casual winter visitor (Oct.–Apr.) in Florida.

Range Breeds in the western United States from Washington, Idaho, and Colorado south to southern Mexico; winters from southern California, Arizona, and northern Mexico to Honduras on the Pacific slope.

230. Great Crested Flycatcher
Myiarchus crinitus
(L-9 W-13)

Brown above; throat and breast gray; belly yellow; rufous tail.

Voice "Wheep."

Similar Species The rare Western Kingbird (coast) also has a gray throat. However, it also has a gray head (not brown), no crest, a greenish back, and a dark tail with a white border on outer tail feathers. The rare Brown-crested Flycatcher of South Florida and the Keys is very similar in pattern to the

Flycatchers, Kingbirds

Great Crested Flycatcher but not as dark brown above or as bright yellow below. Best distinguished by voice.

Habitat Broadleaf and mixed forest.

Abundance and Distribution Common to uncommon transient and summer resident* (Apr.–Sept.) in Georgia, Alabama, Mississippi, the Panhandle, and North Florida; uncommon to rare summer resident* (Apr.–Sept.) and rare to casual winter resident (Oct.–Mar.) in Central and South Florida and the Keys.

Where to Find Chewalla Lake, Holly Springs National Forest, Mississippi; Fort Mountain State Park, Georgia; Tuskegee National Forest, Alabama; Lower Suwannee National Wildlife Refuge, Florida.

Range Breeds in the eastern United States, central and southeastern Canada; winters in South Florida, Cuba, and southern Mexico through Middle America to Colombia and Venezuela.

231. Brown-crested Flycatcher
Myiarchus tyrannulus
(L-9 W-13)

Brownish olive above; gray throat and breast; pale yellow belly; rufous tail.

Voice A series of sharp "quip" notes; also a whistled, "quip quit too."

Similar Species The rare Brown-crested Flycatcher of South Florida and the Keys is very similar in pattern to the Great Crested Flycatcher but not as dark brown above or as bright yellow below. Best distinguished by voice.

Habitat Broadleaf hammocks and mangroves.

Abundance and Distribution Rare winter visitor (Nov.–Apr.) to South Florida and the Keys.

Where to Find Everglades National Park, Florida; DuPuis Management Area, Florida.

Range Breeds from the southwestern United States south along both slopes in Mexico through Middle and South America to Argentina; winters from southern Mexico south through breeding range.

232. Western Kingbird
Tyrannus verticalis
(L-9 W-15)

Pearl gray head and breast; back and belly yellowish; wings dark brown; tail brown with white outer tail feathers; male's red crown patch usually concealed.

Voice Various harsh twitters; call: a sharp "whit."

Similar Species The Western Kingbird has a gray throat, like the Great Crested and Brown-crested flycatchers. However, it also has a gray head (not brown), no crest, a greenish back, and a dark tail with white outer tail feathers.

Habitat Grasslands, pastures, old fields.

Abundance and Distribution Rare to casual fall transient (Sept.–Oct.) along the coast in Georgia, Mississippi, and Alabama, and throughout Florida; common to rare and local winter resident (Oct.–Apr.) in Central and South Florida and the Keys.

Where to Find Everglades National Park, Florida.

Range Breeds in western North America from southern British Columbia and Manitoba to southern Mexico; winters from southern Mexico to Costa Rica.

233. Eastern Kingbird
Tyrannus tyrannus
(L-9 W-15)

Blackish above; white below; terminal white band on tail; red crest is usually invisible.

Voice A harsh, high-pitched rattle, "kit kit kitty kitty" etc., or "tshee" repeated.

Habits The male is very aggressive to intruders on breeding territory. Dive-bombs any large bird that happens to cross his airspace, and harasses mammals, including humans, that trespass.

Habitat Wood margins, open farmland, hedgerows.

Abundance and Distribution Common to rare transient and summer resident* (Apr.–Sept.) throughout the region, although birds summering in the Keys are not known to breed.

Where to Find Natchez State Park, Mississippi; Lake Guntersville State Park, Alabama; Laura S. Walker State Park, Georgia; St. Marks National Wildlife Refuge, Florida.

Range Breeds from central Canada south through eastern and central United States to eastern Texas and Florida; winters in central and northern South America.

Flycatchers, Kingbirds

234. Gray Kingbird
Tyrannus dominicensis
(L-9 W-15)

Grayish above; white below; notched tail; heavy bill; dark ear patch; red crown patch usually not visible.

Voice Harsh "pechurrry."

Similar Species Eastern Kingbird is darker, smaller; slimmer bill.

Habitat Tropical savanna, mangroves.

Abundance and Distribution Uncommon to rare and local summer resident* (Apr.–Sept.) along the Georgia and Florida coast and the Keys; rare to casual inland in Florida as a transient and winter visitor (Aug.–May).

Where to Find Everglades National Park, Florida; Dry Tortugas National Park, Florida; J. N. "Ding" Darling National Wildlife Refuge, Florida; St. Simons Island, Georgia.

Range Caribbean basin, rarely north along the Atlantic coast to South Carolina; winters into northern South America.

Figure 35. Sidney Lanier (1916) described the quiet beauty of oak woodlands on Georgia's barrier islands, such as these on St. Simons, as, "beautiful glooms, soft dusks in the noon-day fire,—wildwood privacies, closets of lone desire." A little overheated, perhaps, in more ways than one for modern tastes, but one cannot doubt his appreciation for this habitat, home to Painted Buntings, Red-bellied Woodpeckers, Blue Grosbeaks, Red-eyed Vireos, Eastern Towhees, and Wood Thrushes.

235. Scissor-tailed Flycatcher
Tyrannus forficatus
(L-14 W-14)

Tail black and white, extremely long, forked. Pearl gray head, back, and breast, washed with rose on belly, crissum, wing lining; bright rose "armpits" (axillaries); wings black. **Immature** Short-tailed; lacks rose color of adult.

Voice Series of "kip," "kyeck," and "keee" notes.

Habitat Savanna, prairie, agricultural lands with scattered trees.

Abundance and Distribution Rare transient (Oct., Apr.), mainly along the Gulf coast of Florida; uncommon to rare and local transient and winter resident (Oct.–Apr.) in Central and South Florida and the Keys; has bred* in natural prairie areas of eastern Mississippi.

Where to Find Everglades National Park, Florida; Florida Keys National Wildlife Refuges, Florida.

Range Breeds in the central and southern Great Plains from Nebraska south to northern Mexico; winters from southern Florida and southern Mexico south to Panama.

Shrikes
Family Laniidae

The New World species of shrikes are medium-sized, stocky, predominantly gray and white birds with hooked beaks and strong feet for grasping and killing insects, small mammals, birds, reptiles, and amphibians.

236. Loggerhead Shrike
Lanius ludovicianus
(L-9 W-13)

Gray above, paler below; black mask, wings, and tail; white outer tail feathers and wing patch.

Habits Hunts from exposed perches; wary, flees observer with rapid wingbeats; larders prey on thorns and barbs.

Voice Song: a series of weak warbles and squeaks; call: a harsh "chaaa," often repeated 3–4 times.

Similar Species The Northern Mockingbird is slighter, lacks heavy, hooked bill, has longer tail, and has no black mask.

Shrikes

Habitat Old fields, farmlands, hedgerows; prefers open, barren areas where perches (such as fenceposts or telephone poles) are available for sallying.

Abundance and Distribution Common to uncommon resident* in the Panhandle, North, and Central Florida and along the coastal plain of Mississippi, Alabama, and Georgia; uncommon to rare resident* in the piedmont; rare resident* in the highlands; uncommon to rare resident* in South Florida, casual in the Keys (winter).

Where to Find Natchez Trace Parkway, Mississippi; Fort Toulouse, Alabama; Ocmulgee National Monument, Georgia; Lower Suwannee National Wildlife Refuge, Florida.

Range Breeds locally over most of the United States and southern Canada south through highlands of Mexico to Oaxaca; winters in all but north portions of breeding range.

Vireos
Family Vireonidae

A predominantly tropical family of small, feisty birds, with most patterned in greens, yellows, grays, and browns. The relatively thick bill has a small, terminal hook. Most vireos are woodland species that deliberately glean twigs, leaves, and branches for insect larvae.

237. White-eyed Vireo
Vireo griseus
(L-5 W-8)

Greenish gray above, whitish washed with yellow below; white eye, yellowish eyering and forehead ("spectacles"); white wing bars. **Immature** Has brown eye until Aug.–Sept. with some remaining grayish until spring.

Habits Solitary and retiring; both sexes sing occasionally in winter.

Voice Song: "tstlik tstlit-a-lur tslik" or variations; call: a whiny "churr" repeated.

Similar Species *Empidonax* flycatchers have whiskers and flattened bill; lack "spectacles" and white eye.

Vireos

Habitat Riparian woodland, thickets, swamp borders, overgrown fields.

Abundance and Distribution Common resident* in Florida; common summer resident* (Apr.–Oct.) and uncommon winter resident (Nov.–Mar.) elsewhere in the region along the coastal plain; common summer resident* (Apr.–Oct.) in the piedmont and highlands.

Where to Find Clear Springs Lake, Homochitto National Forest, Mississippi; Piedmont National Wildlife Refuge, Georgia; Gulf State Park, Alabama; Lake Woodruff National Wildlife Refuge, Florida.

Range Breeds in the eastern United States from southern Minnesota to Massachusetts southward to Florida and eastern Mexico to Veracruz; winters from the southeastern United States south through eastern Mexico and Central America to northern Nicaragua; Bahamas and Greater Antilles.

238. Bell's Vireo
Vireo bellii
(L-5 W-7)

Grayish green above, whitish with yellowish flanks below; white "spectacles" (lores, eyering, forehead); two faint whitish wing bars.

Habits Normally forages in dense thickets.

Voice Song: a mixture of "tsitl tsitl tsee" and "tsitl tsitl tsoo" with pauses between phrases; call: a raspy "tsoo weea tsi."

Similar Species Ruby-crowned Kinglet lacks yellow on flanks and "spectacles."

Habitat Thorn forest, savanna, deciduous woodlands; often near water.

Abundance and Distribution Rare transient (Sept.–Oct., Apr.), mainly in the Panhandle, western Florida Peninsula; rare winter resident (Oct.–Apr.) in South Florida and the Keys.

Range Breeds in central and southwestern United States south through northern Mexico; winters from southern Mexico to Honduras.

Vireos

239. Yellow-throated Vireo
Vireo flavifrons
(L-6 W-10)

Greenish above with gray rump; yellow throat, breast and "spectacles" (lores, forehead, eyering); white belly and wing bars.

Voice Like a hoarse, slow Red-eyed Vireo, "chearee ... chewia ... tsuweet," etc.

Similar Species The smaller, slimmer, more active Pine Warbler has yellow-green rump (not gray), white tail spots, and thin bill.

Habitat Deciduous forest, riparian woodland.

Abundance and Distribution Common to uncommon summer resident* (Apr.–Sept.) in the Panhandle, North, and Central Florida, Georgia, Alabama, and Mississippi; uncommon to rare transient (Aug.–Sept., Apr.) in South Florida and the Keys; rare to casual winter visitor (Oct.–Apr.) in Florida.

Where to Find Bladon Springs State Park, Alabama; John W. Kyle State Park, Mississippi; Grand Bay Wildlife Management Area, Georgia; St. Marks National Wildlife Refuge, Florida.

Range Breeds in the eastern United States; winters from southern Mexico, south through Central and northern South America; Bahamas; Greater Antilles.

240. Blue-headed Vireo
Vireo solitarius
(L-6 W-10)

Greenish on the back with a gray rump; whitish below with yellow flanks; two prominent, white wing bars; gray head and white "spectacles" (lores, forehead, eyering).

Habits A deliberate forager like most vireos but in contrast to most warblers, which forage in much more active fashion.

Voice Song: a rich series of "chu wit ... chu wee ... cheerio," etc., similar to Red-eyed Vireo but with longer pauses between phrases; call: a whiny "cheeer."

Similar Species The gray head and white spectacles of the Blue-headed Vireo are distinctive in this region.

Habitat Coniferous and mixed woodlands.

Abundance and Distribution Common summer resident* (Mar.–Oct.) in the highlands; uncommon to rare transient (Sept.–Oct., Mar.–Apr.) in the piedmont and upper coastal plain;

uncommon to rare winter resident (Oct.–Mar.) along the lower coastal plain and throughout Florida.

Where to Find Brasstown Bald, Georgia; Cheaha State Park, Alabama; Bogue Chitto National Wildlife Refuge, Mississippi; Lake Woodruff National Wildlife Refuge, Florida.

Range Breeds across central and southern Canada, northern and western United States; winters from the southern United States through Mexico and Central America to Costa Rica; Cuba.

241. Warbling Vireo
Vireo gilvus
(L-6 W-9)

Grayish green above, pale yellow below; white eye stripe; no wing bars.

Voice Song: a long wandering series of warbles almost always ending with an upward inflection; call: a hoarse "tswee."

Similar Species Can be difficult to separate from some pale Philadelphia Vireos, most of which are yellower below and have a dark loral spot.

Habitat Riparian woodlands and floodplains; often frequents tall elms and sycamores.

Abundance and Distribution Rare to casual transient (Sept., Apr.–May) throughout.

Range Breeds across North America south of the Arctic region to central Mexico; winters from Guatemala to Panama.

242. Philadelphia Vireo
Vireo philadelphicus
(L-5 W-8)

Grayish green above, variably yellowish below; white eye stripe and dark loral spot; no wingbars.

Habits Deliberate foraging movements with much peering and poking in outer clumps of leaves and twigs; even hanging occasionally like a chickadee.

Voice Song is similar to the Red-eyed Vireo but higher and slower.

Similar Species Some Warbling Vireos can be difficult to separate from pale Philadelphia Vireos, which are yellower below and have a dark loral spot. Could be mistaken for immature Tennessee

Vireos

Warbler or Orange-crowned Warbler except for thick vireo bill and deliberate foraging behavior.

Habitat Deciduous and mixed forest.

Abundance and Distribution Rare transient (Sept.–Oct., Apr.–May) throughout, more numerous in fall (Sept.).

Range Breeds eastern and central boreal North America in Canada and northern United States; winters Guatemala to Panama.

243. Red-eyed Vireo
Vireo olivaceus
(L-6 W-10)

Olive above, whitish below; gray cap; white eyeline; red eye (brown in juvenile).

Voice Song: a leisurely, seemingly endless series of phrases, "cheerup, cherio, chewit, chewee," etc. through the middle of long summer days. Male occasionally sings from nest while incubating. Call: a harsh "cheear."

Similar Species The Red-eyed Vireo is the only gray-capped vireo in the region without wing bars except for the Black-whiskered Vireo, which has a black whisker.

Habitat Deciduous and mixed woodlands.

SUMMER
MIGRATION
WINTER
PERMANENT

Abundance and Distribution Common to uncommon summer resident* (Apr.–Oct.) throughout most of the Southeast; rare and local resident* in South Florida; common transient (Aug.–Oct., Mar.–May) in the Keys.

Where to Find Leaf Wilderness, De Soto National Forest, Mississippi; Chickamauga and Chattanooga National Military Park, Georgia; Dauphin Island, Alabama (transient); St. Vincent National Wildlife Refuge, Florida.

Range Breeds over much of North America (except western United States, Alaska, and northern Canada). Close relatives breed in Central and South America. United States forms winter in northern South America.

244. Black-whiskered Vireo
Vireo altiloquus
(L-6 W-10)

Olive above, whitish below; gray cap; white eyeline; black whisker; red eye (brown in juvenile).

Vireos

Figure 36. Castellow Hammock Preserve, on the fringes of the Greater Miami/Homestead urban sprawl, has some South Florida specialties including White-winged Dove and Black-whiskered Vireo.

Voice Song: similar to Red-eyed Vireo but with repeated phrases.

Habitat Mangroves; coastal scrub.

Abundance and Distribution Uncommon to rare summer resident* (Apr.–Oct.) along the coast of Central and South Florida and the Keys, north on the Gulf side to Levy Co. and the Atlantic side to Brevard Co.

Where to Find J. N. "Ding" Darling National Wildlife Refuge, Florida; Florida Keys National Wildlife Refuges, Florida; Castellow Hammock Preserve, Florida; Dry Tortugas National Park, Florida (spring).

Range South Florida, the Bahamas, West Indies, and northern Venezuela.

Crows and Jays
Family Corvidae

Medium-sized to large songbirds; crows and ravens have generally dark plumages, jays are blues, greens, and grays. Most corvids are social, aggressive, and highly vocal.

245. Blue Jay
Cyanocitta cristata
(L-11 W-16)

Blue above; a dirty white below; blue crest; black nape and lores; white wing bars and tip of tail; black necklace.

Voice A loud harsh cry, jaaaay, repeated; a liquid gurgle; many other cries and calls; mimics hawks.

Habitat Deciduous forest, parklands, residential areas.

Abundance and Distribution Common resident* nearly throughout the Southeast; rare in the Keys.

Where to Find Lake Woodruff National Wildlife Refuge, Florida; Fort Toulouse, Alabama; Fort Mountain State Park, Georgia; Legion State Park, Mississippi.

Range Temperate and boreal North America east of the Rockies.

246. Florida Scrub-Jay
Aphelocoma coerulescens
(L-11 W-16)

Blue crown, face, and neck; white forehead; dark eyeline; blue wings, rump, and tail; gray throat, breast, and belly with dark streaks on throat and breast; grayish back.

Voice A harsh "kuweeep;" "kay kay kay kay kay kay;" "keeaah;" other cries.

Habitat Oak scrub.

Abundance and Distribution Common but local resident* of Central Florida; uncommon to rare and local in North and South Florida.

Where to Find Oscar Scherer State Park, Florida; Archbold Biological Station, Florida; Jonathan Dickinson State Park, Florida; Merritt Island National Wildlife Refuge, Florida

Range Central Florida.

247. American Crow
Corvus brachyrhynchos
(L-18 W-36)

Black throughout.

Voice A series of variations on "caw"—fast, slow, high, low, and various combinations; nestlings and fledglings use an incessant, nasal "caah."

Habitat Deciduous and mixed woodlands, grasslands, farmlands, and residential areas in winter.

Similar Species Ravens croak and have wedged-shaped rather than square tail of crows. Distinguished from the smaller Fish Crow mainly on voice: American Crows usually give the familiar

Crows, Jays

Figure 37. In addition to the pine scrub shown here, Hobe Sound National Wildlife Refuge near Jupiter, Florida, has mangroves, beaches, and dunes. Gray Kingbirds are found at the refuge as well as Florida Scrub-Jays and Common Ground-Doves.

"caw" while Fish Crows have a high-pitched, nasal "caah" (although juvenile American Crows have a similar call).

Abundance and Distribution Common resident* throughout the Southeast except in the Keys where rare or absent.

Where to Find Fort Mountain State Park, Georgia; Vicksburg National Military Park, Mississippi; Oak Mountain State Park, Alabama; Florida Caverns State Park, Florida.

Range Temperate and boreal North America; migratory in northern portion of range.

248. Fish Crow
Corvus ossifragus
(L-15 W-33)

Black throughout.

Voice A high, nasal "cah."

Habitat Flood plain forests, bayous, and coastal waterways.

Similar Species American Crows are best distinguished from the smaller Fish Crow by voice: American Crows usually give the familiar "caw" while Fish Crows have a high-pitched, nasal "caah" (although juvenile American Crows have a similar call).

Abundance and Distribution Common resident* in Florida, except the Keys where uncommon to rare, and along the coastal plain of Georgia, Alabama, and Mississippi; uncommon to rare summer resident* (Mar.–Oct.) in the piedmont.

Where to Find George L. Smith State Park, Georgia; Hobe Sound National Wildlife Refuge, Florida; Battleship Park, Alabama; Buccaneer State Park Mississippi.

Range Coastal plain and parts of the piedmont of the eastern United States from Maine to eastern Texas.

249. Common Raven
Corvus corax
(L-24 W-48)

Black throughout; large heavy bill; shaggy appearance in facial region; wedge-shaped tail.

Voice A variety of harsh, low croaks.

Habitat Rugged crags, cliffs, canyons as well as a variety of forested and open lands.

Similar Species Ravens croak and have wedged-shaped rather than square tail of crows.

Abundance and Distribution Rare and local resident* in the mountains of north Georgia.

Where to Find Brasstown Bald, Georgia; Rabun Bald, Georgia.

Range Arctic and boreal regions of the Northern Hemisphere south through mountainous regions of the Western Hemisphere to Nicaragua, and in the Eastern Hemisphere to North Africa, Iran, the Himalayas, Manchuria, and Japan.

SUMMER
MIGRATION
WINTER
PERMANENT

Larks
Family Alaudidae

Small, terrestrial songbirds with extremely long hind claws. The breeding song of these open country inhabitants is often given in flight.

250. Horned Lark
Eremophila alpestris
(L-7 W-13)

Brown above; white below with black bib; face and throat whitish or yellowish with black forehead and eyeline; black "horns" raised when singing. **Female** Similar pattern but paler. **Immature** Nondescript

brownish above; whitish below with light streaking; has dark tail with white edging and long hind claw like adult.

Voice Series of high-pitched notes, often given in flight; call is a thin "tseet."

Similar Species Immature lark is similar to pipits, but is grayish white rather than buffy on face and underparts.

Habitat Overgrazed pasture, airports, golf courses, plowed fields, surface mines, roadsides, sand flats.

Abundance and Distribution Common to uncommon winter resident (Nov.–Mar.) in the piedmont and highlands, rare to casual elsewhere in the region.

Where to Find Piedmont National Wildlife Refuge, Georgia; Wheeler National Wildlife Refuge, Alabama; Pharr Mounds, Natchez Trace Parkway, Mississippi.

Range Breeds in North America south to southern Mexico; winters in southern portion of breeding range.

Swallows and Martins
Family Hirundinidae

Mostly small, sleek birds with pointed wings. Swallows forage on flying insects caught on the wing.

251. Purple Martin
Progne subis
(L-8 W-16)

Iridescent midnight blue throughout. **Female and Immature** Dark, iridescent blue above; dirty white, occasionally mottled with blue below; grayish collar.

Voice Various squeaky "quik"s and "querks"s repeated in a short harsh series.

Similar Species The male martin is the only entirely dark swallow in the region. The female and immature are variously whitish below, but not pure white as in the Tree Swallow. The Bank Swallow is white below with a brown breast band, and the Northern Rough-winged Swallow, although dingy white below, is brown, not iridescent blue as in martins, above. Martins are much larger than any other swallows found in the area.

Habitat Open areas—limited by nesting sites. Nests colonially,

Swallows, Martins

originally in hollow trees, now often in specially constructed martin houses and gourds.

Abundance and Distribution Common transient and summer resident* (Feb.–Oct.) in the Panhandle, North, and Central Florida, Georgia, Alabama, and Mississippi, somewhat scarcer in South Florida and piedmont; rare in the mountains; common to uncommon transient (Jul.–Nov., Feb.–May) in the Keys; casual winter resident in coastal areas.

Where to Find Altamaha River/Atkinson Tract, Georgia; Weeks Bay National Estuarine Research Reserve, Alabama; Hugh White State Park, Mississippi; St. Andrews Recreation Area, Florida.

Range Breeds in open areas over most of temperate North America south to the highlands of southern Mexico; winters in South America.

252. Tree Swallow
Tachycineta bicolor
(L-6 W-13)

Iridescent blue above; pure white below with slightly forked tail. **Female** Similar in pattern to male, but duller. **Immature** Grayish brown above; whitish below.

Voice Series of "weet tuwit tuweet" with twitters.

Similar Species The stark contrast between dark blue back and white underparts is distinctive among the region's swallows.

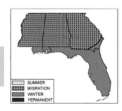

Habitat Lakes, ponds, marshes, open fields—any open area during migration and winter.

Abundance and Distribution Common to uncommon transient (Jul.–Oct., Mar.–May) throughout the region; common to uncommon winter resident (Nov.–Feb.) in Florida and along the coast in Georgia, Alabama, and Mississippi.

Where to Find Laura S. Walker State Park, Georgia; Lower Suwannee National Wildlife Refuge, Florida; Mississippi Sandhill Crane National Wildlife Refuge, Mississippi; Eufaula National Wildlife Refuge, Alabama.

Range Breeds over most of boreal and north temperate North America south to the southern United States; winters from southern United States south to Costa Rica and Greater Antilles.

253. Northern Rough-winged Swallow
Stelgidopteryx serripennis
(L-6 W-12)

Grayish brown above; grayish throat and breast becoming whitish on belly.

Voice A harsh "treet," repeated.

Similar Species Of the two brown-backed swallows, the Bank Swallow has a distinct dark breast band set off by white throat and belly; the roughwing lacks breastband.

Habitat Lakes, rivers, ponds, streams, most open areas during migration. Nests in holes in banks, drain pipes, and abandoned rodent burrows, normally in single pairs.

Abundance and Distribution Uncommon transient (Aug.–Oct., Mar.–Apr.) throughout, most numerous in fall (Aug.–Sept.) in eastern parts of the region and spring in the western parts; uncommon to rare and local summer resident* (May–Aug.) throughout; rare winter resident (Nov.–Feb.) in South Florida and the Keys.

Where to Find Natchez State Park, Mississippi; Blackbeard Island National Wildlife Refuge, Georgia; Eufaula National Wildlife Refuge, Alabama; St. Marks National Wildlife Refuge, Florida.

Range Breeds locally over most of temperate North America; winters from southern Florida, southern Texas and northern Mexico south to Panama.

254. Bank Swallow
Riparia riparia
(L-6 W-12)

Brown above; white below with brown band across breast and down to belly (like a "T").

Voice "Bzzt," repeated in a harsh rattle.

Similar Species Among the brown-backed swallows of the region, the Bank Swallow has a distinct dark breast band set off by white throat and belly; roughwing lacks breast band.

Habitat Lakes, rivers, ponds, most open areas during migration. Nests in holes in banks, normally in colonies.

Abundance and Distribution Uncommon to rare transient (Aug.–Oct., Apr.–May), more numerous in fall in eastern parts of the region; casual summer resident*.

Where to Find Savannah National Wildlife Refuge, Georgia.

Swallows, Martins

Range Cosmopolitan, breeding over much of Northern Hemisphere continents, wintering in the tropics of Asia, Africa, and the New World.

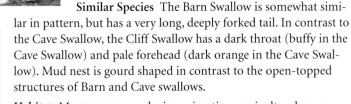

255. Cliff Swallow
Petrochelidon pyrrhonota
(L-6 W-12)

Dark above; whitish below with dark orange or blackish throat; orange cheek; pale forehead; orange rump; square tail. **Immature** Similar to adults but duller.

Voice Song: a series of harsh twitters.

Similar Species The Barn Swallow is somewhat similar in pattern, but has a very long, deeply forked tail. In contrast to the Cave Swallow, the Cliff Swallow has a dark throat (buffy in the Cave Swallow) and pale forehead (dark orange in the Cave Swallow). Mud nest is gourd shaped in contrast to the open-topped structures of Barn and Cave swallows.

Habitat Most open areas during migration; agricultural areas, near water. This species seems to be limited by nesting locations during the breeding season (farm buildings, culverts, bridges, cliffs—near potential mud source).

Abundance and Distribution Uncommon transient (Aug.–Sept., Apr.–May) and uncommon to rare and local summer resident* (May–Aug.) in the piedmont and highlands and at dams at reservoirs in the region; rare transient (Aug.–Sept., Apr.–May) elsewhere in the Southeast.

Where to Find Tenn-Tom Waterway, Natchez Trace Parkway, Mississippi.

Range Breeds over most of North America to central Mexico; winters central and southern South America.

256. Cave Swallow
Petrochelidon fulva
(L-6 W-12)

Dark above; whitish below with pale orange breast and sides; pale orange throat, cheek, and ear; dark orange forehead; orange rump; square tail. **Immature** Similar to adults but duller.

Voice Song: a rapid series of squeaks.

Similar Species In contrast to the Cliff Swallow, the Cave Swallow has buffy (rather than dark) throat and dark orange (rather than

pale) forehead. Mud nest is open topped, like that of the Barn Swallow, rather than the gourdlike structure of the Cliff Swallow.

Habitat Open areas, near water; nests in sinkholes, caves, and most recently, culverts.

Abundance and Distribution Uncommon spring visitor (Feb.–Jun) in the Dry Tortugas; a small breeding* population nests under highway overpasses in the Homestead, Florida area (Jan.–Sept.); scattered records from elsewhere in the region.

Where to Find Dry Tortugas National Park, Florida; Canal Overpass, jct Hainlin Mill Dr. and Florida Turnpike, Homestead, Florida.

Range Breeds from New Mexico and central Texas south through central and southern Mexico, the Greater Antilles, northern South America in Ecuador and Peru; winters in southern portion of breeding range.

257. Barn Swallow
Hirundo rustica
(L-7 W-13)

Dark, iridescent blue above; orange forehead and orange below with partial or completely blue breast band; long, deeply forked tail. **Immature** Paler with shorter tail.

Voice Song: a series of squeaks and twitters, some harsh, some melodic.

Habitat Open areas near water; like most swallows, it requires special sites for nesting, such as bridges, culverts, buildings.

Similar Species The Barn Swallow is somewhat similar in pattern to the Cliff Swallow, but has a very long, deeply forked tail. The mud nest of the Cliff Swallow is gourdlike while that of the Barn Swallow is open topped; both are placed under eaves, bridges, culverts, dams, and similar protected walls.

Abundance and Distribution Common to uncommon transient (Apr.–May, Aug.–Sept.) throughout the Southeast; common to uncommon summer resident* (May–Aug.) in Georgia, Alabama, Mississippi, the Panhandle, North and Central Florida; rare and local summer resident* in South Florida and the Upper Keys.

Where to Find Historic Blakeley State Park, Alabama; Tenn-Tom Waterway, Natchez Trace Parkway, Mississippi; Arrowhead Public Fishing Area, Georgia; Wakulla Springs State Park, Florida.

Swallows, Martins

Range Cosmopolitan—breeds over much of the Northern Hemisphere; winters in South America, Africa, northern Australia, Micronesia.

Chickadees and Titmice
Family Paridae

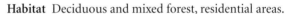

Small, perky, active birds with plumages of gray and white; generally chickadees and titmice forage in small groups, feeding on arthropods and seeds.

258. Carolina Chickadee
Poecile carolinensis
(L-5 W-8)

Black cap and throat contrasting with white cheek, dark gray back, and grayish white breast and belly.

Habits Hangs upside down from branches and twigs while foraging.

Voice "See dee see doo"; "chick a dee dee dee."

Habitat Deciduous and mixed forest, residential areas.

Abundance and Distribution Common resident* in Georgia and Alabama, Mississippi, the Panhandle, and North Florida; increasingly scarce as a resident southward in the Florida Peninsula, and absent from South Florida and the Keys.

Where to Find Watson Mill Bridge State Park, Georgia; Little River Canyon National Preserve, Alabama; Leaf Wilderness, De Soto National Forest, Mississippi; Tall Timbers Reserach Station, Florida.

Range Eastern United States from Kansas east to New Jersey south to central Florida and east Texas.

259. Tufted Titmouse
Baeolophus bicolor
(L-6 W-9)

Gray above; white below with buffy sides; gray crest; black forehead.

Habits Hangs upside down in chickadee fashion from branches and twigs while foraging.

Voice "Peter peter peter"; also "peet peet peet" on occasion; various chickadee-like calls.

Habitat Broadleaf and mixed forest, residential areas.

Abundance and Distribution Common resident* in Georgia, Alabama, Mississippi, the Panhandle, and North Florida; increasingly uncommon to rare and local in Central Florida; rare to casual in South Florida and absent from the Keys.

Where to Find Fort Mountain State Park, Georgia; Little River Canyon National Preserve, Alabama; Lower Suwannee National Wildlife Refuge, Florida; J. P. Coleman State Park, Mississippi.

Range Eastern United States west to Nebraska, Iowa, Oklahoma and west Texas, and in Mexico south to Hidalgo and northern Veracruz.

Nuthatches
Family Sittidae

Nuthatches are peculiar birds in both appearance and behavior. Long-billed, hunched little beasts, built for probing bark on tree trunks, they creep along the trunks, usually from the top down (not bottom up like Brown Creepers).

260. Red-breasted Nuthatch
Sitta canadensis
(L-5 W-8)

Gray above; orange buff below; dark gray cap with white line over eye; black line through eye. **Female and Immature** Paler buff below.

Habits Inches along, often head down, probing bark for invertebrates on inner branches and trunks.

Voice A nasal, high-pitched series of "anh"s.

Habitat Coniferous forest.

Abundance and Distribution Uncommon to rare winter visitor (Sept.–Apr.), varying markedly in numbers from year to year, in Georgia, Alabama, Mississippi the Panhandle, and North Florida.

Where to Find Vicksburg National Military Park, Mississippi; Dauphin Island, Alabama; Piedmont National Wildlife Refuge, Georgia.

Range Breeds across the northern tier of Canada and the United States south to North Carolina in the Appalachians and to New

Figure 38. Old second growth forest now covers much of the Vicksburg battlefield where Union and Confederate forces fought fiercely for months over control of the heights commanding the Mississippi River. Formerly the lynchpin holding eastern and western portions of the Confederacy together, the park presently serves as a memento mori and lovely nature walk.

Mexico in the Rockies; winters throughout breeding range and most of the United States to northern Mexico.

261. White-breasted Nuthatch

Sitta carolinensis
(L-6 W-11)

Gray above; white below with black cap; buffy flanks. **Female** Cap is gray or dull black.

Habits Forages on tree trunks, generally working from higher up on the trunk down toward the base.

Voice A series of "yank"s.

Habitat Deciduous and mixed forest, parklands, residential areas.

Abundance and Distribution Uncommon resident* in the highlands and piedmont; uncommon to rare and local resident* in the coastal plain of Georgia, Alabama, and Mississipi, and in the Tallahassee region of North Florida.

Where to Find Vogel State Park, Georgia; DeSoto State Park, Alabama; Tall Timbers Research Station, Florida; John W. Kyle State Park, Mississippi.

Range Southern tier of Canada and most of the United States; local in Great Plains region; highlands of Mexico south to Oaxaca.

262. Brown-headed Nuthatch

Sitta pusilla
(L-5 W-8)

Gray above; buffy white below; brown cap; white cheeks, throat, and nape.

Habits Inches along, often upside down, probing bark for invertebrates on branches and trunks.

Voice "Ki tee"; also various "kit" calls.

Habitat Pine forest.

Similar Species The bird is clearly a nuthatch from its foraging behavior, and the brown cap and white nape distinguish it from other nuthatches in the region.

Abundance and Distribution Common resident* nearly throughout in Georgia, Alabama, Mississippi, the Panhandle, and North Florida; rare in mountains; increasingly scarce as a resident southward in the Florida Peninsula, rare in South Florida and absent from the Keys.

Where to Find Okefenokee National Wildlife Refuge, Georgia; Lake Guntersville State Park, Alabama; Big Lagoon State Recreation Area, Florida; Black Creek Trail, Mississippi.

Range Southeastern United States from Delaware to east Texas.

Creepers
Family Certhiidae

The creepers are a small family with only five representatives worldwide, one of which, the Brown Creeper, occurs in the New World. Creepers, like nuthatches, are built for probing tree trunks. These no-necked bits of brown and white fluff have long, decurved bills and stiff tails for foraging over tree trunks, picking arthropod larvae from bark. They usually forage upright, beginning from the bottom of a tree trunk and moving up, opposite to the way a nuthatch works a trunk.

263. Brown Creeper
Certhia americana
(L-5 W-8)

Brown streaked and mottled with white above; white below; white eyeline; decurved bill.

Habits Creeps nuthatch-like over trunks, but usually begins at the base of the trunk and works up.

Voice A high-pitched "tseeee."

Habitat Breeds in a variety of forest types, seemingly

wherever loose bark provides suitable nesting sites; most woodlands in winter.

Similar Species There is no other small, brown and white bird that forages on tree trunks in the region.

Abundance and Distribution Uncommon to rare winter visitor (Oct.–Mar.) in the highlands and piedmont, scarcer in the coastal plain of Georgia, Alabama, and Mississippi, and the Florida Panhandle; increasingly rare and irregular as a winter visitor southward in the Florida Peninsula, and absent from South Florida and the Keys.

Where to Find Vogel State Park, Georgia; Lake Guntersville State Park, Alabama; Noxubee National Wildlife Refuge, Mississippi.

Range Breeds in boreal, montane, and transitional zones of North America south through the highlands of Mexico and Central America to Nicaragua; winters nearly throughout in temperate, boreal, and montane regions of the continent.

Wrens
Family Troglodytidae

Wrens are a large, mostly tropical family of superb songsters. Most species have plumages of brown and white, sharp, decurved bills, and short, cocked tails. Nests are often built in a cavity or a completely closed structure of grasses.

264. Carolina Wren
Thryothorus ludovicianus
(L-6 W-8)

A rich brown above; buff below with prominent white eyeline and whitish throat.

Voice Song: a loud, clearly whistled "tea kettle tea kettle tea kettle" or variations on this theme; call: a sharp trill.

Habitat Thickets, tangles, and undergrowth of moist woodlands, riparian forest, swamps; residential areas.

Abundance and Distribution Common resident* nearly throughout the Southeast, although uncommon to rare in the Upper Keys and absent from the Lower Keys.

Where to Find Clear Springs Lake, Homochitto National Forest,

Mississippi; George L. Smith State Park, Georgia; Oak Mountain State Park, Alabama; Myakka River State Park, Florida.

Range Eastern North America from Iowa, Minnesota, New York, and Massachusetts south through the southeastern states, eastern Mexico and Central America along the Caribbean slope to Nicaragua.

265. House Wren
Troglodytes aedon
(L-5 W-7)

Brown above, buff below; buff eyeline; barred flanks.

Voice A rapid, descending trill, "chipy-chipy-chipy-chipy," with associated buzzes and churrs.

Habitat Thickets, undergrowth, and tangles in riparian forest, woodlands, hedgerows, and residential areas.

Similar Species Winter Wren is a richer brown below, has shorter tail and more prominent barring on flanks and belly. Songs and calls are very different.

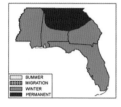

Abundance and Distribution Uncommon summer resident* (Apr.–Sept.) in the upper piedmont and highlands; uncommon transient and winter resident (Sept.–Apr.) nearly throughout the region, although rare in the Lower Keys.

Where to Find Savannah National Wildlife Refuge, Georgia; Fort Toulouse, Alabama; Three Lakes Wildlife Management Area, Lake Marian Highlands, Florida; Wall Doxey State Park, Mississippi.

Range Breeds in temperate North America from southern Canada south to south-central United States; winters in southern United States south to southern Mexico. The Southern House Wren, now considered to be conspecific with the Northern, is resident over much of Mexico, Central and South America, and the Lesser Antilles.

Wrens

266. Winter Wren
Troglodytes troglodytes
(L-4 W-6)

Brown above; brownish buff below; buffy eyeline; barred flanks and belly; short tail.

Voice A rich, cascading series of trills and warbles; call: staccato "chuck"s, "kip"s, "churr"s.

Habitat Thickets, tangles, undergrowth of coniferous fens, bogs, and swamps; lowland riparian thickets in winter.

Similar Species Winter Wren is a richer brown below, has shorter tail, and has more prominent barring on flanks and belly than House Wren. Songs and calls are very different for the two species.

Abundance and Distribution Uncommon to rare winter resident (Oct.–Apr.) in Georgia, Alabama, Mississippi, the Panhandle, and North Florida.

Where to Find Harris Neck National Wildlife Refuge, Georgia; Rabun Bald, Georgia (has been heard singing during the breeding season); Fort Toulouse, Alabama; St. Marks National Wildlife Refuge, Florida; Bogue Chitto National Wildlife Refuge, Mississippi.

Range Breeds from Alaska and British Columbia to Labrador, south along the Pacific coast to central California and in the Appalachians to north Georgia; winters from the central and southern United States to northern Mexico.

267. Sedge Wren
Cistothorus platensis
(L-4 W-6)

Crown and back brown streaked with white; pale buff below; indistinct white eyeline.

Voice A weak series of gradually accelerating "tsip"s; call: a sharp "chip" or "chip chip."

Similar Species Marsh Wren has plain brown (unstreaked) crown, distinct white eyeline; black back streaked with white.

Habitat Low, wet marshes, grasslands; estuaries.

Abundance and Distribution Uncommon to rare winter resident (Oct.–Apr.) in the Panhandle and Peninsula of Florida and along the coastal plain of Georgia, Alabama, and Mississippi; uncommon to rare transient (Aug.–Sept., Apr.–May) in the piedmont and highlands; absent from the Florida Keys.

Where to Find Seminole State Park, Georgia; Mississippi Sandhill Crane National Wildlife Refuge, Mississippi; Bon Secour National Wildlife Refuge, Alabama; St. Andrews Bay State Recreation Area, Florida.

Range Breeds across the northeastern United States and southeastern Canada from southeastern Saskatchewan to New Brunswick, south to Virginia and Oklahoma; winters along Atlantic and Gulf Coastal Plain from New Jersey to northern Mexico.

Wrens

Scattered resident populations in Mexico and Central and South America.

268. Marsh Wren
Cistothorus palustris
(L-5 W-7)

Brown above; black back prominently streaked with white; white eyeline and throat; buff underparts.

Voice A rapid series of dry "tsik"s, like the sound of an old sewing machine; call: a sharp "tsuk."

Habitat Cattail and bulrush marshes, wet grasslands; saltwater marshes.

Similar Species Marsh Wren has plain brown (unstreaked) crown, distinct white eyeline; black back streaked with white. The crown and back of the Sedge Wren are streaked with white; also, the Sedge Wren has no black on the back.

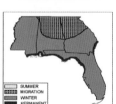

Abundance and Distribution Common to rare and local resident* along the immediate coast in Georgia, Alabama, Mississippi, and Florida from the mouth of the St. Johns River north on the Atlantic side and from Pasco County north and west on the Gulf side; common to rare and local winter resident (Oct.–Apr.) elsewhere in the coastal plain; uncommon to rare transient (Sept.–Oct., Apr.–May) in the highlands and piedmont.

Where to Find Cumberland Island National Seashore, Georgia; Bon Secour National Wildlife Refuge, Alabama; Gulf Islands National Seashore, Mississippi; Canaveral National Seashore, Florida.

Range Breeds across central and southern Canada and northern United States, southward along both coasts to northern Baja California and southeastern Texas; rare and local in inland United States; winters along both coasts and southern United States to southern Mexico.

Bulbuls
Family Pycnonotidae

The bulbuls are an Old World family. Many members are brightly colored, vocal, and gregarious. No species is native to the New World, but several occur as escapes, and two, the Red-vented Bulbul and the Red-whiskered Bulbul (discussed below), have established breeding populations in Hawaii and South Florida respectively.

269. Red-whiskered Bulbul
Pycnonotus jocosus
(L-7 W-12)

Dark brown above with a long crest; white below; red and white cheek patch; red vent; dark streak from shoulder to center of breast; dark tail with white terminal tips. **Immature** Patterned like adult but with paler brown above, orange vent, and no red on cheek.

Voice "A chatter; also 'a distinctive whistle, *Queep kwil-ya* and *queek-kay*'" (King and Dickinson 1975).

Habitat Residential parklands.

Abundance and Distribution Feral populations of this exotic species can be found in the Kendall suburb of the Greater Miami area of South Florida.

Where to Find Tennis courts at the corner of SW 98th St. and SW 72nd Ave. in Kendall suburb of Greater Miami, Florida.

Range Southern Asia from India east to Southeast Asia and southern China. Introduced in southeast Florida, Hawaiian Islands, Australia, and the Nicobar Islands.

Kinglets
Family Regulidae

A small, New World family of birds containing only two species, as described below.

270. Golden-crowned Kinglet
Regulus satrapa
(L-4 W-7)

Greenish above, whitish below; dark wings with yellow edges of primaries and secondaries; white wing bars, white eyeline; male has orange crown bordered by yellow and black; female has yellow crown bordered in black.

Habits Continually flicks wings while foraging.

Voice Call: a very high-pitched "tse tse tse"; song: a series of "tsee"s first rising, then descending in pitch.

Similar Species Rubycrown has broken white eyering which goldencrown lacks; goldencrown has white eyeline which rubycrown lacks.

Habitat Breeds in mature boreal spruce-fir forest; found in a variety of woodland habitats in winter.

Abundance and Distribution Common winter resident (Oct.–Apr.) in the piedmont and highlands; uncommon to rare winter resident (Oct.–Mar.) in the coastal plain of Georgia, Alabama, Mississippi, the Panhandle, and North Florida.

Where to Find Lake Guntersville State Park, Alabama; Tallahatchie National Wildlife Refuge, Mississippi; Black Rock Mountain State Park, Georgia.

Range Breeds in boreal North America (except Great Plains) and in the Appalachians south to North Carolina; south in Rockies to Guatemala; winters from southern Canada and the United States south through highland breeding range in Mexico and Guatemala.

271. Ruby-crowned Kinglet
Regulus calendula
(L-4 W-7)

Greenish above, whitish below; white wing bars, broken white eyering; adult male has scarlet crown. **Immature and Female** Lack scarlet crown.

Habits Continually flicks wings while foraging.

Voice Song: begins with a series of "tsee" notes followed by lower pitched "tew" notes, terminated by a series of "teedadee"s; call: distinctive "tsi tit."

Similar Species Rubycrown has broken white eyering which goldencrown lacks; goldencrown has white eyeline which rubycrown lacks.

Habitat Coniferous forests of the boreal zone in summer; a variety of woodlands during winter.

Abundance and Distribution Common to uncommon winter resident (Oct.–Apr.) in Georgia, Alabama, Mississippi, and Florida south to Central Florida; rare in South Florida and casual in the Keys.

Where to Find Okefenokee National Wildlife Refuge, Georgia; Oak Mountain State Park, Alabama; Lake Woodruff National

Kinglets

Wildlife Refuge, Florida; Clear Springs Lake, Homochitto National Forest, Mississippi.

Range Breeds in boreal North America from Alaska to Labrador south to northern New York, Michigan, and Minnesota, and in the Rockies south to New Mexico and Arizona; winters over most of the United States, Mexico and Guatemala; resident populations on Guadalupe Island (Baja California), and in Chiapas.

Old World Warblers and Gnatcatchers
Family Sylviidae

The sylviids are a group of mainly Old World species, mostly slim, arboreal birds comparable in size to the New World warblers (Parulidae). The family is represented in the Southeast region by one species, the Blue-gray Gnatcatcher, as described below.

272. Blue-gray Gnatcatcher
Polioptila caerulea
(L-5 W-7)

Bluish gray above, white below; tail black above with white outer feathers (tail appears white from below); white eyering. Adult male in breeding plumage (Apr.–Aug.) has black forehead and eyeline. Sexes nearly identical in nonbreeding plumage.

Voice Song: a barely audible string of high-pitched warbles and squeaks; call: "tsee."

Habitat Deciduous woodlands and riparian forest; residential areas.

Abundance and Distribution Common to uncommon summer resident* (Mar.–Oct.) in Georgia, Alabama, Mississippi, the Panhandle, North and Central Florida; increasingly rare and local in summer in South Florida and absent from the Keys; uncommon to rare winter resident (Nov.–Mar.) along the lower coastal plain of Georgia, Alabama, Mississippi, and North Florida, common in Central and South Florida and the Keys.

Where to Find Ocmulgee National Monument, Georgia; Choctaw National Wildlife Refuge, Alabama; Freedom Hills Overlook, Natchez Trace Parkway, Mississippi; St. Joseph Peninsula State Park, Florida.

Range Breeds in the temperate United States south through

Figure 39. The quiet beauty of Mississippi's historic Natchez Trace provides a lovely ride through many of the state's richest natural habitats.

Mexico to Guatemala; winters in the southern Atlantic (from Virginia south) and Gulf states; and in the west from California, Arizona, New Mexico, and Texas south throughout Mexico and Central America to Honduras. Resident in the Bahamas.

Thrushes and Bluebirds
Family Turdidae

A group of medium-sized birds, most cryptically colored in browns and grays. The thrush family is considered by many to contain the most beautiful singers in the bird world. Though you may debate whether the Wood Thrush, Hermit Thrush, Slate-colored Solitaire or Nightingale holds the top position, few would contest their place in the Top Ten.

273. Eastern Bluebird
Sialia sialis
(L-7 W-12)

Blue above, brick red below with white belly. **Female** Similar but paler.

Voice A whistled "cheer cheerful farmer"; call: "tur lee."

Habitat Old fields, orchards, parkland, open woodlands, open country with scattered trees—appears limited by the availability of suitable nest sites (cavities in posts and nest boxes).

Abundance and Distribution Common to uncommon resident* in Georgia, Alabama, Mississippi, the Panhandle,

North and Central Florida; rare to casual in South Florida and absent from the Keys.

Where to Find Tombigbee State Park, Mississippi; Laura S. Walker State Park, Georgia; Oak Mountain State Park, Alabama; Wekiwa Springs State Park, Florida.

Range Breeds in eastern North America from southern Saskatchewan to New Brunswick south to Florida and Texas; through highlands of Mexico and Central America to Nicaragua; Bermuda; winters in southern portion of breeding range (central and eastern United States southward).

274. Veery
Catharus fuscescens
(L-7 W-12)

Russet above; throat buff with indistinct spotting; whitish belly.

Voice Song: a whistled, wheezy, descending "zheew zheew zhoo zhoo"; call: "zink."

Similar Species Breast spotting is more distinct in Swainson's and Gray-cheeked thrushes; Swainson's has distinct eyering; russet tail of Hermit Thrush contrasts with gray-brown back.

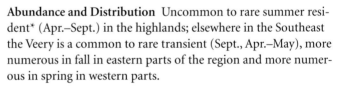

Habitat Mature deciduous and mixed forest; residential areas as a transient.

Abundance and Distribution Uncommon to rare summer resident* (Apr.–Sept.) in the highlands; elsewhere in the Southeast the Veery is a common to rare transient (Sept., Apr.–May), more numerous in fall in eastern parts of the region and more numerous in spring in western parts.

Where to Find Brasstown Bald, Georgia (breeding); Rabun Bald, Georgia (breeding); Dauphin Island, Alabama; Bogue Chitto National Wildlife Refuge, Mississippi.

Range Breeds across southern Canada and northern United States, south in mountains to Georgia in the east and Colorado in the west; winters in northern South America.

275. Gray-cheeked Thrush
Catharus minimus
(L-8 W-12)

Grayish brown above, whitish below; heavy dark spotting at throat diminishing to smudges at belly and flanks.

Voice Song: "zhee zheeoo titi zhee"; call: "zheep."

Similar Species The Gray-cheeked Thrush is distinguished from the other *Catharus* thrushes more by what it does not have than what it does. It does not have a rich buff eyering or buffy underparts like the Swainson's Thrush; it does not have a rusty tail like the Hermit Thrush; and it does not have a rusty back and head like the Veery. In our region, if you see a grayish brown thrush with no eyering, it is likely to be this bird.

Habitat Breeding: coniferous forest and shrubby taiga; migration and winter: riparian forest, deciduous and mixed woodlands, scrub, and residential areas.

Abundance and Distribution Uncommon to rare transient (Sept.–Oct., Apr.–May), more numerous in fall in eastern parts of the region and more numerous in spring in western parts.

Range Breeds from northeastern Siberia across Alaska and the northern tier of Canada; winters in northern South America.

276. Bicknell's Thrush
Catharus bicknelli
(L-8 W-12)

Grayish brown above, whitish below; heavy dark spotting at throat diminishing to smudges at belly and flanks; tail rustier (on average) than in Gray-cheeked Thrush.

Voice Song: "zhee zheeoo titi zhee"; call: "zheep."

Similar Species Bicknell's Thrush is virtually indistinguishable from the Gray-cheeked Thrush in the field, although the tail is somewhat rustier in Bicknell's (on average). Both are distinguished from the other *Catharus* by lack of a rich buff eyering and underparts (Swainson's); lack of a bright rusty rump and tail (Hermit) or a rusty back and head (Veery).

Habitat Breeding: coniferous forest; migration and winter: riparian forest, deciduous and mixed woodlands and scrub.

Abundance and Distribution Status unknown, but perhaps similar to that of the Gray-cheeked Thrush.

Range Breeds in the northeastern United States and southeastern Canada; winters in Greater Antilles.

Thrushes, Bluebirds

277. Swainson's Thrush

Catharus ustulatus
(L-7 W-12)

Brown or grayish brown above, buffy below with dark spotting; lores and eyering buffy.

Voice Song: "zhoo zhoo zhee zhee" with rising pitch; call: "zheep."

Similar Species The whitish or buff eyering of the Swainson's Thrush distinguishes this bird from the Gray-cheeked Thrush and western populations of the Veery. Also, flanks of the Swainson's Thrush are buffy, not grayish as in western Veeries.

Habitat Breeding: thickets in coniferous forest, bogs, alder swamps; migration and winter: moist woodlands, riparian thickets.

Abundance and Distribution Common to uncommon transient (Sept.–Oct., Apr.–May) throughout, more numerous in fall in eastern parts of the region and more numerous in spring in western parts.

Where to Find Mississippi Sandhill Crane National Wildlife Refuge, Mississippi; Oak Mountain State Park, Alabama; Harris Neck National Wildlife Refuge, Georgia; Gulf Islands National Seashore, Florida.

Range Breeds in boreal North America from Alaska across Canada to Labrador south to the northern United States; south in mountains and along coast to southern California and in mountains to northern New Mexico; winters from southern Mexico to the highlands of South America.

278. Hermit Thrush

Catharus guttatus
(L-7 W-12)

Grayish brown above; whitish below with dark spotting; whitish eyering; rusty tail, often flicked.

Voice Distinct phrases, each beginning with a long, whistled note followed by a trill; trills of different phrases have different inflection; call: "tuk tuk tuk" or a raspy "zhay."

Similar Species The bright rusty rump and tail of the Hermit Thrush distinguishes this bird from the other *Catharus* thrush species (Swainson's, Veery, Bicknell's, and Gray-cheeked), although Bicknell's has a somewhat rusty tail.

Habitat Breeding: Spruce-fir and hemlock forest; migration and winter: riparian thickets, broadleaf woodlands.

Abundance and Distribution Common to uncommon winter resident (Nov.–Apr.) in the coastal plain and piedmont of Georgia, Alabama, and Mississippi, scarce in the highlands; uncommon winter resident (Nov.–Apr.) in the Panhandle and North and Central Florida, rare to casual in South Florida and the Keys.

Where to Find Fort Toulouse, Alabama; Altamaha River/Atkinson Tract, Georgia; Roosevelt State Park, Mississippi; Tall Timbers Research Station, Florida.

Range Breeds in boreal Canada and northern United States, south in mountains to southern California, Arizona, New Mexico, and west Texas; winters from the southern United States north along coasts to southern British Columbia and New Jersey, and south through Mexico (excluding Yucatan Peninsula) to Central America. Resident population in Baja California.

279. Wood Thrush
Hylocichla mustelina
(L-8 W-13)

Russet above, white below with distinct black spots; reddish brown crown and nape.

Voice Distinct phrases of buzzy trills separated by pauses; call: "bup bup bup."

Similar Species None of the *Catharus* thrushes have clear white underparts and distinct, black spots.

Habitat Deciduous or mixed forest, riparian woodland.

Abundance and Distribution Common to uncommon transient and summer resident* (Apr.–Oct.) in Georgia, Alabama, Mississippi, the Panhandle, and North Florida; uncommon to rare transient (Sept.–Oct., Apr.–May) in Central and South Florida and the Keys.

Where to Find Wall Doxey State Park, Mississippi; Cloudland Canyon State Park, Georgia; Blackwater River State Park, Florida; Choctaw National Wildlife Refuge, Alabama.

Range Breeds in the eastern United States and southeastern Canada; winters from southern Mexico to Panama and northwestern Colombia.

Thrushes, Bluebirds

280. American Robin
Turdus migratorius
(L-10 W-17)

Dark gray above, orange brown below; white lower belly; white throat with dark streaks; partial white eyering.

Voice Song: a varied series of whistled phrases, "cheerily cheerup cheerio" etc.; call: "tut tut."

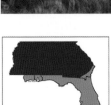

Habitat A wide variety of forest and parkland will serve as breeding habitat so long as there is rich, moist soil containing earthworms for foraging and mud available for nest construction. Deciduous and mixed forest, scrub, parkland, riparian forest, oak woodlands, and residential areas in winter.

Abundance and Distribution Common resident* in the highlands, piedmont, and upper coastal plain; common winter resident (Nov.–Mar.), rare in summer*, in the lower coastal plain of Georgia, Alabama, and Mississippi, and throughout Florida (casual or absent in summer in Central and South Florida and the Keys).

Where to Find Chickamauga and Chattanooga National Military Park, Georgia; Panther Swamp National Wildlife Refuge, Mississippi; Wheeler National Wildlife Refuge, Alabama; Jaycee Park, Lake Okeechobee, Florida.

Range Breeds nearly throughout Canada and United States south through central highlands of Mexico; winters from southern half of breeding range into Guatemala; western Cuba; Bahamas. Resident population in Baja California.

Thrashers and Mockingbirds
Family Mimidae

Long-tailed, medium-sized birds; several have a somewhat fierce appearance because of their decurved bills and colored eyes (orange, yellow, white). Some of the mimids include phrases from the songs of other birds in their own songs.

281. Gray Catbird
Dumetella carolinensis
(L-9 W-12)

Slate gray throughout, black cap and tail, rusty undertail coverts.

Voice A stream of whistles, mews, squeaks; sometimes mimics other species; call: a nasal, catlike mew.

Habitat Thickets in riparian areas; tangles, heavy undergrowth in coniferous and broadleaf woodlands; second growth, hedgerows.

Abundance and Distribution Common transient and summer resident* (Apr.–Oct.) and rare winter resident (Nov.–Mar.) in the highlands and piedmont; uncommon to rare summer resident* (Apr.–Oct.) and common winter resident* in the lower coastal plain of Georgia, Alabama, and Mississippi, the Panhandle, and North Florida; common winter resident (Nov.–Mar.) in Central and South Florida and the Keys.

Where to Find Chickamauga and Chattanooga National Military Park, Georgia; St. Andrews State Recreation Area, Florida; Hillside National Wildlife Refuge, Mississippi; Fort Toulouse, Alabama.

Range Breeds throughout eastern, central, and northwestern United States and southern Canada; winters along central and southern Atlantic and Gulf coasts south through the Gulf and Caribbean lowlands of Mexico to Panama; Bahamas, Greater Antilles. Resident in Bermuda.

Figure 40. Just north of Montgomery, Alabama, is Fort Toulouse at the junction of the Coosa and Talapoosa rivers. The great botanist and naturalist William Bartram traveled through this region in the late 1700s, and a nature walk has been built here in his honor, passing through mixed deciduous forest and swamp.

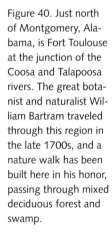

Thrashers, Mockingbirds

282. Northern Mockingbird
Mimus polyglottos
(L-10 W-14)

Gray body, paler below; black tail with white outer tail feathers; white wing bars and white patches on wings.

Habits Often flies to the ground and spreads wings and tail in a very mechanical fashion while foraging.

Voice A variety of whistled phrases, repeated several times and including pieces of other bird songs.

Similar Species Loggerhead Shrike has heavy, hooked bill, short tail, and black mask.

Habitat Old fields, hedgerows, agricultural areas, residential areas.

Abundance and Distribution Common resident* nearly throughout the Southeast although scarcer in the highlands.

Where to Find Gulf State Park, Alabama; Natchez State Park, Mississippi; Ocmulgee National Monument, Georgia; McKay Bay Nature Park, Florida.

Range Resident in central and southern United States and Mexico to Oaxaca; Bahamas, Greater Antilles.

283. Brown Thrasher
Toxostoma rufum
(L-11 W-13)

Rufous above, buff below with dark streaking; yellowish eye.

Voice A long sequence of brief phrases of squeaky warbles, each phrase given twice.

Habitat Tangles, undergrowth, and thickets of forests, old fields, hedgerows.

Abundance and Distribution Common resident* nearly throughout the Southeast except in Central and South Florida and the Keys where uncommon to rare; numbers increase across most of the region in winter with the influx of migrants from the north.

Where to Find Fort Toulouse, Alabama; Big Lagoon State Recreation Area, Florida; Fort Yargo State Park, Georgia; Wall Doxey State Park, Mississippi.

Range Breeds across eastern and central North America from southern Canada west to Alberta and south to east Texas and southern Florida; winters in southern portion of breeding range.

Starlings
Family Sturnidae

Starlings are an Old World family with no members native to the New World. They are medium-sized, relatively long-billed songbirds, often with iridescent plumage. Many of the species mimic the songs of other birds.

284. European Starling
Sturnus vulgaris
(L-9 W-15)

Plump, short tailed, and glossy black with purple and green highlights and long, yellow bill in summer. **Winter** Dark billed and speckled with white.

Habits Erect waddling gait when foraging on ground; forms large roosting flocks during nonbreeding season.

Voice Various squeaks, harsh "churr"s, whistles, and imitations of other bird songs, often with repeated phrases; call: a high-pitched, rising "tseee."

Similar Species Other black birds are shorter billed, longer tailed; winter bird is speckled with white; summer bird has yellow bill.

Habitat Towns, farmland.

Abundance and Distribution Common resident* throughout the Southeast.

Where to Find Miami, Florida; Atlanta, Georgia; Jackson, Mississippi; Birmingham, Alabama.

Range New World, resident from southern Canada to northern Mexico; Bahamas and Greater Antilles; Old World, breeds in temperate and boreal regions of Eurasia; winters in southern portions of breeding range into north Africa, Middle East, and southern Asia.

Starlings

Pipits
Family Motacillidae

Chaff-colored, long-tailed birds of open country. Like larks, pipits have an extremely long hind claw, and often call and sing on the wing. They pump their tails with each step as they walk along the ground in search of seeds and insects.

285. American Pipit
Anthus rubescens
(L-7 W-11)

Sparrowlike in size and coloration but sleek and erect in posture, walking rather than hopping, and with a thin bill; grayish brown above; buffy below streaked with brown; whitish throat and eyeline; white outer tail feathers; dark legs; wags tail as it walks; undulating flight.

Voice Flight song: a sibilant "chwee" repeated; call: "tsee-eet."

Similar Species American Pipit has unstreaked back and dark legs; Sprague's Pipit has streaked back and flesh-colored legs; Vesper Sparrow has cone-shaped bill (not narrow); hops rather than walks.

Habitat Short grassland, plowed fields, swales, mudflats, roadsides; pond, stream and river margins.

Abundance and Distribution Uncommon to rare winter visitor (Oct.–Apr.) in Georgia, Alabama, Mississippi, the Panhandle, and North Florida; increasingly scarce southward along the Peninsula from Central to South Florida and rare to casual in the Keys.

Where to Find Harris Neck National Wildlife Refuge, Georgia; Eufaula National Wildlife Refuge, Alabama; Natchez Trace Parkway, Mississippi; Orange County Eastern Water Reclamation Facility, Florida.

Range Breeds in Arctic regions of the New World, and in mountainous areas and high plateaus of temperate regions; winters in temperate regions and high, arid portions of the tropics.

286. Sprague's Pipit
Anthus spragueii
(L-7 W-11)

Streaked brown above; whitish below streaked with brown; pale legs; white outer tail feathers; walks rather than hops; bobs tail.

Voice Flight song: a series of high, sweet notes, descending in pitch; call: a hoarse "tsip."

Similar Species See American Pipit.

Habitat Shortgrass prairie, dunes, pastures.

Abundance and Distribution Rare and local winter visitor (Oct.–Apr.), mainly in the eastern Florida Panhandle.

Where to Find Apalachicola Municipal Airport, Florida.

Range Breeds in the northern Great Plains of Canada and the north-central United States; winters in the southern United States and Mexico south to southern Veracruz, Puebla, and Michoacan.

Waxwings
Family Bombycillidae

Waxwings are a small family of sleek, brown, crested birds with bright waxy tips on their secondaries. They are highly social during the nonbreeding season, feeding mostly in flocks on tree fruits and berries.

287. Cedar Waxwing
Bombycilla cedrorum
(L-7 W-11)

Natty brown above and below with sharp crest; black face and throat; yellow wash on belly; tail tipped with yellow; red waxy tips to secondaries. **Immature** faint streaking below, lacks waxy tips.

Voice A thin, gurgling "tseee."

Habitat Open coniferous and deciduous woodlands, bogs, swamps, and shrubby, overgrown fields; cemeteries, arboreta, residential areas where fruiting trees are found.

Abundance and Distribution Common to uncommon winter visitor (Sept.–Apr.) in Georgia, Alabama, Mississippi, the Panhandle, and North Florida; increasingly irregular in occurrence southward along the Peninsula from Central to South Florida and the Keys; rare summer resident* (May–Aug.) in the highlands and upper piedmont.

Where to Find Little River Canyon National Preserve, Alabama; Patterson Gap Road, Georgia; Dahomey National Wildlife Refuge, Mississippi; Lake Woodruff National Wildlife Refuge, Florida.

Range Breeds across southern Canada and northern United States south to northern California, Kansas, and New York; winters in temperate United States south through Mexico and Central America to Panama and the Greater Antilles.

Wood Warblers
Family Parulidae

The wood warblers are a large group of mostly small species, many of which are migratory. Males of several species are brightly colored.

288. Blue-winged Warbler
Vermivora pinus
(L-5 W-8)

Greenish yellow above, yellow below; head yellow with black line through eye; bluish gray wings and tail with white wing bars and tail spots. **Female** More greenish on head.

Voice Song: a dry, buzzy "beee bizzz."

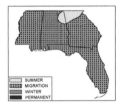

Habitat Deciduous scrub, old fields.

Abundance and Distribution Uncommon to rare transient (Aug.–Oct., Apr.–May) throughout the region; uncommon to rare summer resident* (May–Aug.) in the highlands.

Where to Find Crockford-Pigeon Mountain Wildlife Management Area, Georgia; Dauphin Island, Alabama; Lake Arbuckle Nature Trail, Avon Park Air Force Range, Florida; Bogue Chitto National Wildlife Refuge, Mississippi.

Range Breeds in the eastern United States; winters from southern Mexico to Panama. Interbreeds with Golden-winged Warbler to produce hybrid Brewster's (patterned like bluewing but with whitish underparts) and Lawrence's (patterned like goldenwing but yellow below) warblers.

289. Golden-winged Warbler
Vermivora chrysoptera
(L-5 W-8)

Gray above, white below; golden crown and epaulets; black throat and ear patch; white tail spots. **Female**

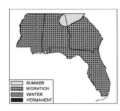

and Immature Patterned like male but with gray throat and ear patch.

Voice Song: "bee biz biz biz."

Habitat Deciduous scrub, old fields.

Abundance and Distribution Uncommon to rare transient (Aug.–Oct., Apr.–May) throughout the region; uncommon to rare summer resident* (May–Aug.) in the highlands.

Where to Find Ocmulgee National Monument, Georgia; Oak Mountain State Park, Alabama; Vicksburg National Military Park, Mississippi; Fort De Soto County Park, Florida.

Range Breeds in the northeastern and north-central United States; winters from southern Mexico to Colombia and Venezuela. See Blue-winged Warbler for discussion of hybrids.

290. Tennessee Warbler
Vermivora peregrina
(L-5 W-8)

Olive above, white below with gray cap, white eye stripe, and dark line through eye. **Immature** Tinged with yellow.

Voice Song: a series of rapid "tsip"s followed by a series of rapid "tsi"s; call: a strong "tsip."

Similar Species The Tennessee Warbler lacks streaking on breast and has white undertail coverts. The Orange-crowned Warbler has faint streaking on breast and yellow undertail coverts. Also, the Tennessee is greener above than the Orange-crowned Warbler, and has a more prominent eye stripe.

Habitat Breeds in coniferous forest; deciduous and mixed forest on migration.

Abundance and Distribution Common to uncommon transient (Sept.–Oct., Apr.–May) throughout, more numerous in fall in eastern parts of the region and more numerous in spring in western parts.

Where to Find Palm Point Park, Gainesville, Florida; Mississippi Sandhill Crane National Wildlife Refuge, Mississippi; Bon Secour National Wildlife Refuge, Alabama; Ocmulgee National Monument, Georgia.

Range Breeds across boreal North America; winters from southern Mexico to northern South America.

Wood Warblers

291. Orange-crowned Warbler
Vermivora celata
(L-5 W-8)

Greenish gray above, dingy yellow faintly streaked with gray below; grayish head with faint whitish eye stripe; orange crown visible on some birds at close range.

Voice Song: a weak, fading trill; call: a strong "cheet."

Similar Species The Orange-crowned Warbler has faint streaking on the breast and yellow undertail coverts while the breast of the Tennessee Warbler is unstreaked and the undertail coverts are white; the Tennessee Warbler is greener above than the Orange-crowned Warbler and has a more prominent eye stripe. Immatures of some Yellow Warblers are similar but have yellow (not gray) undertail lining.

Habitat Old fields, forest thickets, coastal scrub.

Abundance and Distribution Uncommon to rare transient and winter resident (Oct.–Apr.) throughout the region; scarcer as a winter resident in the highlands and piedmont.

Where to Find Legion State Park, Mississippi; Conecuh National Forest, Open Pond, Alabama; Gulf Islands National Seashore, Florida; Jekyll Island, Georgia.

Range Breeds in western and northern North America; winters from the southern United States into Mexico, Belize, and Guatemala.

292. Nashville Warbler
Vermivora ruficapilla
(L-4 W-7)

Olive above, yellow below; gray head; white eyering; rufous cap. **Female** Dingier; lacks reddish cap.

Voice Song: "tsepit tsepit tsepit" followed by a trilled "tseeeeeeeeeeee"; call: "tsip."

Habitat Coniferous bogs; scrub; old fields, overgrown strip mines, clearcuts, and pine barrens.

Abundance and Distribution Uncommon to rare transient (Sept.–Oct., Apr.–May) throughout, more numerous in fall in eastern parts of the region and more numerous in spring in western parts.

Where to Find Yazoo National Wildlife Refuge, Mississippi.

Range Breeds across extreme north-central and northeastern

United States, south-central and southeastern Canada, and north-western United States; winters from south Texas to Honduras.

293. Northern Parula
Parula americana
(L-5 W-8)

Bluish above; yellow throat and breast with black collar rimmed below with rust; white eyering, belly, and wing bars; greenish yellow on back. **Female and Immature** Lack collar.

Voice Song: "brrrrrzzeeit," like running a thumbnail up a comb; also a slower, rising "zhe zhe zhe zeeeeit."

Habitat Swampy deciduous and mixed forest.

Abundance and Distribution Common to uncommon transient and summer resident* (Mar.–Sept.) in Georgia and Alabama (scarcer in summer in the highlands), Mississippi, the Panhandle, North and Central Florida; common to uncommon transient (Aug.–Sept., Mar.–Apr.) and rare to casual winter resident (Oct.–Mar.) in South Florida and the Keys.

Where to Find Leaf Wilderness, De Soto National Forest, Mississippi; Okefenokee National Wildlife Refuge, Georgia; Choctaw National Wildlife Refuge, Alabama; Lake Woodruff National Wildlife Refuge, Florida.

Range Breeds in the eastern United States and southeastern Canada; winters from southern Mexico to Panama; West Indies.

Figure 41. This railroad cut through southeastern Mississippi's Leaf Wilderness seems to beckon the traveler into the magnificent mixed broadleaf forests and bottomlands. Leaf Wilderness is good for Prothonotary Warbler, Northern Parula, Hooded Warbler, Swainson's Warbler, and Boone-and-Crocket-size mosquitoes.

294. Yellow Warbler
Dendroica petechia
(L-5 W-8)

Yellow throughout, somewhat dingier on the back; yellow tail spots. Male variably streaked below with reddish.

Voice Song: "tseet tseet tseet tsitsitsi tseet" (sweet, sweet, sweet, I'm so sweet); call: "chip."

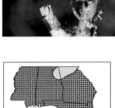

Similar Species Some immature Yellow Warblers are quite greenish, resembling immature Orange-crowned Warblers, but they have yellow (not gray) undertail lining.

Habitat Old fields, riparian thickets.

Abundance and Distribution Common to uncommon transient (Aug.–Oct., Apr.–May) throughout, more numerous in fall in eastern parts of the region and more numerous in spring in western parts; uncommon to rare summer resident* (May–Aug.) in the upper piedmont and highlands; uncommon to rare and local resident* in mangroves of the Keys and the southern tip of the Florida Peninsula; rare to casual in winter, mainly along the coast, elsewhere in Florida.

Where to Find Florida Keys National Wildlife Refuges, Florida; Vogel State Park, Georgia; St. Catherine Creek National Wildlife Refuge, Mississippi; Dauphin Island, Alabama.

Range Breeds across most of North America; winters from extreme southern United States through Mexico and Central America to northern and central South America. Resident races in mangroves of West Indies, Central and South America.

295. Chestnut-sided Warbler
Dendroica pensylvanica
(L-5 W-8)

Greenish streaked with black and white above; white below with chestnut sides (more extensive in male); yellow cap; white cheek and wing bars; black eye stripe and malar stripe. **Winter Adult and Immature** Spring green above, white below with whitish yellow eyering, wing bars and tail spots; adults males have some chestnut on flanks.

Voice Song: "pleased pleased pleased ta meetcha" and variations; call: "tsip."

Similar Species Bay-breasted Warbler is chestnut (male) or buffy (female) on breast, not white. Bright yellow-green back and white

Wood Warblers

underparts separate the winter adult and immature from immatures of other warblers.

Habitat Scrub, thickets, second growth, hedgerows.

Abundance and Distribution Common to rare transient (Sept.–Oct., Apr.–May) throughout, more numerous in fall in eastern parts of the region and more numerous in spring in western parts; uncommon summer resident* (May–Aug.) in the highlands.

Where to Find Black Rock Mountain State Park, Georgia; Cheaha State Park, Alabama; Noxubee National Wildlife Refuge, Mississippi; St. Andrews State Recreation Area, Florida.

Range Breeds in southeastern Canada and the northeastern United States south, in the Appalachians to Georgia.

296. Magnolia Warbler
Dendroica magnolia
(L-5 W-8)

Black back, gray cap; yellow below broadly streaked with black; yellow rump; white wing and tail patches. **Female and Winter Male** More brownish above than breeding male; breast streaking is faint and grayish.

SUMMER
MIGRATION
WINTER
PERMANENT

Habits Continually fans tail, showing white patches; often sallies for insects during foraging.

Voice Song: "tsweeta tsweeta tsweetee;" call: a hoarse, vireolike "eeeeeh," very different from most other warblers.

Similar Species No other warbler has broken white band across the middle of the tail.

Habitat Thickets in coniferous forest, especially young spruce and hemlock, on the breeding ground; various woodlands and scrub at other times of the year.

Abundance and Distribution Common to rare transient (Sept.–Oct., Apr.–May) throughout, more numerous in eastern parts of the region in fall and in western parts in the spring; rare to casual in Florida in winter (Nov.–Mar.).

Where to Find Dauphin Island, Alabama; Everglades National Park, Florida; Savannah National Wildlife Refuge, Georgia; Dahomey National Wildlife Refuge, Mississippi.

Range Breeds across much of boreal Canada and the northeastern United States; winters from central Mexico to Panama; West Indies.

Wood Warblers

297. Cape May Warbler
Dendroica tigrina
(L-5 W-8)

Greenish with black streakings above; dark sreaking on crown; yellow breast with black streaks; yellowish rump; chestnut face with black line through eye; white undertail coverts, wing patch, and tail spots. **Female and Immature** Dingier; yellowish or grayish face.

Voice Song: a weak, high-pitched "tsee tsee tsee tsee."

Similar Species Female Yellow-rumped Warbler lacks distinct streaking on throat and breast. Palm Warbler has yellow (not white) undertail coverts and wags tail.

Habitat Coniferous, mixed, and deciduous forest; riparian and oak woodland.

Abundance and Distribution Common to rare transient (Sept.–Oct., Apr.–May) in Georgia and Florida, concentrated along the Atlantic coast in fall, more widespread and numerous in spring; rare winter resident (Oct.–Apr.) in extreme South Florida and the Keys.

Where to Find Blackbeard Island National Wildlife Refuge, Georgia; Easterlin Park, Fort Lauderdale, Florida.

Range Breeds in boreal regions of central and eastern Canada and northeastern United States; winters in southern Florida and the West Indies.

298. Black-throated Blue Warbler
Dendroica caerulescens
(L-5 W-8)

Dark grayish blue above; black face, throat, and sides; white breast, belly, and spot on primaries. **Female** Brownish above, dingy white below with whitish eye stripe, dark ear patch, and (usually) white patch on primaries.

Voice Song: a rising "tsee tsee tsee tsuree"; call: "tsik."

Similar Species Female resembles Philadelphia Vireo and Tennessee Warbler, but dark cheek patch and white wing patch (when present) are distinctive.

Habitat Mixed woodlands, often with laurel or rhododendron understory, during the breeding season; various woodlands on migration and in winter.

Wood Warblers

Abundance and Distribution Common to rare transient (Sept.–Oct., Apr.–May) in Georgia, peninsular Florida, and the Keys; rare transient in Alabama, Mississippi, and the Florida Panhandle; common summer resident* (May–Aug.) in the highlands.

Where to Find Black Rock Mountain State Park, Georgia.

Range Breeds from southeastern Canada and the northeastern United States south along the Appalachian chain to northern Georgia; winters in the Caribbean basin.

299. Yellow-rumped Warbler
Dendroica coronata
(L-5 W-8)

Blue gray streaked, with black above; black breast and sides; white belly; yellow cap, rump, and shoulder bars; white wing patch. Breeding males of the eastern and northern race have white throat; western race has yellow throat. **Female, Winter Male, and Immature** Brownish above, dingy below with faint streaking; yellow rump.

Voice Song: a weak trill, rising at the end, "tsitsitsitsitsitsitsee"; "chit" call note often given in flight.

Habitat Breeds in coniferous and mixed forest; various woodlands and scrub on migration and in winter.

Abundance and Distribution Common transient and winter resident (Oct.–May) throughout the Southeast.

Where to Find DeSoto State Park, Alabama; Lake Woodruff National Wildlife Refuge, Florida; Leaf Wilderness, De Soto National Forest, Mississippi; Chickamauga and Chattanooga National Military Park, Georgia.

Range Breeds across northern boreal North America and in mountains of the west south to southern Mexico; winters from central and southern United States to Panama and the West Indies.

300. Black-throated Gray Warbler
Dendroica nigrescens
(L-5 W-8)

Dark gray above, whitish below with white wing bars; distinct facial pattern of black crown, white eye stripe, black eyeline and ear stripe, white chin stripe, and yellow loral spot; black throat and breast. **Female**

Wood Warblers

and **Immature** More grayish throughout; throat and breast are whitish with variable amounts of gray or black.

Voice Song: "tseta tseta tseta tseeet cha" with rising inflection on penultimate syllable.

Similar Species Female Cerulean Warbler has bluish cap and buffy (not gray) cheek patch.

Habitat Arid pinyon, oak, and juniper scrub.

Abundance and Distribution Rare winter visitor (Oct.–Apr.), mainly in South Florida and the Keys.

Range Breeds in the western United States and northwestern Mexico; winters from the southwestern United States into southern Mexico.

301. Black-throated Green Warbler
Dendroica virens
(L-5 W-8)

Green above; black bib; green crown; golden face; white belly. **Female and Immature** Usually with some gray or black across breast.

Voice Song: a lazy, insectlike "zee zee zee zoo zee" or "zoo zee zeezee zoo"; call: "chip."

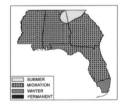

Habitat Breeds in coniferous and mixed forest; found in broadleaf forest and scrub on migration and in winter.

Abundance and Distribution Common to rare transient (Sept.–Oct., Apr.–May) throughout, more numerous in fall in eastern parts of the region and more numerous in spring in western parts; uncommon summer resident* (May–Aug.) in the highlands; uncommon to rare winter resident in South Florida and the Keys.

Where to Find Unicoi Gap, Georgia; Cheaha State Park, Alabama; Yazoo National Wildlife Refuge, Mississippi; Sawgrass Lake County Park, Florida; Everglades National Park (winter).

Range Breeds across central and southern Canada and north-central and northern United States, also south in the Appalachians to north Georgia and along the coastal plain to South Carolina; winters from south Texas and South Florida through Mexico and Central America to Panama; West Indies.

302. Blackburnian Warbler

Dendroica fusca

(L-5 W-8)

Black above, white below; orange bib; black and orange facial pattern. **Female and Immature** Patterned like male but black areas of adult male are grayish in female and immature, and orange areas are yellowish.

Voice Song: very high-pitched, rising "tsip tsip tsip tsip tsitsi tseeee"; call: "tsip."

Similar Species Female Black-throated Green is greenish or mottled black and green on the back. Female Blackburnian has pale striping on dark back.

Habitat Breeds in spruce-fir, mixed, and deciduous forest (in the Appalachians); found in various forest types on migration and in winter.

Abundance and Distribution Common to rare transient (Sept.–Oct., Apr.–May) throughout, more numerous in fall in eastern parts of the region and more numerous in spring in western parts; uncommon summer resident* (May–Aug.) in the highlands.

Where to Find Brasstown Bald, Georgia; Dauphin Island, Alabama (transient); Bogue Chitto National Wildlife Refuge, Mississippi; Sawgrass Lake County Park, Florida.

Range Breeds in southeastern Canada and the northeastern United States south, in the Appalachians to Georgia; winters in Costa Rica, Panama, and northern South America.

303. Yellow-throated Warbler

Dendroica dominica

(L-5 W-8)

Dark gray above, white below with yellow bib; black mask; white eye stripe (yellow in some individuals); black streaks on sides.

Habits Often forages by creeping along tree branches.

Voice Song: a strong, slurred series of notes ending with an upward inflection, "tew tew tew tew teweesee."

Habitat Conifers, cypress, sycamores; riparian woodland.

Abundance and Distribution Common to rare summer resident* (Mar.–Sept.) in Georgia, Alabama, Mississippi (scarce in the piedmont), the Panhandle, North and Central Florida; common to

Wood Warblers

Figure 42. Fakahatchee Strand Preserve viewed from the Big Cypress Bend boardwalk on south Florida's Tamiami Trail (FL 41) is a unique habitat that must be seen if you visit the region. It represents one of the few remaining stands of virgin cypress in the southeastern United States. I have seen only one other that can match it—Minnie's Island in the middle of south Georgia's Okefenokee Swamp, a much more remote and difficult place to visit. The Fakahatchee cypresses are a fifteen-minute stroll from the highway visitor center down a nice boardwalk. Unfortunately there aren't any Ivory-billed Woodpeckers there, but other cypress denizens, like Yellow-throated Warbler, are common.

uncommon transient (Aug.–Sept., Mar.–Apr.) and winter resident (Oct.–Mar.) in the lower coastal plain of Georgia, Alabama, Mississippi, and Florida (rare in western Panhandle).

Where to Find Noxubee National Wildlife Refuge, Mississippi; Tuskegee National Forest, Alabama; Big Cypress Bend, Fakahatchee Strand Preserve State Park, Florida; Reed Bingham State Park, Georgia.

Range Breeds in the eastern United States; winters from the Gulf coast of the United States south through Central America to Costa Rica; Bahamas and Greater Antilles.

304. Pine Warbler
Dendroica pinus
(L-6 W-9)

Olive above, yellow below with faint, grayish streaking; whitish belly and undertail coverts; yellow eye stripe; white wing bars; white tail spots. **Female and Immature** Patterned like male but olive areas above are tinged brownish or grayish and yellowish underparts are a dingy white.

Voice Song: a series of chips similar to the Chipping Sparrow but slower, each chip distinct.

Similar Species Immature similar to immature Blackpoll and Bay-breasted but plain (not streaked) back. Could be confused with Yellow-throated Vireo, but the slimmer, smaller, more active Pine Warbler has yellow-green rump (not gray), white tail spots, and thin bill.

Habitat Pine forest.

Abundance and Distribution Common to uncommon resident* nearly throughout the Southeast, although rare or absent in the highlands and the Florida Keys.

Where to Find Legion State Park, Mississippi; Bladon Springs State Park, Alabama; Tall Timbers Research Station, Florida; Laura S. Walker State Park, Georgia.

Range Breeds in the eastern half of the United States and south-central and southeastern Canada; Bahamas, Hispaniola; winters in southern portion of breeding range.

305. Prairie Warbler

Dendroica discolor
(L-5 W-7)

Greenish yellow above streaked with chestnut; yellow below with black markings on sides; yellow face with black eyeline and chin stripe; yellowish wing bars. **Immature** Similarly patterned but much dingier.

Habits Wags tail while foraging.

Voice Song: a rising series of buzzy "zee"s.

Similar Species Tail wagging habit separates this species from all but the immature Palm Warbler, which is brownish (not green) above and has grayish streaking on breast (not restricted to sides).

Habitat Scrubby coniferous and deciduous second growth; clearcuts; pine plantations; mangroves of South Florida and the Keys.

Abundance and Distribution Common to uncommon transient and summer resident* (Mar.–Oct.) in the Panhandle and North Florida, Alabama, Mississippi, and Georgia; common to uncommon resident* in Central and South Florida (north to Pasco and Volusia counties) and the Keys. The resident race of the Prairie Warbler in Florida is found mainly in mangroves of coastal areas; inland birds in this area are likely to be transients or winter residents.

Where to Find Skidaway Island State Park, Georgia; Gulf State

Wood Warblers

Park, Alabama; Florida Keys National Wildlife Refuges, Florida; Mississippi Sandhill Crane National Wildlife Refuge, Mississippi.

Range Breeds in the eastern half of the United States; winters in South Florida and the Caribbean basin.

306. Palm Warbler
Dendroica palmarum
(L-5 W-7)

Olive with dark streaks above; yellowish or creamy below with brownish streaks; yellow undertail coverts; chestnut cap in breeding plumage; yellow eye stripe and eye ring.

Habits Wags tail while foraging. Often forages low or on the ground.

Voice Song: a weak series of buzzy notes on the same pitch.

Similar Species The immature Palm Warbler is similar to the immature Pine Warbler but has grayish streaking on breast (not restricted to sides) and yellowish (not whitish) undertail coverts.

Habitat Spruce bogs on breeding ground; marshes, swampy thickets, and mangroves on migration and in winter.

Abundance and Distribution Common transient (Sept.–May) throughout the region; common (south) to rare (north) winter resident (Oct.–Apr.) nearly throughout, although rare or absent from the piedmont and highlands.

Where to Find Harris Neck National Wildlife Refuge, Georgia; J. N. "Ding" Darling National Wildlife Refuge, Florida; Blakely Island, Alabama; Bogue Chitto National Wildlife Refuge, Mississippi.

Range Breeds across central and eastern Canada and extreme north-central and northeastern United States; winters along the Atlantic and Gulf Coastal Plain and the northern Caribbean basin.

307. Bay-breasted Warbler
Dendroica castanea
(L-6 W-9)

Gray above with heavy, dark streaking; chestnut cap, throat, and sides; black mask; beige neck patch; dark wings with two white wing bars; dark tail with white patches (from below); dark legs. **Female, Winter Male, and Immature** Olive above with dark streak-

Wood Warblers

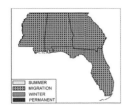

ing, beige or dingy olive below, often with some buff or chestnut on sides; dark wings with two white wing bars; dark tail with white patches (from below); dark legs.

Voice Song: a very high-pitched "wesee wesee wesee."

Similar Species Immature Blackpoll Warbler has faintly streaked (not plain) breast and pale (not dark) legs.

Habitat Breeds in coniferous forest; various woodlands on migration and in winter.

Abundance and Distribution Common to rare transient (Sept.–Oct., Apr.–May) throughout, more numerous in fall in eastern parts of the region and more numerous in spring in western parts.

Where to Find Gulf Islands National Seashore, Mississippi; Eufaula National Wildlife Refuge, Alabama.

Range Breeds across central and eastern Canada and extreme north-central and northeastern United States; winters in Panama, Colombia, and northwestern Venezuela.

308. Blackpoll Warbler
Dendroica striata
(L-6 W-9)

Grayish green streaked with black above, white below; black cap; white cheek; black chin stripe and streakings on side; dark wings with two white wing bars; dark tail with white patches (from below); pale legs. **Female, Winter Male, and Immature** Olive cap more or less streaked with black or grayish; faint white or yellowish eye stripe; greenish or yellowish cheek; whitish below with variable amounts of gray streaking; dark wings with two white wingbars; dark tail with white patches (from below); pale legs.

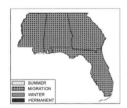

Voice Song: a weak series of "tsi"s, building in volume and then trailing off; call: a soft "chuk."

Similar Species Black-and-white Warbler resembles male Blackpoll Warbler but crown has white median stripe (not solid black). Immature and winter Blackpoll has faintly streaked breast (not plain as in Bay-breasted Warbler) and pale legs (not dark).

Habitat Breeds in coniferous forest; various forest and scrub sites on migration and in winter.

Abundance and Distribution Common to rare transient (Sept.–Oct., Apr.–May) throughout, more numerous in fall along the Georgia coast and more numerous in spring elsewhere in the region except western Panhandle, where rare to casual.

Wood Warblers

Where to Find Skidaway Island State Park, Georgia; Noxubee National Wildlife Refuge, Mississippi; Canaveral National Seashore, Florida.

Range Breeds in northern boreal regions of North America; winters in South America to northern Argentina.

309. Cerulean Warbler
Dendroica cerulea
(L-5 W-8)

A delicate bluish gray above, white below; black bar across chest and streakings down side; white wing bars. **Female** Olive more or less tinged with blue above; whitish below with faint grayish streakings; blue-gray or greenish crown; creamy eye stripe.

Voice Song: a series of 6–8 buzzy "tsee" notes, the last with an upward inflection; call: "tsip."

Similar Species Black throat band is distinctive for male. Female resembles female and immature Blackpoll Warbler but has unstreaked back, prominent eye stripe, and dark legs (not pale).

Habitat Deciduous forest, often tall oaks or sycamores; various types of woodlands on migration.

Abundance and Distribution Common to rare transient (Sept.–Oct., Apr.–May) throughout, more numerous in fall in eastern parts of the region and more numerous in spring in western parts; uncommon to rare summer resident* (Apr.–Aug.) in northern and central Mississippi, Alabama, and (rarely) Georgia.

Where to Find Little River Canyon National Preserve, Alabama; Rock Spring, Natchez Trace Parkway, Mississippi; Piedmont National Wildlife Refuge, Georgia; Sawgrass Lake County Park, Florida.

Range Breeds in the eastern United States except southeastern coastal plain; winters in northern South America.

310. Black-and-white Warbler
Mniotilta varia
(L-5 W-9)

Boldly striped with black and white above and below; black throat. **Female** Similar to male but with faint grayish streaking below; white throat.

Habits Clambers up and down tree trunks and branches, nuthatch fashion.

Voice Song: a weak "wesee wesee wesee"; call: "pit."

Similar Species This is the only warbler species with white median stripe in black cap, and peculiar trunk-foraging behavior.

Habitat Deciduous and mixed forest; various woodland types during migration and winter.

Abundance and Distribution Common to uncommon transient (Aug.–Sept., Mar.–May) throughout; uncommon to rare summer resident* (Apr.–Aug.) in the highlands and upper piedmont; uncommon winter resident (Oct.–Mar.) in Florida and along the coastal plain in Mississippi, Alabama, and Georgia.

Where to Find Little River Canyon National Preserve, Alabama; Rock Spring, Natchez Trace Parkway, Mississippi; Cumberland Island National Seashore, Georgia; St. Marks National Wildlife Refuge, Florida.

Range Breeds across Canada east of the mountains and in the eastern half of the United States; winters from extreme southern United States, eastern Mexico and Central America to northern South America; West Indies.

311. American Redstart
Setophaga ruticilla
(L-5 W-9)

Black above and below with brilliant orange patches on tail, wings, and sides of breast; white undertail coverts. **Female** Grayish brown above, whitish below with yellow patches on tail, wings, and sides of breast. **Immature Male** Similar to female but with salmon-colored patches on sides of breast.

Habits This species catches much of its insect prey on the wing in brief sallies; often fans tail and droops wings while foraging.

Voice One individual may have three or four different songs, even alternating song types from one phrase to the next. Some common phrases are "tsee tsee tsee tsee tseet," "tsee tsee tsee tsee tsee-o," "teetsa teetsa teeetsa teetsa teet." Call: a strong "chip."

Habitat Deciduous and mixed forest.

Abundance and Distribution Common to uncommon summer resident* (May–Aug.) in the highlands, piedmont, and rarely, locally, in parts of the coastal plain (e.g., western Panhandle—Okaloosa Co.); common to rare transient (Sept.–Oct., Apr.–May) throughout, more numerous in fall in eastern parts of the region and more numerous in spring in western parts; rare to casual winter resident (Oct.–Apr.) in Florida.

Wood Warblers

Figure 43. Snowfall is rare in most parts of the Southeast, but not on Rabun Bald at the southern end of the Appalachians in the Georgia highlands. Forests here support Canada Warblers, Rose-breasted Grosbeaks, Chestnut-sided Warblers, and Blackburnian Warblers in summer, Pine Siskins and Evening Grosbeaks in winter (occasionally), and Ruffed Grouse and Common Ravens year round.

Where to Find Wall Doxey State Park, Mississippi; Little River Canyon National Preserve, Alabama; Rabun Bald, Georgia; Florida Keys National Wildlife Refuge, Florida.

Range Breeds across Canada south of the Arctic region and in the eastern half of the United States except the southeastern coastal plain; winters from central Mexico south to northern South America; West Indies.

312. Prothonotary Warbler

Protonotaria citrea

(L-6 W-9)

Golden head and breast; yellow-green back; blue-gray wings; white belly and undertail coverts. **Female** Similar but yellow rather than orange on head.

Voice Song: a loud, ringing "peeet weeet weeet weeet weeet weeet weeet"; call: "tsip."

Similar Species Female Wilson's Warbler has brownish green (not gray) wings and yellow (not white) undertail coverts. Yellow Warbler has yellow wing bars (none on Prothonotary).

SUMMER
MIGRATION
WINTER
PERMANENT

Habitat Wooded swamps.

Abundance and Distribution Common summer resident* (Apr.–Aug.) in the Panhandle, North, and Central Florida and along the coastal plain of Georgia, Alabama, and Mississippi, scarce or absent in the piedmont and highlands, rare to casual summer resident* in South Florida; common to uncommon transient (Mar.–

Wood Warblers

Apr., Sept.–Oct.) throughout, more numerous in spring in the mountains and piedmont.

Where to Find Mathews Brake National Wildlife Refuge, Mississippi; Tuskegee National Forest, Alabama; Blackwater River State Park, Florida; Grand Bay Wildlife Management Area, Georgia.

Range Breeds in the eastern half of the United States; winters in mangroves along coast, from southeastern Mexico, the Caribbean basin of Central America, Costa Rica, Panama, and northern South America.

313. Worm-eating Warbler
Helmitheros vermivorum
(L-6 W-9)

Olive above, buffy below; crown striped with black and buff.

Habits Forages in dead leaf clumps in trees or on the ground.

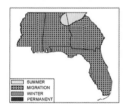

Voice Song: an insectlike, buzzy trill; call: a strong "chip."

Habitat Deciduous and mixed forest, often on west-facing slopes.

Abundance and Distribution Uncommon summer resident* (May–Aug.) in the highlands and (rarely) the upper piedmont; also a rare and local summer resident in Okaloosa County in the western Florida Panhandle; common to uncommon transient (Aug.–Oct., Apr.–May) throughout; rare winter resident in South Florida and the Keys.

Where to Find Cheaha State Park, Alabama; Crockford-Pigeon Mountain Wildlife Management Area, Georgia; Sebastian Inlet State Recreation Area, Florida.

Range Breeds in the eastern United States; winters from southern Mexico to Panama; West Indies.

314. Swainson's Warbler
Limnothlypis swainsonii
(L-6 W-9)

Brown above, buff below with chestnut cap; whitish eye stripe.

Habits Feeds mainly on the ground.

Voice Song: a loud, clear "whee whee whitoo whee"; call: a ringing "chip."

Wood Warblers

SUMMER
MIGRATION
WINTER
PERMANENT

Habitat Canebrakes, swampy thickets; also in rhododendron thickets in the southern Appalachians.

Abundance and Distribution Uncommon to rare and local summer resident* (Apr.–Aug.) in the highlands, the coastal plain of Alabama, Mississippi, and Georgia, and, locally, the Panhandle and North Florida (to Duval and Dixie counties); uncommon to rare transient (Aug.–Oct., Mar.–May) in Central and South Florida and the Keys.

Where to Find Ocmulgee National Monument, Georgia; Conecuh National Forest, Alabama; Blackwater River State Park, Florida; Leaf Wilderness, De Soto National Forest, Mississippi.

Range Breeds in the southeastern United States; winters in the Bahamas, Greater Antilles, eastern Mexico and Yucatan.

315. Ovenbird
Seiurus aurocapilla
(L-6 W-10)

Olive above, white below with heavy dark streaks; orange crown stripe bordered in black; white eyering.

Habits Walks on forest floor, flicking leaves and duff while foraging for invertebrates.

Voice Song: a loud "teacher teacher teacher teacher" etc.

Similar Species Northern and Louisiana waterthrushes have a prominent white or yellowish eye stripe. Also, Ovenbirds do not bob while walking as do waterthrushes.

SUMMER
MIGRATION
WINTER
PERMANENT

Habitat Deciduous and mixed forest.

Abundance and Distribution Common to rare transient (Sept.–Oct., Apr.–May) throughout, more numerous in fall in eastern parts of the region and more numerous in spring in western parts; common to uncommon summer resident* (May–Aug.) in the highlands and upper piedmont; uncommon to rare winter resident (Nov.–Mar.) in Central and South Florida and the Keys.

Where to Find Black Rock Mountain State Park, Georgia; Cheaha State Park, Alabama; Tallahatchie National Wildlife Refuge, Mississippi; St. Andrews Bay State Recreation Area, Florida.

Range Central and eastern Canada and central and eastern United States south to east Kansas and north Georgia; winters from South Florida and southern Mexico south through Central America to northern Venezuela; West Indies.

316. Northern Waterthrush
Seiurus noveboracensis
(L-6 W-10)

Brown above, white or yellowish below with dark streaking on throat and breast; prominent creamy or yellowish eye stripe.

Habits Forages on the ground, bobbing as it walks, usually in boggy or wet areas.

Voice Song: "chi chi chi chewy chewy will will"; call: "chink."

Similar Species The Louisiana Waterthrush has a clear white throat (not streaked) and buffy flanks.

Habitat Swamps, bogs, swales, ponds, rivers, lakes, usually near stagnant water; mangrove swamp in South Florida and the Keys.

Abundance and Distribution Common to rare transient (Aug.–Oct., Mar.–May) throughout, more numerous in fall in eastern parts of the region and more numerous in spring in western parts; uncommon to rare winter resident (Oct.–Mar.) in Central and South Florida and the Keys.

Where to Find Everglades National Park, Florida; Dauphin Island, Alabama; Noxubee National Wildlife Refuge, Mississippi; Ocmulgee National Monument, Macon, Georgia.

Range Breeds in boreal North America south of the Arctic Circle; winters from central Mexico south through Central America to northern South America; southern Florida; Caribbean basin.

317. Louisiana Waterthrush
Seiurus motacilla
(L-6 W-10)

Brown above, creamy below with dark streaking on breast and sides; prominent white eye stripe.

Habits Forages on the ground, bobbing as it walks, usually near running water.

Voice Song: "tsepit tsepit tsepit tsew titit ti ti."

Similar Species The Northern Waterthrush has streaking on the throat (not clear white as in Louisiana Waterthrush) and flanks are same color as breast and belly (not buffy as in the Louisiana).

Habitat Streams, rivers, swales, ponds.

Abundance and Distribution Common to uncommon summer resident* (Mar.–Aug.) in the highlands, piedmont, and, locally, in the Panhandle and North Florida (to Alachua Co.); uncommon to rare transient (Aug.–Oct., Mar.–Apr.) throughout; rare to casual

Wood Warblers

in winter (Nov.–Feb.) in Florida except western Panhandle, where absent.

Where to Find Wall Doxey State Park, Mississippi; Conecuh National Forest, Open Pond, Alabama; Blackwater River State Park, Florida; Beaverdam Wildlife Management Area, Georgia.

Range Breeds in the eastern United States; winters from Mexico to northern South America; West Indies.

318. Kentucky Warbler
Oporornis formosus
(L-5 W-8)

Green above, yellow below; yellow spectacles (forehead, eye stripe, eyering); black crown, lores, earpatch. **Female** Similar to male but with black more or less replaced by green.

Habits Forages by hopping (not walking) on the ground, picking insects from overhanging vegetaion.

Voice Song: a clear, loud "choree choree choree choree choree"; call: a series of "chip"s, repeated as the bird hops, rising and falling in volume as the bird turns one way and then another.

Similar Species Male Common Yellowthroat has a black mask— no yellow spectacles.

Habitat Moist forest.

Abundance and Distribution Common to rare transient and summer resident* (Apr.–Oct.) in Georgia, Alabama, Mississippi, and the Florida Panhandle; rare transient (Sept., Apr.) in peninsular Florida and the Keys.

Where to Find Bladon Springs State Park, Alabama; Donivan Slough, Natchez Trace, Mississippi; Beaverdam Wildlife Management Area, Georgia; Paynes Prairie Preserve State Park, Florida.

Range Breeds in the eastern United States; winters from southern Mexico to northern Colombia and northwestern Venezuela.

319. Connecticut Warbler

Oporornis agilis
(L-6 W-9)

Olive above, yellow below; gray hood; complete, white eyering. **Female** Similar to male but with brownish yellow head.

Habits Forages low and on the ground.

Voice Song: a loud, clear "chipychip chipychip chipychipchipit"; call: "chink."

Similar Species Spring male has a complete white eyering (lacking in Mourning Warbler), and gray breast (blackish in Mourning). Females and immatures of these species are safely separable only in the hand on the basis of wing measurement minus tail measurement (Lanyon and Bull 1967).

Habitat Bogs, thickets.

Abundance and Distribution Rare transient (Sept.–Oct., Apr.–May) throughout, more numerous in fall in the eastern portions of the region and spring in the western portions.

Range Breeds in central Canada and extreme north-central United States; winters in northern South America.

320. Mourning Warbler

Oporornis philadelphia
(L-6 W-9)

Olive above, yellow below; gray hood with black on breast. **Female** Brownish yellow head and partial eyering.

Habits Forages low and on the ground.

Voice Song: a loud, clear "chewy chewy chewy chewy chewit"; call: a dry "chit."

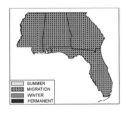

Similar Species Spring male Connecticut has a complete white eyering (lacking in Mourning Warbler), and gray breast (blackish in Mourning). Females and immatures of these species are safely separable only in the hand on the basis of wing measurement minus tail measurement (Lanyon and Bull 1967).

Habitat Dense thickets and tangles of second-growth woodlands.

Abundance and Distribution Rare transient (Sept.–Oct., Apr.–May) throughout.

Range Breeds in central and eastern Canada and extreme north-central and northeastern United States; winters from Nicaragua to northern South America.

Wood Warblers

Figure 44. The traffic can be brutal driving north from Orlando to Wekiwa Springs State Park so that by the time you reach it all you can think about is getting into the spring-fed pool as quickly as possible and cooling off a bit. You can drip-dry while looking for Common Yellowthroat, Eastern Bluebird, Carolina Wren, Florida Scrub-Jay, Great Crested Flycatcher, and Pileated Woodpecker, all of which are common at this or one of the neighboring public lands in the "Wekiva [*sic*] Basin Geopark."

321. Common Yellowthroat
Geothlypis trichas
(L-5 W-7)

Olive above, yellow below with black mask. **Female** Brownish above, bright yellow throat fading to whitish on belly; brownish on sides.

Habits Skulks in low, marsh vegetation.

Voice Song: "wichity wichity wichit"; call: a harsh "chuk."

Similar Species Lack of eyeline, eyering, and wing bars plus whitish belly separates female from other warblers.

Habitat Marshes, streams, estuaries, wet meadows, riparian areas; reed beds bordering rivers, ponds, and streams.

Abundance and Distribution Common to uncommon resident* in Florida (doesn't breed in the Keys) and the piedmont and coastal plain of Georgia, Mississippi, and Alabama; common to uncommon transient and summer resident* (Mar.–Oct.) in the highlands.

Where to Find Skidaway Island State Park, Georgia; Oak Mountain State Park, Alabama; Yazoo National Wildlife Refuge, Mississippi; Wekiwa Springs State Park, Florida.

Range Breeds from Canada south throughout the continent to the southern United States, and in the highlands to southern Mexico. Winters from the southern United States through Mexico and Central America to Costa Rica; Bahamas, Greater Antilles.

Wood Warblers

322. Hooded Warbler
Wilsonia citrina
(L-5 W-8)

Olive above, yellow below with black hood, yellow forehead and face; white tail spots. **Female** Usually lacks hood but has greenish cap, yellow forehead and eye stripe.

Habits Sallies from low perches for insects; often fans tail, exposing white spots.

Voice Song: "sweeta wee teeoo"; call: a clear musical "chip," usually given repeatedly for up to a minute.

Similar Species Female resembles female Wilson's Warbler, but Wilson's Warbler lacks the white tail marks of the Hooded Warbler and does not fan tail.

Habitat Dense thickets, tree falls in lowland deciduous, swamp, and riparian forest.

Abundance and Distribution Common to uncommon summer resident* (Apr.–Sep.) in Georgia, Alabama, Mississippi, the Panhandle, and North Florida; common to rare transient (Mar.–Apr., Aug.–Oct.) throughout, more numerous in the eastern portions of the region in fall and the western portions in the spring.

Where to Find Leaf Wilderness, De Soto National Forest, Mississippi; Watson Mill Bridge State Park, Georgia; Tuskegee National Forest, Alabama; Blackwater River State Forest, Florida.

Range Breeds in the eastern United States. Winters from southern Mexico to Panama.

323. Wilson's Warbler
Wilsonia pusilla
(L-5 W-7)

Olive above, yellow below with a black cap. **Female** Often has only a partially black or completely greenish yellow crown.

Habits Flycatches at mid- to upper canopy level, using short, sallying flights.

Voice Song: "chee chee chee chee chipy-chipy-chipy-chipy" (almost a trill); call: a hoarse "ship."

Similar Species In some female Wilson's, the dark cap may be completely lacking. These birds can be distinguished from female Yellow Warblers by the brownish tail, lacking yellow spots. Also the larger, chunkier female Hooded Warbler can resemble the female Wilson's Warbler, but Wilson's Warbler lacks the white tail marks of the Hooded Warbler and does not fan tail.

Habitat Brushy thickets (willow, alder, aspen, dogwood).

Abundance and Distribution Rare transient (Sep.–Oct., Apr.–May) throughout, more numerous in fall in the eastern portions of the region and spring in the western portions; rare to casual in Florida in winter (Nov.–Mar.).

Where to Find Bogue Chitto National Wildlife Refuge, Mississippi.

Range Breeds in boreal regions of northern and western North America; winters from southern California, Texas, and Florida south to Panama.

324. Canada Warbler
Wilsonia canadensis
(L-5 W-8)

Slate gray above, yellow below with black "necklace" across breast; yellow lores and eyering. **Female** Similar but necklace is usually fainter.

Voice Song: a high, thin, slurred series of notes, "tsi tsi tsi tsewy tsi," etc.

SUMMER
MIGRATION
WINTER
PERMANENT

Habitat A variety of coniferous and mixed forests and thickets.

Abundance and Distribution Uncommon to rare transient (Sep.–Oct., Apr.–May) throughout; rare summer resident* in the highlands.

Where to Find Brasstown Bald, Georgia; Bogue Chitto National Wildlife Refuge, Mississippi; DeSoto State Park, Alabama.

Range Breeds in eastern and central Canada from Labrador to northeastern British Columbia and in boreal United States from Minnesota to New England; south in the Appalachians to northern Georgia. Winters in northern South America.

325. Yellow-breasted Chat
Icteria virens
(L-7 W-10)

A nearly thrush-sized warbler; brown above; yellow throat and breast (orangish in some races); white belly and undertail coverts; white eyering and supraloral stripe; lores black or grayish.

Habits Very shy; has flight song.

SUMMER
MIGRATION
WINTER
PERMANENT

Voice A varied series of clear whistles and harsh, scolding "chak"s and "jeer"s .

Habitat Dense thickets, brushy pastures, forest undergrowth.

Abundance and Distribution Common to uncommon summer resident* (Apr.–Aug.) in the piedmont, coastal plain, the Panhandle, and North Florida; uncommon to rare transient (Aug.–Sep., Apr.–May) and rare summer resident* in the mountains; uncommon to rare transient and winter resident (Sep.–May) in Central and South Florida and the Keys, decreasing in numbers as a winter visitor northward.

Where to Find Piedmont National Wildlife Refuge, Georgia; Choctaw National Wildlife Refuge, Alabama; St. Catherine National Wildlife Refuge, Mississippi; Blackwater River State Forest, Florida.

Range Breeds in scattered regions nearly throughout the United States and southern Canada south to central Mexico. Winters in southern Florida and from central Mexico to Panama.

Tanagers
Family Thraupidae

Most tanagers are neotropical in distribution. Only four species are native to the United States, with three found regularly in the Southeast. Males are predominantly red (Hepatic Tanager, Summer Tanager, Scarlet Tanager) or yellow and red (Western Tanager). Females are brownish or greenish.

326. Summer Tanager
Piranga rubra
(L-8 W-13)

Red. **Female and Immature Male** Tawny brown above, more yellowish below; second year males and some females are blotched with red.

Voice Song: slurred, robinlike phrases; call: "pit-a-chuk."

Similar Species The female Baltimore Oriole is somewhat similar to the female Summer Tanager, but has white wing bars and a long, pointed oriole bill. The female Summer Tanager lacks wing bars and has a relatively blunt, tanager bill. The female Scarlet Tanager is olive green above, not tawny as in the female Summer Tanager.

Tanagers

Habitat Open deciduous and mixed woodlands.

Abundance and Distribution Common to uncommon summer resident* (May–Aug.) in Georgia, Alabama, Mississippi, the Panhandle, North and Central Florida; common to uncommon transient (Sep.–Oct., Apr.–May) throughout; rare to casual winter resident (Nov.–Mar.) in Florida.

Where to Find Chewalla Lake, Holly Springs National Forest, Mississippi; Laura S. Walker State Park, Georgia; Lake Guntersville State Park, Alabama; Lettuce Lake Regional Park, Florida.

Range Breeds across eastern and southern portions of the United States and northern Mexico; winters from southern Mexico through Central America to northern South America.

327. Scarlet Tanager

Piranga olivacea
(L-8 W-13)

Red with black wings. **Winter Male** Greenish above with black wings and tail; splotched with red during molt. **Female and Immature Male** Olive above, yellowish below.

Voice Song: hoarse, loud, robinlike phrases; call: "chik-burr."

Similar Species Female is distinguished from other female tanagers by greenish (rather than brownish or grayish) cast to plumage, and whitish (not greenish or yellowish) wing linings.

Habitat Deciduous and mixed forest; oak and riparian woodland.

Abundance and Distribution Uncommon summer resident* (May–Sep.) in the highlands and upper piedmont; uncommon to rare transient throughout; more numerous eastward in fall (Sep.–Oct.) and westward in spring (May).

Where to Find Unicoi Gap, Georgia; Cheaha State Park, Alabama; Arkabutla Lake, Mississippi; Dry Tortugas National Park (spring).

Range Breeds in the northeastern United States and southeastern Canada; winters in northern South America.

328. Western Tanager
Piranga ludoviciana
(L-8 W-13)

Red head; yellow below with yellow rump, neck and shoulder; black back, wings, and tail with two white wing bars. **Winter Male** Lacks red on head. **Female and Immature Male** Similar to winter male but

duller.

Voice Song: hoarse and robinlike with pauses between phrases; call: "chit-it" or "chit-a-chit."

Similar Species Female resembles some female orioles but has heavy tanager bill, and yellowish rump and nape contrast with olive back.

Habitat Montane fir, pine, and pine-oak forest; nonbreeders in arid thorn and riparian forest

Abundance and Distribution Rare winter resident (Aug.–May) throughout Florida with scattered records from elsewhere in the region; feeders are a significant draw.

Range Breeds in the mountains of western North America from Alaska to northwestern Mexico; winters from central Mexico through Central America to Costa Rica.

Towhees and Sparrows
Family Emberizidae

Small to medium-sized birds with conical bills. The towhees have brightly patterned males, while most sparrows are cryptically colored in various shades and patterns of browns and grays.

329. Eastern Towhee
Pipilo erythrophthalmus
(L-8 W-11)

Red eye (white in some Florida birds); black head, breast, and back; rufous sides; white belly; tail black and rounded with white corners. **Female** Patterned similarly but brown instead of black.

Habits This bird spends most of its time on the ground, using backward kick-hops to scatter duff and expose seeds and invertebrate prey.

Towhees, Sparrows

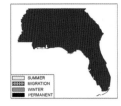

SUMMER
MIGRATION
WINTER
PERMANENT

Voice Song: "drink your teeee" and variations; call: "chewink," "shrrinnk."

Habitat Undergrowth and thickets of deciduous and mixed woodlands.

Abundance and Distribution Common to uncommon resident* throughout the region except in the Florida Keys where scarce or absent.

Where to Find Piedmont National Wildlife Refuge, Georgia; Fort Toulouse, Alabama; Big Lagoon State Recreation Area, Florida; Lake Woodruff National Wildlife Refuge, Florida; Dahomey National Wildlife Refuge, Mississippi.

Range Breeds from extreme southern Canada across the United States (except most of Texas) and in the highlands of Mexico and Guatemala; winters from central and southern United States to Mexico and Guatemala.

330. Bachman's Sparrow
Aimophila aestivalis
(L-6 W-8)

Grayish streaked with brown above; pale gray below; dark malar stripe; gray cheek; central crown stripe bordered by brown.

Habits Secretive.

SUMMER
MIGRATION
WINTER
PERMANENT

Voice Song: "tseee chi chi chi," "tsoooo chew chew chew," and other variations on a similar theme.

Similar Species The Field Sparrow is rustier with a pinkish (not dark) bill; Grasshopper Sparrow is yellowish buff with creamy central crown stripe (not gray).

Habitat Open pine woods and savanna; brushy, overgrown fields.

Abundance and Distribution Common to uncommon resident* in the coastal plain of Alabama, Mississippi, Georgia, the Panhandle, North and Central Florida; rare to casual resident* in South Florida, not recorded in the Florida Keys; rare summer resident* (Mar.–Oct.) in the piedmont.

Where to Find Reed Bingham State Park, Georgia; Okefenokee National Wildlife Refuge, Georgia; Lake Guntersville State Park, Alabama (winter); Three Lakes Wildlife Management Area, Florida.

Range Southeastern United States.

Towhees, Sparrows

331. American Tree Sparrow
Spizella arborea
(L-6 W-9)

Streaked brownish above; dingy white below with dark breast spot; rufous crown; two white wing bars.

Voice Song: a rapid, high-pitched series of notes, "tse tse tse tsetl tse" and similar variations; call: "tsetl-de."

Similar Species This is the largest rufous-capped sparrow, and the only one with a dark spot on an unstreaked breast.

Habitat Open, shrubby areas; weedy fields; overgrown pastures; grasslands.

Abundance and Distribution Rare winter visitor (Nov.–Mar.) in central and northern Mississippi and western Alabama.

Where to Find Noxubee National Wildlife Refuge, Mississippi; Choctaw National Wildlife Refuge, Alabama.

Range Breeds in bog, tundra, and willow thickets of northern North America; winters in southern Canada, northern and central United States.

332. Chipping Sparrow
Spizella passerina
(L-5 W-8)

A small sparrow, streaked rusty brown above, dingy white below with two white wing bars; rufous cap (somehat streaked in winter); white eyebrow; black eyeline. **Immature** Streaked crown; gray or buffy eyebrow; brown cheek patch.

Voice Song: a rapid, metallic trill; call: "tsip."

Similar Species Adult facial pattern is distinctive; immature is similar to Clay-colored Sparrow, but has grayish rather than buffy rump.

Habitat Open pine forests, woodlands, orchards, parks, suburbs, and cemeteries with scattered coniferous trees.

Abundance and Distribution Common resident* in the piedmont; uncommon summer resident* (Mar.–Oct.) and rare in winter in the highlands; common to uncommon winter resident (Nov.–Feb.) in the coastal plain of Mississippi, Alabama, Georgia, the Panhandle, North and Central Florida (has bred); increasingly rare winter resident southward in South Florida and scarce or absent in the Florida Keys.

Where to Find Ocmulgee National Monument, Georgia; Lake Guntersville State Park, Alabama; Vicksburg National Military Park, Mississippi; St. Marks National Wildlife Refuge, Florida.

Range Breeds over most of North America south of the tundra, south through Mexico and Central America to Nicaragua; winters along coast and in southern portions of the breeding range.

333. Clay-colored Sparrow
Spizella pallida
(L-5 W-8)

Streaked brown above, buffy below; streaked crown with central gray stripe; grayish eyebrow; buffy cheek patch outlined in dark brown; gray nape; two white wing bars.

Voice Song: a buzzy "zee zee zee," with the number and speed of the "zee"s varying; call: "sip."

Similar Species The immature Clay-colored Sparrow has a buffy rump rather than grayish as in the immature Chipping Sparrow.

Habitat Grasslands, brushy pastures.

Abundance and Distribution Rare transient (Sep.–Nov.) along the Georgia coast; rare winter visitor (Sep.–May) in Florida (numbers increasing?).

Range Breeds from central Canada to the north-central United States; winters from Texas south to Guatemala.

334. Field Sparrow
Spizella pusilla
(L-6 W-8)

Pink bill; streaked brown above, buff below; crown with gray central stripe bordered by rusty stripes; two white wing bars.

Voice Song: a series of "tew"s, beginning slowly and accelerating to a trill; call: "tsee."

Similar Species No other plain-breasted sparrow has pink bill.

Habitat Old fields, brushy pastures.

Abundance and Distribution Common resident* in the mountains and piedmont and rare resident* in the Florida Panhandle; common to uncommon winter resident (Nov.–Feb.) in the coastal plain of Mississippi, Alabama, Georgia, and North Florida; increasingly scarce southward in Central and South Florida in winter and absent from the Florida Keys.

Figure 45. Savannah National Wildlife Refuge on the Georgia/South Carolina border is a good place for raptors, including Swallow-tailed Kite, Osprey, Mississippi Kite, Bald Eagle, and Northern Harrier (winter).

Where to Find Oak Mountain State Park, Alabama; Tallahatchie National Wildlife Refuge, Mississippi; St. Andrews State Recreation Area, Florida; Savannah National Wildlife Refuge, Georgia.

Range Breeds across the eastern half of the United States and southeastern Canada; winters in the southern half of the breeding range south to Florida and northeastern Mexico.

335. Vesper Sparrow
Pooecetes gramineus
(L-6 W-10)

Grayish streaked with brown above; white with brown streaks below; rusty shoulder patch; white outer tail feathers.

Voice Song: "chew chew chee chi-chi-chi titititi" etc.; call: "chip."

Similar Species Savannah Sparrow has yellow lores and brown (not white) outer tail feathers.

Habitat Grasslands, pastures, scrub, agricultural fields.

Abundance and Distribution Common to uncommon winter resident (Oct.–Apr.) in the piedmont and coastal plain of Georgia, Alabama, Mississippi, the Panhandle, and North Florida; rare winter visitor in the highlands, and increasingly rare from Central Florida south into the Florida Keys.

Where to Find Moundville Archaeological State Park, Alabama; Vicksburg National Military Park, Mississippi; Grand Bay Wildlife Management Area, Georgia; Gulf Islands National Seashore, Florida.

Range Breeds across much of northern North America to the central United States; winters in the southern United States and Mexico.

336. Lark Sparrow
Chondestes grammacus
(L-7 W-11)

Streaked brown above; dingy below; distinctive chest-nut, white and black face pattern; white throat; black breast spot; white corners on black, rounded tail.

Voice Song: towhee-like "drink-your-teee," often followed by various trills; call: "tseek."

Habitat Grasslands, pastures, coastal prairie and dunes, agricultural fields.

Abundance and Distribution Rare and local summer resident*(Apr.–Sep.) in Alabama and Mississippi; rare and local transient (mainly fall) throughout Florida, and winter resident in Central and South Florida.

Where to Find Noxubee National Wildlife Refuge, Mississippi.

Range Breeds in the Canadian prairie states and across most of the United States except eastern, forested regions, south into northern Mexico; winters from the southern United States to southern Mexico.

337. Savannah Sparrow
Passerculus sandwichensis
(L-6 W-9)

Buff striped with brown above; whitish variously streaked with brown below; yellow or yellowish lores; whitish or yellowish eyebrow; often with dark, central breast spot. Plumage is highly variable in amount of yellow on face and streaking on breast according to subspecies, several of which winter in the region.

Habits Often in flocks.

Voice Song: a high-pitched, insectlike "tseet tsitit tsee tsoo"; call: "tsee."

Similar Species Savannah Sparrow has yellow lores and brown (not white) outer tail feathers; Vesper Sparrow has white outer tail feathers and lacks yellow lores.

Habitat Grasslands, pastures, agricultural fields, coastal marshes.

Abundance and Distribution Common to uncommon winter resident (Sep.–May) throughout.

Where to Find Moundville Archaeological State Park, Alabama; Newcomer Treatment Facility, Georgia; Shepard State Park, Mississippi; St. Andrews Recreation Area, Florida.

Range Breeds throughout the northern half of North America south to the central United States; also breeds in the central highlands of Mexico and Guatemala; winters in the coastal and southern United States south to Honduras.

338. Grasshopper Sparrow
Ammodramus savannarum
(L-5 W-8)

A stubby, short-tailed bird; streaked brown above; creamy buff below; buffy crown stripe; yellow at bend of wing; yellowish or buffy lores and eyebrow.

Voice Song: an insectlike "tsi-pi-ti-zzzzzzzzz"; call: a weak "kitik."

Habitat Overgrazed pasture (prefer short stubble).

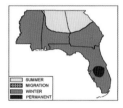

Abundance and Distribution Rare and local summer resident* (Mar.–Oct.) in the piedmont and highlands, and in Central Florida; uncommon to rare winter resident in the coastal plain of Mississippi, Alabama, Georgia, and throughout Florida including the Keys.

Where to Find Avon Park Bombing Range, Florida (Florida race); Three Lakes Wildlife Management Area, Florida; Eufaula National Wildlife Refuge, Georgia/Alabama; Noxubee National Wildlife Refuge, Mississippi.

Range Breeds across the northern and central United States and central Florida; southern Mexico to northwestern South America; Bahamas, and Cuba; winters in the southern United States, Mexico, and elsewhere within its tropical breeding range.

339. Henslow's Sparrow
Ammodramus henslowii
(L-5 W-7)

Streaked rusty brown above with rusty wings; buffy breast with dark streaks; whitish belly; grayish green head with dark brown crown and malar stripes. **Immature** Breast streaking is faint or absent.

Voice Song: a high-pitched, repeated "tse-ik"; call: "tsip"

Similar Species The Henslow's Sparrow has rusty wings (not grayish brown) and lacks the yellow lores of Savannah Sparrow and yellow bend of wing of Grasshopper Sparrow.

Towhees, Sparrows

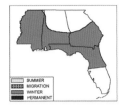

Habitat Wet meadows, sedge marshes, weedy fields.

Abundance and Distribution Uncommon to rare winter resident (Oct.–Apr.) in the coastal plain of Mississippi, Alabama, Georgia, the Panhandle, North, and Central Florida.

Where to Find Meaher State Park, Alabama; Savannah National Wildlife Refuge, Georgia; St. Marks National Wildlife Refuge, Florida.

Range Breeds in the northeastern and north-central United States and southeastern Canada; winters in the southeastern United States

340. LeConte's Sparrow
Ammodramus leconteii
(L-5 W-7)

Streaked brown above; whitish below with dark streaking on sides; whitish central crown stripe bordered by dark brown stripes; buffy yellow eyebrow stripe; gray cheek patch outlined by buffy yellow.

Voice Song: a high-pitched, insectlike buzz, "tsi tsi tzzzzz"; call: "tseak"

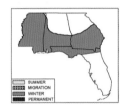

Similar Species Unstreaked breast like the Grasshopper Sparrow and sharp-tailed sparrows, but the Grasshopper Sparrow has yellow at the bend of the wing, and lacks streaking on flanks; Sharp-tailed sparrows have gray nape (LeConte's is buffy).

Habitat Tall grasslands, wet meadows, salt marsh, rank fields.

Abundance and Distribution Rare winter resident (Nov.–Mar.) in the coastal plain of Mississippi, Alabama, and Georgia; rare winter resident in North and Central Florida, increasingly scarce southward.

Where to Find Weeks Bay National Estuarine Research Reserve, Alabama; Okaloosa County Holding Ponds, Florida.

Range Breeds in central Canada (British Columbia to Quebec) and extreme north-central United States (Montana to Michigan); winters in the southeastern United States.

341. Nelson's Sharp-tailed Sparrow
Ammodramus nelsoni
(L-6 W-8)

Streaked dark brown above; buffy throat and buffy-orange breast; belly whitish; gray crown stripe bordered by dark brown crown stripes; buffy orange eyebrow; gray nape.

Voice Song: a hoarse, buzzy "chur-chur-aaaaa zee-zurr zee-zurr"; often uses a flight song as well; call: "tsuk."

Similar Species Nelson's Sharp-tailed Sparrow has buffy throat, tawny, unstreaked breast, and lacks gray cheek patch; Salt Marsh Sharp-tailed Sparrow has white throat, buffy, streaked breast, and gray cheek patch. Both species of sharp-tailed sparrows have a gray nape (LeConte's is buffy).

Habitat Wet grasslands and inland marshes (breeding and transient); coastal marshes (winter).

Abundance and Distribution Rare transient throughout; uncommon to rare and local winter resident along the immediate coast.

Where to Find Skidaway Island State Park, Georgia; Meaher State Park, Alabama; Okaloosa County Holding Ponds, Florida; Gulf Islands National Seashore, Mississippi.

Range Breeds in central Canada and northeastern and north-central United States (North Dakota, Minnesota, Maine); winters along the coast of the southeastern United States from Virginia to Texas and northeastern Mexico.

342. Saltmarsh Sharp-tailed Sparrow
Ammodramus caudacutus
(L-6 W-8)

Streaked dark brown above; buffy breast and flanks with faint brown streaks; belly whitish; gray crown stripe bordered by dark brown crown stripes; buffy orange eyebrow; gray cheek outlined by buffy orange stripes above and below; white throat; gray nape.

Voice Song: a "whisper song" involving a prolonged series of soft, wheezy twitters and trills.

Similar Species Salt Marsh Sharp-tailed Sparrow has white throat, buffy, streaked breast, and gray cheek patch. Nelson's Sharp-tailed Sparrow has buffy throat, tawny, unstreaked breast, and lacks gray cheek patch. Sharp-tailed Sparrow has gray nape (LeConte's is buffy).

Habitat Coastal salt marsh.

Abundance and Distribution Uncommon to rare and local winter resident along the immediate coast throughout the region.

Where to Find Harris Neck National Wildlife Refuge, Georgia; Meaher State Park, Alabama; Okaloosa County Holding Ponds, Florida; Gulf Islands National Seashore, Mississippi.

Range Breeds along the Atlantic Coast of the United States from Maine to North Carolina; winters along the Atlantic and Gulf coasts from New York to the Texas coastal bend.

Towhees, Sparrows

343. Seaside Sparrow

Ammodramus maritimus
(L-6 W-8)

Yellow lores; white throat; grayish streaked with dark brown above; buffy breast and whitish belly streaked with brown; a stocky bird with longish bill and short tail.

Voice Song: "brrrt zee zzurr zee," reminiscent of Red-winged Blackbird; call: "kak"

Similar Species LeConte's and sharp-tailed sparrows lack yellow lores and clear, white throat of Seaside Sparrow.

Habitat Salt marshes.

Abundance and Distribution Common to uncommon resident* in marshes along the immediate coast in Georgia, Alabama, Mississippi, and locally in Florida in the northeast corner (north of St. Johns River), central and northern Gulf Coast, and in parts of the southernmost counties of the Peninsula (Dade and Monroe); winters along the Florida east coast.

Where to Find Shepard State Park, Mississippi; Cumberland Island National Seashore, Georgia; Meaher State Park, Alabama; Everglades National Park, Florida ("Cape Sable" race).

Range Resident along the coast of the eastern United States from Maine to Texas.

344. Fox Sparrow

Passerella iliaca
(L-7 W-11)

Hefty, for a sparrow - nearly thrush-sized; streaked dark or rusty brown above; whitish below with heavy dark or rusty streakings that often coalesce as a blotch on the breast; rusty rump and tail.

Habits Forages in towhee fashion, jump-kicking its way through forest duff.

Voice Song: whistled, with long (3–4 sec) varied phrases; call: "tshek."

Similar Species Hermit Thrush has long, thrush bill (not short, conical bill of sparrow), and unstreaked back.

Habitat Thickets and undergrowth of deciduous, mixed, and coniferous woodlands; hedgerows; scrub, brush piles.

Abundance and Distribution Rare to casual winter visitor (Oct.–

Apr.) in the highlands and piedmont region, and in the Panhandle and North Florida.

Where to Find Moundville Archaeological State Park, Alabama; Vicksburg National Military Park, Mississippi; Piedmont National Wildlife Refuge, Georgia.

Range Breeds across the northern tier of North America and in the mountains of the west; winters in the coastal and southern United States.

345. Song Sparrow
Melospiza melodia
(L-6 W-9)

Streaked brown above; whitish below with heavy brown streaks and central breast spot; gray eyebrow; dark whisker and post-orbital stripe.

Voice Song: "chik sik-i-sik choree k-sik-i-sik"; many variations; call: a nasal "chink."

SUMMER
MIGRATION
WINTER
PERMANENT

Similar Species Fox Sparrow head is un-striped brownish—lacks light/dark striping of Song Sparrow.

Habitat Swamps; inland and coastal marshes; riparian thickets (reeds, sedges); wet meadows; brushy fields.

Abundance and Distribution Common to uncommon resident* in the piedmont and highlands; common to rare winter resident (Oct.–Apr.) in the coastal plain of Mississippi, Alabama, Georgia, the Panhandle, North, and Central Florida; rare to casual in South Florida and absent from the Keys.

Where to Find Lake Guntersville State Park, Alabama; Vicksburg National Military Park, Mississippi; Piedmont National Wildlife Refuge, Georgia; St. Marks National Wildlife Refuge, Florida.

Range Breeds across temperate and boreal North America; winters in temperate breeding range, southern United States and northern Mexico; resident population in central Mexico.

346. Lincoln's Sparrow
Melospiza lincolnii
(L-6 W-8)

Streaked brown above; patterned gray and brown face; white throat and belly; distinctive finely streaked, buffy breast band.

Voice Song: a series of brief trills at different pitches; call: "shuk."

Towhees, Sparrows

Similar Species Finely streaked, buffy breast band is unique.

Habitat Brushy fields, hedgerows.

Abundance and Distribution Uncommon to rare transient and winter resident (Oct.–May) throughout.

Where to Find Fort Toulouse, Alabama; Mississippi Sandhill Crane National Wildlife Refuge, Mississippi; Harris Neck National Wildlife Refuge, Georgia; Paynes Prairie Preserve State Park, Florida.

Range Breeds across the northern tier of North America and in the mountains of the west; winters in the coastal and southern United States south to Honduras.

347. Swamp Sparrow
Melospiza georgiana
(L-6 W-8)

Rusty crown with central grayish stripe; gray face; streaked brown above with rusty wings; whitish throat but otherwise grayish below with tawny flanks—faintly streaked.

Voice Song: long "chipy-chipy-chipy" trills at various pitches and speeds; call: "chip."

Similar Species Only the Swamp Sparrow among rusty-crowned sparrows of the region lacks white wingbars.

Habitat Northern peat bogs (summer); coastal and inland marshes, wet grasslands, brushy pastures (winter).

Abundance and Distribution Common to uncommon winter resident (Oct.–May) nearly throughout, somewhat scarcer in the highlands and South Florida; rare and irregular in the Keys.

Where to Find Merritt Island National Wildlife Refuge, Florida; Weeks Bay National Estuarine Research Reserve, Alabama; Shepard State Park, Mississippi; Arrowhead Public Fishing Area, Georgia.

Range Breeds in central and eastern Canada and north-central and northeastern United States; winters in eastern and south-central United States south to Mexico.

348. White-throated Sparrow
Zonotrichia albicollis
(L-7 W-9)

White throat; alternating black and white (or black and buff) crown stipes; yellow lores; streaked brown above; grayish below.

SUMMER
MIGRATION
WINTER
PERMANENT

Voice Song: a thin, wavering whistle, often heard in March in thickets, "poor sam peabody peabody"; call: "seet."

Habitat Coniferous bogs (breeding); woodland thickets, brushy fields, feeders (migration, winter).

Abundance and Distribution Common to uncommon winter resident (Oct.–May) nearly throughout the region; rare in Central and South Florida and casual in the Keys.

Where to Find Fort Toulouse, Alabama; Yazoo National Wildlife Refuge, Mississippi; Piedmont National Wildlife Refuge, Georgia; St. Andrews State Recreation Area, Florida.

Range Breeds across most of boreal Canada and northeastern and north-central United States; winters in eastern and southern United States and northern Mexico.

349. White-crowned Sparrow
Zonotrichia leucophrys
(L-7 W-10)

Black and white striped crown; gray neck, breast, and belly; streaked gray and brown back; pinkish bill. **Immature** Crown stripes are brown and gray.

Voice Song: "tsee tsee tsee zzeech-i chi-i-i"; call: "chip."

Similar Species The White-throated Sparrow is also a large, plain-breasted, striped-crowned sparrow, but it has a white throat and yellow lores.

SUMMER
MIGRATION
WINTER
PERMANENT

Habitat Thickets in coniferous and deciduous woodlands, brushy fields.

Abundance and Distribution Uncommon to rare winter resident (Oct.–Apr.) throughout the region, somewhat more prevalent in the piedmont.

Where to Find Vicksburg National Military Park, Mississippi; Oak Mountain State Park, Alabama; Eufaula National Wildlife Refuge, Alabama/Georgia; Paynes Prairie Preserve State Park, Florida.

Range Breeds in northern and western North America; winters across most of the United States south to central Mexico.

Towhees, Sparrows

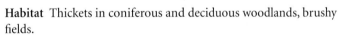

350. Dark-eyed Junco
Junco hyemalis
(L-6 W-10)

Entirely dark gray except for white belly and outer tail feathers, and pinkish bill. **Female** Similar but brownish rather than gray.

Voice Song: a trill, given at different speeds and pitches; call: "tsik."

Habitat Coniferous and mixed forests (breeding); open mixed woodlands; grasslands; agricultural fields, feeders (migration, winter).

Abundance and Distribution Common resident* in the highlands; common to uncommon winter resident (Oct.–Apr.) in the piedmont and upper coastal plain; rare winter resident in the lower coastal plain, the Panhandle, and North Florida; casual or absent in Central and South Florida and the Keys.

Where to Find Black Rock Mountain State Park, Georgia (breeding); Lake Guntersville State Park, Alabama (winter); Dahomey National Wildlife Refuge, Mississippi; Okaloosa County Holding Ponds, Florida.

Range Breeds across northern North America and in the eastern and western United States, south in the mountains; winters from southern Canada south through the United States to northern Mexico.

351. Lapland Longspur
Calcarius lapponicus
(L-6 W-11)

Black head and breast with white or buff face pattern; rusty nape; streaked brown above; white belly; tail is all dark except for outermost tail feathers. **Winter Male and Female** Brownish crown; buffy eyebrow, nape, and throat with darker brown mottlings on breast and flanks; buffy cheek outlined by darker brown.

Voice Song: short phrases of squeaky, slurred notes, given in flight; call: "tseeu."

Habitat Plowed fields, overgrazed pasture.

Abundance and Distribution Rare winter visitor (Nov.–Mar.) to the highlands and piedmont.

Where to Find Wheeler National Wildlife Refuge, Alabama.

Towhees, Sparrows

Range Breeds in tundra of extreme northern North America and Eurasia; winters in temperate regions of the Old and New World.

Cardinals, Grosbeaks, and Buntings
Family Cardinalidae

Small to medium-sized songbirds with conical bills; several species have brightly colored males and cryptic females.

352. Northern Cardinal
Cardinalis cardinalis
(L-9 W-12)

Red with crest; black face patch at base of red bill. **Female and Immature Male** Crested like male but greenish brown, paler below, bill brownish or reddish

Voice Song: loud, ringing whistle, "whit-chew," repeated; call: a sharp "peak."

Habitat Thickets and tangles of open deciduous forest and second growth, hedgerows, residential parklands.

SUMMER
MIGRATION
WINTER
PERMANENT

Abundance and Distribution Common resident* nearly throughout except in Lower Keys.

Where to Find Big Lagoon State Recreation Area, Florida; Leaf Wilderness, De Soto National Forest, Mississippi; Oakmulgee District, Talladega National Forest, Alabama; Ocmulgee National Monument, Georgia.

Range Eastern United States and southeastern Canada; southwestern United States, Mexico, Guatemala, and Belize.

353. Rose-breasted Grosbeak
Pheucticus ludovicianus
(L-8 W-13)

Black head, back, wings, and tail; brownish in winter; red breast; white belly, rump, wing patches, and tail spots. **Female** Mottled brown above, buffy below heavily streaked with dark brown; white eyebrow and wing bars. **First Year Male** Like female but shows rose tints on breast and underwing coverts. **Second Year Male** Patterned much like adult male but splotched brown and black on head and back.

Cardinals, Grosbeaks, Buntings

Figure 46. Brasstown Bald is Georgia's highest mountain (4,768'), and as a result, it has some of the state's few remaining spruce-fir stands, home to breeding populations of Veerys, Dark-eyed Juncos, Common Ravens, and Blue-headed Vireos.

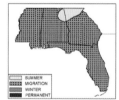

Voice Song: rapid, robinlike phrases; call: a sharp "keek" or "kik."

Habitat Deciduous forest and parklands.

Abundance and Distribution Uncommon summer resident* (Apr.–Sep.) in the highlands; uncommon to rare transient (Sep.–Oct., Apr.–May) elsewhere throughout the region.

Where to Find Brasstown Bald, Georgia (breeding); St. Andrews Recreation Area, Florida; Bon Secour National Wildlife Refuge, Alabama; Bogue Chitto National Wildlife Refuge, Mississippi.

Range Breeds in northeastern United States, central and southeastern Canada; winters from southern Mexico south through Central America to northern South America and western Cuba.

354. Blue Grosbeak
Passerina caerulea
(L-7 W-11)

Dark blue with two rusty wing bars. **Female and Immature Male** Brownish above, paler below with tawny wing bars, often with a blush of blue on shoulder or rump.

Habits Flicks and fans tail.

Voice Song: a rapid series of up and down warbles, some notes harsh, some slurred; call: "chink."

Similar Species Male and female Indigo Bunting re-

semble corresponding sex of Blue Grosbeak but are smaller and lack tawny wing bars and massive grosbeak bill.

Habitat Thickets, scrub, brushy pastures, hedgerows.

Abundance and Distribution Common to uncommon summer resident* (Apr.–Oct.) in piedmont and coastal plain of Georgia, Alabama, Mississippi, the Panhandle, and North Florida; uncommon to rare summer resident* in the highlands and Central Florida; common to uncommon transient (Sep.–Oct., Mar.–May) throughout; rare and irregular winter visitor (Nov.–Mar.) in Florida.

Where to Find Altamaha River/Atkinson Tract, Georgia; Little River Canyon National Preserve, Alabama; Mississippi Sandhill Crane National Wildlife Refuge, Mississippi; Paynes Prairie Preserve State Park, Florida.

Range Breeds from central and southern United States through Mexico and Central America to Costa Rica; winters from northern Mexico to Panama; rarely Florida and Cuba.

355. Indigo Bunting
Passerina cyanea
(L-6 W-9)

Indigo blue. **Female and Immature Male** Brown above, paler below with faint streaking on breast. **Winter Adult and Second Year Male** Bluish with variable amounts of brown on back and wings.

Voice Song: Warbled phrases of paired or triplet notes; call: "tsink."

Similar Species Male and female Indigo Bunting resemble corresponding sex of Blue Grosbeak but are smaller and lack tawny wing bars and massive grosbeak bill.

Habitat Thickets, hedgerows, brushy fields.

Abundance and Distribution Common to uncommon summer resident* and transient (Apr.–Oct.) in Mississippi, Alabama, Georgia, the Panhandle, and North Florida, scarcer in the highlands and Central Florida; common to rare transient (Sep.–Oct., Mar.–May) and rare winter resident (Nov.–Feb.) throughout Florida.

Where to Find Trace State Park, Mississippi; Cheaha State Park, Alabama; Kingsley Plantation, Florida; Ocmulgee National Monument, Georgia.

Range Breeds from extreme southeastern and south-central Canada south through eastern and southwestern United States; winters from central Mexico to Panama and the West Indies.

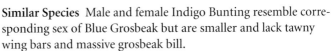

Cardinals, Grosbeaks, Buntings

356. Painted Bunting
Passerina ciris
(L-6 W-9)

Purple head, red underparts and rump; green back; dark wings and tail. **Female and Immature Male** Bright green above, paler below; dark wings and tail.

Voice Song: a prolonged series of rapid warbles; call: "tsip."

Similar Species Other female buntings are brownish or grayish, not green.

Habitat Riparian and thorn forest, oak woodlands, savanna, brushy pastures, hedgerows.

Abundance and Distribution Common to rare and local summer resident* (Apr.–Oct.) along the coast of Georgia and northeastern Florida; also along the immediate coast of Mississippi and southwestern Alabama; rare to casual in summer (nonbreeding) in the Florida Panhandle, Gulf Coast, and Atlantic Coast north to Putnam Co.; common to rare transient (Sep.–Oct., Mar.–Apr.) and rare to casual winter resident (Nov.–Feb.) throughout Florida.

Where to Find Blackbeard Island National Wildlife Refuge, Georgia; Kingsley Plantation, Florida; Dauphin Island, Alabama; Bogue Chitto National Wildlife Refuge, Mississippi.

Range Breeds in coastal South Carolina, Georgia, and extreme northeastern Florida; also in the south-central United States east to southwestern Alabama and south to northeastern Mexico; winters from northern Mexico to western Panama; also Florida, the Bahamas, and Cuba.

357. Dickcissel
Spiza americana
(L-6 W-9)

Patterned like a miniature meadowlark—black bib (gray in winter) and yellow breast; streaked brown above; grayish head with creamy eyebrow; rusty red wing patch. **Female and Immature Male** Patterned like male but paler yellow below and without black bib.

Voice Song: a dry "chik sizzzle," also a "brrrzeet" given in flight.

Similar Species Pale females and immatures resemble House Sparrow female but usually have traces of yellow on pale white

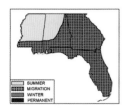

(not dirty white) breast, a clear, whitish or yellowish eyebrow, and some chestnut on shoulder.

Habitat Grasslands, agricultural fields.

Abundance and Distribution Uncommon to rare transient (Aug.–Oct., Apr.–May) throughout; rare to casual winter visitor (Nov.–Mar.) in Florida; uncommon summer resident* (Apr.–Oct.) in northern and central Mississippi and Alabama; has bred* in the Georgia piedmont and Central Florida (1999—Orange Co., *fide* B. H. Anderson).

Where to Find Moundville Archaeological State Park, Alabama (breeding); Dahomey National Wildlife Refuge, Mississippi (breeding).

Range Breeds across the eastern and central United States and south-central Canada; winters mainly in northern South America.

Orioles and Blackbirds
Family Icteridae

Most migratory icterids are dimorphic with large, strikingly colored males, and smaller, more cryptically colored females.

358. Bobolink
Dolichonyx oryzivorus
(L-7 W-12)

Black with creamy nape, white rump and shoulder patch. **Winter Male and Female** Streaked brown and yellow buff above; yellow buff below; crown with central buff stripe bordered by dark brown stripes; buff eyebrow.

Voice Song: twittering, bubbling series of squeaks, cherks, inks, along with a few "bob-o-link"s and other, similar phrases thrown in, given in flight; call: "tink"

Similar Species Blackbird size and bill separate this bird from sparrows and buntings.

Habitat Grasslands, grain and hay fields, brushy pastures.

Abundance and Distribution Common to rare transient (Aug.–Oct., Apr.–Jun.) throughout; more numerous in fall along the Georgia coast; more numerous in spring elsewhere in the region.

Where to Find Merritt Island National Wildlife Refuge, Florida;

Orioles, Blackbirds

Savannah National Wildlife Refuge, Georgia; Fort Toulouse, Alabama; Arkabutla Lake, Mississippi.

Range Breeds in the northern United States and southern Canada; winters in South America.

359. Red-winged Blackbird
Agelaius phoeniceus
(L-8 W-14)

Black with red epaulets bordered in orange. **Female and Immature Male** Dark brown above, whitish below heavily streaked with dark brown; whitish eyebrow and malar stripes. **Second Year Male** Intermediate between female and male: black blotching, some orange on epaulet.

SUMMER
MIGRATION
WINTER
PERMANENT

Voice Song: "konk-ka-ree"; call: a harsh "shek."

Similar Species Blackbird size and bill separate females from female Purple and House finches, which are also heavily streaked.

Habitat Inland and coastal marshes (breeding); brushy fields; tall grasslands; grain and hay fields; grain storage areas and feeders, marshes (winter).

Abundance and Distribution Common to uncommon resident* nearly throughout; somewhat scarcer in winter in the highlands and very rare in the Dry Tortugas.

Where to Find Fort Yargo State Park, Georgia; Pharr Mounds, Natchez Trace Parkway, Mississippi; Choctaw National Wildlife Refuge, Alabama; Chassahowitzka National Wildlife Refuge, Florida.

Range Breeds nearly throughout North America from the Arctic Circle south to Costa Rica; winters from temperate portions of breeding range south; resident populations in Bahamas and Cuba.

360. Eastern Meadowlark
Sturnella magna
(L-10 W-15)

Streaked brown and white above; yellow below with a black or brownish "V" on the breast; crown striped with buff and dark brown; tail is dark in center, white on outer edges.

Voice Song: a plaintive "see-ur see-ur," the second phrase at a lower pitch than the first; call: a rattling, harsh "ka-kak-kak-kak-kak-kak."

Similar Species Western Meadowlark is paler on the back; malar stripe is white in the Eastern Meadowlark, yellow in the Western Meadowlark.

Habitat Grasslands; grain and hay fields; overgrown pastures.

Abundance and Distribution Common to uncommon resident* nearly throughout; somewhat scarcer in the lower coastal plain in summer (May–Aug.) and very rare in the Florida Keys during any season.

Where to Find Pharr Mounds, Natchez Trace Parkway, Mississippi; Chickamauga and Chattanooga National Military Park, Georgia; Wheeler National Wildlife Refuge, Alabama; Lake Woodruff National Wildlife Refuge, Florida.

Range Breeds from southeastern Canada and the eastern and southern United States west to Arizona and south through Mexico, Central America, and northern South America; Cuba; winters through most of breeding range except northern portions.

361. Yellow-headed Blackbird
Xanthocephalus xanthocephalus
(L-10 W-16)

Black body with yellow head and breast; white wing patch. **Female and Immature Male** Brown body; yellowish breast and throat; yellowish eyebrow.

Voice Song: "like a buzz saw biting a hard log" (Edwards in Oberholser 1974:808); call: a croak.

Habitat Marshes, brushy pastures, agricultural fields. Favorite sites for these and several other blackbird species are cattle feedlots and grain elevators in winter.

Abundance and Distribution Rare winter visitor (Sep.–May) in most of peninsular Florida.

Where to Find Lake Apopka Restoration Area, Florida; Biscayne National Park, Florida.

Range Breeds in south-central and southwestern Canada, north-central and northwestern United States; winters from southern California, Arizona, and New Mexico south to central Mexico.

Orioles, Blackbirds

362. Rusty Blackbird
Euphagus carolinus
(L-9 W-14)

Entirely black with creamy yellow eye. **Breeding Female** Grayer. **Winter Male** Black is tinged with rusty; often shows a buffy eyebrow. **Winter Female** Rusty above, buffy below with prominent buffy eyebrow.

Voice Song: "curtl seee" repeated; call: "chik."

Similar Species Prominent creamy eye separates this bird from female Brewer's Blackbirds. The few fall male Brewer's that show some rusty are black (not rusty as in Rusty Blackbird) along the trailing edge of the secondaries.

Habitat Deciduous and coniferous forests, swamps, wooded edges of marshes.

Abundance and Distribution Uncommon to rare winter resident (Sep.–Apr.) in Georgia, Alabama, Mississippi, the Panhandle, and North Florida; rare to casual in Central and South Florida.

Where to Find Blackwater River State Park, Florida; Piedmont National Wildlife Refuge, Georgia; Eufaula National Wildlife Refuge, Alabama/Georgia; Shepard State Park, Mississippi.

Range Breeds in boreal coniferous forest and bogs across the northern tier of North America; winters in the eastern United States.

363. Brewer's Blackbird
Euphagus cyanocephalus
(L-9 W-15)

Entirely black with purplish gloss on head (in proper light); yellow eye; some fall males are tinged rusty. **Female** Dark brown above with dark brown eye, slightly paler below.

Voice Song: "chik-a-chik-a-perzee chik-a-chik-a-perzee" etc.; call: "chik."

Similar Species The male Brewer's Blackbird is similar in color pattern to the Common Grackle (black with purplish gloss on head), but is much smaller (about the size of a Red-winged Blackbird) than the grackle (Blue Jay-size), and has a relatively short, square-tipped tail, not a long, graduated tail like the grackle. The female Brewer's Blackbird is solid brownish gray below (not buffy with faint gray streaking as in the smaller female Brown-headed Cowbird).

Habitat Grasslands, pastures, agricultural fields; feedlots, grain elevators.

Orioles, Blackbirds

Abundance and Distribution Uncommon to rare winter resident (Oct.–Apr.) in central and southern Mississippi, Alabama, southwestern Georgia and the Florida Panhandle; rare to casual in winter elsewhere in the region.

Where to Find Tallahatchie National Wildlife Refuge, Mississippi; Bogue Chitto National Wildlife Refuge, Mississippi; Noxubee National Wildlife Refuge, Mississippi.

Range Breeds in the western and central United States and Canada; winters in the breeding range from southwestern Canada and the western United States southward into the southern United States to central Mexico.

364. Common Grackle

Quiscalus quiscula
(L-12 W-17)

Entirely black with purple gloss on head and iridescent sheen on body in proper light; tail long and rounded; cream-colored eye. **Female** Dull black; whitish eye; tail not as long as male's.

Voice Song: a repeated squeak, like a rusty hinge, with "chek"s interspersed; call: "chek."

Similar Species Cowbirds and blackbirds have short, square tails (not long and rounded as in grackles). The female Boat-tailed Grackle has a longer tail, and is buffy rather than black.

SUMMER
MIGRATION
WINTER
PERMANENT

Habitat Open woodlands, urban areas, agricultural fields, pastures; feeders; grain storage areas.

Abundance and Distribution Common resident* nearly throughout; common summer resident* (Mar.–Oct.), rare to casual winter resident (Nov.–Feb.) in the Florida Keys.

Where to Find Residential parks in towns and cities.

Range Breeds east of the Rockies in Canada and United States; winters in the southern half of the breeding range.

365. Boat-tailed Grackle

Quiscalus major
(*Male* L-17 W-23; *Female* L-13 W-18)

Entirely black with purplish gloss on head (in proper light) and iridescent sheen on body; tail wedge-shaped and longer than body; eye color ranges from creamy (Atlantic coast south to St. Johns River), to

yellowish (Gulf coast from the western Panhandle westward), to dark brown (most of Florida). **Female** Brown above, paler below; buffy eyebrow; wedge-shaped tail not as long as male's.

Voice Song: a series of harsh "eeek"s, "aaahhks," and similar squawks.

Similar Species The female Boat-tailed Grackle has a longer tail than the female Common Grackle, and is buffy rather than black.

Habitat Coastal marshes.

Abundance and Distribution Common resident* along the immediate coast in Georgia and peninsular Florida but rare winter visitor (Nov.–Mar.) in the Panhandle interior and casual in the Keys; common to uncommon resident along the coast of Alabama and Mississippi and on barrier islands.

Where to Find Gulf Islands National Seashore, Mississippi; Everglades National Park, Florida; Cumberland Island National Seashore, Georgia.

Range Coastal eastern United States from New York to Texas.

366. Shiny Cowbird
Molothrus bonariensis
(L-7 W-13)

Entirely black with purple sheen on head, breast, and back; dark eye. **Female** Dingy grayish brown throughout with somewhat paler eyebrow and throat.

Habits A recent (1985), apparently natural invader of Florida from the Greater Antilles that lays its eggs in the nests of other bird species.

Voice An abrupt bubbling trill accompanied by whistles.

Similar Species The female Brown-headed Cowbird has dark streaks on the breast and lacks the pale eyeline of the female Shiny Cowbird.

Habitat Found in a variety of open, agricultural, residential, and scrub habitats.

Abundance and Distribution Rare to casual and local resident* throughout Florida; mainly in the Florida Keys and extreme southern peninsular Florida; scattered records elsewhere.

Where to Find Everglades National Park, Florida; Florida Keys National Wildlife Refuges, Florida.

Range From Panama south throughout South America to central Chile and Argentina; West Indies; south Florida.

Orioles, Blackbirds

367. Brown-headed Cowbird
Molothrus ater
(L-7 W-13)

Black body; brown head. **Female** Brown above, paler below with grayish streakings.

Habits A social parasite, laying its eggs in other birds' nests.

Voice Song: a series of high-pitched whistles (tseee), guttural chatters, and rising squeaks; call: "chek."

Similar Species The female Brown-headed Cowbird is pale buff or gray below with faint grayish streaks; the larger female Brewer's Blackbird is solid grayish brown below. The female Shiny Cowbird has a pale eyebrow and also lacks streaking on the breast.

Habitat Pastures, agricultural fields, feedlots, grain elevators, scrub, open woodlands.

Abundance and Distribution Common resident* nearly throughout although scarcer in southern peninsular Florida and not yet known to breed in the Florida Keys.

Where to Find Feedlots, cattle pastures, and residential feeders.

Range Breeds across most of North America from south of the Arctic to central Mexico; winters in the southern half of its breeding range.

368. Orchard Oriole
Icterus spurius
(L-7 W-10)

Black hood, wings, and tail; chestnut belly, wing patch, lower back and rump. **Female** Greenish yellow above, yellow below with two white wing bars; blue-gray legs. **Second Year Male** Like female but with black throat and breast.

Voice Song: "tsee tso tsee tsoo tewit tewit tewit tseerr" and similar wandering twitters; call: "kuk."

Similar Species The female Orchard Oriole has an unstreaked greenish yellow back; the larger female Baltimore Oriole is mottled tawny brown and black on the back.

Habitat Riparian woodlands, orchards, brushy pastures, scrub.

Abundance and Distribution Common to uncommon summer resident* (Apr.–Aug.) in Mississippi, Alabama, Georgia, the Panhandle, and North Florida, rare to casual in Central Florida south

Orioles, Blackbirds

to Seminole Co. (*fide* B. H. Anderson); uncommon to rare transient (Jul.–Oct., Mar.–May) throughout mainland Florida and the Keys.

Where to Find Noxubee National Wildlife Refuge, Mississippi; Dauphin Island, Alabama; Chattahoochee River and Nature Center, Georgia; Lower Suwannee National Wildlife Refuge, Florida.

Range Breeds across the eastern and central United States south into central Mexico; winters from central Mexico south to northern South America.

369. Spot-breasted Oriole
Icterus pectoralis
(L-10 W-14)

Orange head, belly, and rump; black face, throat, and center of breast; black spotting on sides of breast; black upper back and tail; wings black with orange shoulder patch, white patch on primaries, and broad white patch on black secondaries. **Immature** Brownish above, yellowish or orange yellow below with blackish throat; yellowish rump; broad white patch on secondaries.

Voice "Calls include loud, nasal notes, singly or in a jerky series; song of male a prolonged, caroling liquid series of rich, clear, slow whistles, often quite beautiful; female's song simpler with a thinner note" (Stiles and Skutch 1989:412).

Similar Species Baltimore Oriole has a black or brownish head and lacks white patch on secondaries.

Figure 47. Urban parks in South Florida act like a magnet for exotics. Reports for Monk and White-winged parakeets, Red-crowned Parrots, Spot-breasted Orioles, and Stripe-headed Tanagers have been made at Ft. Lauderdale's Hugh Taylor Birch State Park, and similar lists can be compiled for other such city sites.

Orioles, Blackbirds

Habitat Suburban residential areas.

Abundance and Distribution Uncommon to rare and local resident* in southeastern Florida (Palm Beach, Broward, and Dade counties). The population is apparently derived from cage birds that escaped in the late 1940s.

Where to Find Hugh Taylor Birch State Park, Florida.

Range Central Mexico south to Costa Rica; southeastern Florida (introduced).

370. Baltimore Oriole
Icterus galbula
(L-8 W-12)

Black hood, back, and wings; tail black at base and center but outer terminal portions orange; orange belly, rump, and shoulder patch. **Female and Immature** Orange brown above, yellow orange below with varying amounts of black on face and throat; white wing bars.

SUMMER
MIGRATION
WINTER
PERMANENT

Voice Slurred rapid series of easily imitated whistles; call: a chatter; also, "wheweee."

Similar Species The female of the Baltimore Oriole has an orangish belly; the smaller female Orchard Oriole is yellowish or greenish yellow on the belly.

Habitat Riparian woodland (sycamore, cottonwood, willow), orchards, open deciduous woodlands, hedgerows, second growth; residential areas.

Abundance and Distribution Rare summer resident* (Apr.–Sep.) in the highlands; uncommon to rare transient (Aug.–Oct., Apr.–May) throughout; rare winter resident (Nov.–Mar.) in southeastern Georgia and Florida (has bred—Key West, 1972, *fide* B. H. Anderson).

Where to Find Cumberland Island National Seashore, Georgia; Bogue Chitto National Wildlife Refuge, Mississippi/Louisiana; Dauphin Island, Alabama; St. Andrews Recreation Area, Florida.

Range Breeds in the eastern United States and southeastern Canada; winters from central Mexico to northern South America; also in the Greater Antilles.

Orioles, Blackbirds

Old World Finches

Family Fringillidae

Like many of the emberizids, finches are small to medium-sized birds with thick, conical bills for eating seeds and fruits.

371. Purple Finch
Carpodacus purpureus
(L-6 W-10)

Rosy head and breast; whitish belly; brown above suffused with rose; rose rump; tail is notched; undertail coverts white. **Female and Immature Male** Brown above; white below heavily streaked with brown; brown head with white eyebrow and malar stripes; undertail coverts white.

Voice Song: a rapid, tumbling series of slurred notes and trills; call: "chit."

Similar Species The "chit" call note of the Purple Finch is dintinct from the nasal "wink" call note of the House Finch. The male Purple Finch is rosier overall and lacks the brown streaking on the flanks of the male House Finch. The female Purple Finch has a pronounced dark jaw stripe and white eyeline, which the female House Finch lacks.

Habitat Coniferous forest and parklands; feeders in winter.

Abundance and Distribution Uncommon (highlands) to rare (elsewhere) winter resident (Oct.–Apr.) in Georgia, Alabama, Mississippi, the Panhandle, and North Florida; casual winter visitor to the remainder of Florida.

Where to Find Little River Canyon National Preserve, Alabama; Black Rock Mountain State Park, Georgia; Dahomey National Widlife Refuge, Mississippi.

Range Breeds across Canada, northern United States, western coastal mountains south into Baja California, and the Appalachians south to Virginia; winters throughout much of the United States except in the Great Plains and western deserts.

372. House Finch
Carpodacus mexicanus
(L-6 W-10)

Brown above with red brow stripe; brown cheeks; rosy breast; whitish streaked with brown below. **Female and Immature** Brown above; buffy head and underparts finely streaked with brown; buffy preorbital stripe in some.

SUMMER
MIGRATION
WINTER
PERMANENT

Voice Song: a long series of squeaks and warbles; call: a nasal "wink."

Similar Species The nasal "wink" call note of the House Finch is easily distinguishable from the whistled "wit" of the Purple Finch. The House Finch has a square tail and prominent streaking on flanks and undertail coverts; Purple Finch has a notched tail and white (unstreaked) undertail coverts. The male Purple Finch is rosier overall and lacks the brown streaking on the flanks of the male House Finch. The female Purple Finch has a pronounced dark jaw stripe and white eyeline, which the female House Finch lacks.

Habitat Scrub, old fields; agricultural, residential, and urban areas; usually nests in scrubby conifers, including ornamentals; common at feeders.

Abundance and Distribution This western species has expanded nearly throughout eastern North America within the past half century, evidently from birds released on Long Island in 1940 (Aldrich and Weske 1978). At present, it is a common to uncommon resident* nearly throughout the region, although rare and local in the highlands and in Central and South Florida.

Where to Find Piedmont National Wildlife Refuge, Georgia; Vicksburg National Military Park, Mississippi; Oak Mountain State Park, Alabama.

Range Resident from southwestern Canada throughout much of the United States except Great Plains, south to southern Mexico.

373. Pine Siskin
Carduelis pinus
(L-5 W-9)

Streaked brown above; whitish below with brown streaks; yellowish wing bar, yellow wing patch, and yellow at base of tail.

Voice Song: a sequence of "chipy chipy" notes inter-

Old World Finches

spersed with raspy, rising "zeeeech" calls; call: a nasal "schreee."

Similar Species The heavily streaked body and yellow patches on wings and base of tail distinguish this bird from other small finches.

Habitat A wide variety of coniferous and mixed forests. Feeders in winter.

Abundance and Distribution Uncommon (highlands) to rare (elsewhere) and highly irregular winter visitor (Oct.–Apr.) in Georgia, Alabama, Mississippi, the Panhandle, and North Florida, present in some years but not in others; casual winter visitor to the remainder of Florida.

Where to Find Lake Guntersville State Park, Alabama; Vicksburg National Military Park, Mississippi; Black Rock Mountain State Park, Georgia.

Range Breeds in boreal regions of northern North America, and in western mountains south through the United States and highlands of Mexico to Veracruz; winters in all except the extreme northern portions of the breeding range and in most of the temperate United States.

374. American Goldfinch
Carduelis tristis
(L-5 W-9)

Yellow body; black cap, wings, and tail; white at base of tail and wing bar; yellow shoulder patch. **Female and Winter Male** Brownish above; yellowish or buff breast; whitish belly; dark wings with white wing bars.

Habits Usually in flocks; dipping-soaring flight, like a roller coaster; almost always giving characteristic flight call: "ker-chik ker-chik-chik-chik."

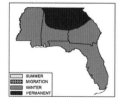

Voice Song: a sequence of trills, whiny "tsoowee"s, and "ker-chik"s; flight call: a characteristic and unmistakable "ker-chik ker-chik-chik-chik."

Similar Species The American Goldfinch female is the only small bird in the region with a conical bill that is brownish above and whitish below.

Habitat Grasslands, brushy pastures, old fields; feeders in winter and spring.

Abundance and Distribution Common resident* in the piedmont and highlands, has bred* in Mississippi; common to uncommon winter resident (Oct.–May) elsewhere in the region except South Florida and the Keys, where uncommon to rare.

Where to Find Ocmulgee National Monument, Georgia; DeSoto State Park, Alabama; Tallahatchie National Wildlife Refuge, Mississippi; St. Andrews State Recreation Area, Florida.

Range Breeds across southern Canada, northern and central United States to southern California and northern Baja California in the west; winters in the central and southern United States and northern Mexico.

375. Evening Grosbeak
Coccothraustes vespertinus
(L-8 W-13)

A chubby bird with heavy, yellowish or whitish bill; yellow body; black crown and brownish head with yellow forehead and eyebrow; black tail and wings with white wing patch. **Female** Grayish above, buffy below; dark malar stripe; white wing patch.

Habits Usually in flocks.

SUMMER
MIGRATION
WINTER
PERMANENT

Voice Calls: a sharp "peak" and a hoarse "peer."

Habitat Coniferous and mixed forest; often at feeders in winter.

Abundance and Distribution Uncommon (highlands) to rare (elsewhere) and highly irregular winter visitor (Oct.–Apr.) in Georgia, Alabama, Mississippi, the Panhandle, and North Florida, present in some years but not in others.

Where to Find Black Rock Mountain State Park, Georgia; Newman Wetlands Center, Atlanta, Georgia; Rabun Bald, Georgia.

Range Breeds in boreal portions of central and southern Canada, northern and western United States, south in western mountains to western and central Mexico; winters in breeding range and in temperate and southern United States.

House Sparrows
Family Passeridae

376. House Sparrow
Passer domesticus
(L-6 W-10)

A chunky, heavy-billed bird; brown above with heavy dark brown streaks; dingy gray below; gray cap; chestnut nape; black lores, chin, and bib. **Female** Streaked buff and brown above; dingy gray below; pale buff postorbital stripe.

Voice Song: "chip cheap chip chip chi-chi-chi chip" etc.; call: "cheap."

Similar Species Pale female and immature Dickcissels resemble House Sparrow female but usually have traces of yellow on pale white (not dirty white) breast, a clear, whitish or yellowish eyebrow, and some chestnut on shoulder.

Habitat Urban areas, pastures, agricultural fields, feedlots, farms, grain elevators.

Abundance and Distribution A Eurasian species introduced into the United States in Brooklyn, New York, in 1850; reached Florida in 1882; now a common resident* nearly throughout, uncommon in the Florida Keys.

Where to Find Urban and agricultural areas throughout.

Range Resident in boreal, temperate, and subtropical regions of the Old and New World; currently expanding into tropical regions.

House Sparrows

Appendix 1. Hypothetical, Casual, Accidental, Escaped Exotic, or Extinct Species

This list represents birds you should not expect to see in the Southeast. Definitions for the various levels of scarcity for the birds is as follows:

Casual (C): A few records for the species (3–40). The bird does occur in the region but is not seen every year.

Accidental (A): One or two records for the species. Not expected to recur.

Hypothetical (H): Not confirmed (photo or specimen), and ornithological listing authorities do not accept reported sightings as fact.

Escaped Exotic (E): There are many escaped exotics in the region. Several have established breeding populations and can be found reliably in the wild. These are listed in the body of the text accompanied by a photo. However, another large group of exotics has been seen in the wild, but are not yet reported as breeding. These are listed below.

Extirpated or Extinct (X): Extirpated species are those that formerly occurred regularly in the region, but can no longer be found. Extinct species are those believed to no longer be in existence, such as the Carolina Parakeet.

Nomenclature and taxonomic order follows the American Ornithologists' Union *Check-List*, 7th ed. and revisions through 2004, where possible; otherwise, Sibley and Monroe (1990).

Spotted Nothura *Nothura maculosa* E
White-faced Whistling Duck *Dendrocygna viduata* E
Bean Goose *Anser fabalis* E
Greylag Goose *Anser anser* E
Swan Goose *Anser cygnoides* E
Ross's Goose *Chen rossii* C
Egyptian Goose *Alpochen aegyptiaca* E
Orinoco Goose *Neochen jubata* E
Mute Swan *Cygnus olor* E
Black Swan *Cygnus atratus* E
Whooper Swan *Cygnus cygnus* E

Ruddy Shelduck *Tadorna ferruginea* E
Ringed Teal *Callonetta leucophrys* E
Mandarin Duck *Aix galericulata* E
Cinnamon Teal *Anas cyanoptera* C
White-cheeked Pintail *Anas bahamensis* C
Hottentot Teal *Anas punctata* E
Spot-billed Duck *Anas poecilorhyncha* E
Rosy-billed Pochard *Netta peposaca* E
King Eider *Somateria spectabilis* C
Common Eider *Somateria mollissima* C
Harlequin Duck *Histrionicus histrionicus* C
Masked Duck *Nomonyx dominicus* C
Chukar *Alectoris chukar* E
Red Junglefowl *Gallus gallus* E
Ring-necked Pheasant *Phasianus colchicus* E
Helmeted Guineafowl *Numida meleagris* E
Arctic Loon *Gavia arctica* H
Pacific Loon *Gavia pacifica* C
Red-necked Grebe *Podiceps grisegena* C
Western Grebe *Aechmophorus occidentalis* C
Clark's Grebe *Aechmophorus clarkii* H
Black-browed Albatross *Thalassarche melanophris* A
Wandering Albatross *Diomedea exulans* H
Northern Fulmar *Fulmarus glacialis* H
Bulwer's Petrel *Bulweria bulwerii* H
Little Shearwater *Puffinus assimilis* H
White-bellied Storm-Petrel *Fregetta grallaria* H
Red-billed Tropicbird *Phaethon aethereus* C
Neotropic Cormorant *Phalacrocorax brasilianus* H
Great Cormorant *Phalacrocorax carbo* C
Scarlet Ibis *Eudocimus ruber* C
White-faced Ibis *Plegadis chihi* C
Black-necked Stork *Ephippiorhynchus asiaticus* E
King Vulture *Sarcoramphus papa* E
Chilean Flamingo *Phoenicopterus chilensis* E
Northern Goshawk *Accipiter gentilis* C
Common Black-Hawk *Buteogallus anthracinus* E
Ferruginous Hawk *Buteo regalis* C
Rough-legged Hawk *Buteo lagopus* C
Prairie Falcon *Falco mexicanus* C
Gray-necked Wood-Rail *Aramides cajanea* E
Purple Swamphen *Porphyrio porphyrio* E
Gray-crowned Crane *Balearica regulorum* E
Sarus Crane *Grus antigone* E
Northern Lapwing *Vanellus vanellus* A

Southern Lapwing *Vanellus chilensis* E
Mountain Plover *Charadrius montanus* C
Eurasian Curlew *Numenius arquata* H
Black-tailed Godwit *Limosa limosa* C
Hudsonian Godwit *Limosa haemastica* C
Bar-tailed Godwit *Limosa lapponica* A
Surfbird *Aphriza virgata* C
Sharp-tailed Sandpiper *Calidris acuminata* A
Curlew Sandpiper *Calidris ferruginea* C
Ruff *Philomachus pugnax* C
Eurasian Woodcock *Scolopax rusticola* H
South Polar Skua *Stercorarius maccormicki* C
Long-tailed Jaeger *Stercorarius longicaudus* C
Little Gull *Larus minutus* C
Black-headed Gull *Larus ridibundus* C
Heermann's Gull *Larus heermanni* A
Band-tailed Gull *Larus belcheri* C
Thayer's Gull *Larus thayeri* C
Iceland Gull *Larus glaucoides* C
Sabine's Gull *Xema sabini* C
Elegant Tern *Sterna elegans* C
Arctic Tern *Sterna pardisaea* C
White-winged Tern *Chlidonias leucopterus* H
Dovekie *Alle alle* C
Razorbill *Alca torda* C
Long-billed Murrelet *Brachyramphus perdix* C
Atlantic Puffin *Fratercula arctica* A
Scaly-naped Pigeon *Patagioenas squamosa* A
Band-tailed Pigeon *Patagioenas fasciata* C
European Turtle-Dove *Streptopelia turtur* A
Spotted Dove *Streptopelia chinensis* E
Diamond Dove *Geopelia cuneata* E
Passenger Pigeon *Ectopistes migratorius* X
Inca Dove *Columbina inca* E?
Key West Quail-Dove *Geotrygon chrysia* C
Ruddy Quail-Dove *Geotrygon montana* C
Red Lory *Eos bornea* E
Ornate Lorikeet *Trichoglossus ornatus* E
Rainbow Lorikeet *Trichoglossus haematod* E
Scaly-breasted Lorikeet *Tricholglossus chlorolepidotus* E
Chattering Lory *Lorius garrulus* E
Galah *Eolophus roseicapillus* E
Great Sulphur-crested Cockatoo *Cacatua galenta* E
Salmon-crested Cockatoo *Cacatua moluccensis* E
White Cockatoo *Cacatua alba* E

Tanimbar Cockatoo *Cacatua goffini* E
Cockatiel *Nymphichs hollandicus* E
Eclectus Parrot *Eclectus roratus* E
Gray Parrot *Psittacus erithacus* E
Senegal Parrot *Poicephalus senegalus* E
Rueppell's Parrot *Poicephallus rueppellii* E
Peach-faced Lovebird *Agapornis roseicollis* E
Fischer's Lovebird *Agapornis fischeri* E
Masked Lovebird *Agapornis personata* E
Rose-ringed Parakeet *Psittacula krameri* C
Plum-headed Parakeet *Psittacula cyanocephala* E
Blossom-headed Parakeet *Psittacula roseata* E
Maroon-bellied Parakeet *Pyrrhura frontalis* E
Green-cheeked Parakeet *Pyrrhura molinae* E
Carolina Parakeet *Conuropsis carolinensis* X
Green Parakeet *Aratinga holochlora* E
Scarlet-fronted Parakeet *Aratinga wagleri* E
Mitred Parakeet *Aratinga mitrata* E
Crimson-fronted Parakeet *Aratinga finschi* E
White-eyed Parakeet *Aratinga leucopthalmus* E
Hispaniolan Parakeet *Aratinga chloroptera* E
Dusky-headed Parakeet *Aratinga weddellii* E
Orange-fronted Parakeet *Aratinga canicularis* E
Peach-fronted Parakeet *Aratinga aurea* E
Brown-throated Parakeet *Aratinga pertinax* E
Hyacinth Macaw *Anodorhynchus hyacinthinus* E
Chestnut-fronted Macaw *Ara severa* E
Military Macaw *Ara militaris* E
Scarlet Macaw *Ara macao* E
Blue-and-yellow Macaw *Ara ararauna* E
Yellow-collared Macaw *Ara auricollis* E
Red-shouldered Macaw *Ara nobilis* E
Maroon-fronted Parrot *Rhynchopsitta terrisi* E
Burrowing Parrot *Cyanoliseus patagonus* E
Orange-chinned Parakeet *Brotogeris jugularis* E
Tui Parakeet *Brotogeris sanctithomae* E
White-crowned Parrot *Pionus senilis* E
White-fronted Parrot *Amazona albifrons* E
Hispaniolan Parrot *Amazona ventralis* E
Lilac-crowned Parrot *Amazona finschi* E
Red-spectacled Parrot *Amazona pretrei* E
Red-lored Parrot *Amazona autumnalis* E
Mealy Parrot *Amazona farinosa* E
Turquoise-fronted Parrot *Amazona aestiva* E
Orange-winged Parrot *Amazona amazonica* E

Yellow-headed Parrot *Amazona oratrix* E
Yellow-naped Parrot *Amazona auropalliata* E
Yellow-crowned Parrot *Amazona ochrocephala* E
Violet Touraco *Musophaga violacea* E
Flammulated Owl *Otus flammeolus* C
Spectacled Owl *Pulsatrix perspicillata* E
Snowy Owl *Bubo scandiacus* C
Long-eared Owl *Asio otus* C
Northern Saw-whet Owl *Aegolius acadicus* C
White-collared Swift *Streptoprocne zonaris* C
Antillean Palm-Swift *Tachornis phoenicobia* A
Buff-bellied Hummingbird *Amazilia yucatanensis* C
Magnificent Hummingbird *Eugenes fulgens* A
Bahama Woodstar *Calliphlox evelynae* C
Anna's Hummingbird *Calypte anna* A
Calliope Hummingbird *Stellula calliope* C
Broad-tailed Hummingbrid *Selasphorus platycercus* A
Allen's Hummingbird *Selashporus sasin* C
Abyssinian Ground-Hornbill *Bucorvus abyssinicus* E
Citron-throated Toucan *Ramphastos citreolaemus* E
Toco Toucan *Ramphastos toco* E
Golden-fronted Woodpecker *Melanerpes aurifrons* A
Ivory-billed Woodpecker *Campephilus principalis* X ?
Western Wood-Pewee *Contopus sordidulus* A
Black Phoebe *Sayornis nigricans* C
Say's Phoebe *Sayornis saya* C
La Sagra's Flycatcher *Myiarchus sagrae* C
Sulphur-bellied Flycatcher *Myiodynastes luteiventris* C
Variegated Flycatcher *Empidonomus varius* H
Tropical Kingbird *Tyrannus melancholicus* C
Couch's Kingbird *Tyrannus couchii* C
Cassin's Kingbird *Tyrannus vociferans* C
Loggerhead Kingbird *Tyrannus caudifasciatus* H
Fork-tailed Flycatcher *Tyrannus savana* C
Banded Pitta *Pitta guajana* E
Thick-billed Vireo *Vireo crassirostris* C
Yellow-green Vireo *Vireo flavoviridis* C
Azure Jay *Cyanocorax caeruleus* E
Green Jay *Cyanocorax yncas* E
Black-billed Magpie *Pica hudsonia* E
Cuban Martin *Progne cryptoleuca* A
Southern Martin *Progne elegans* A
Bahama Swallow *Tachycineta cyaneoviridis* C
Rock Wren *Salpinctes obsoletus* C
Bewick's Wren *Thryomanes bewickii* C

Asian Fairy-Bluebird *Irena puella* E
Northern Wheatear *Oenanthe oenanthe* C
Varied Thrush *Ixoreus naevius* C
Greater Necklaced Laughingthrush *Garrulax pectoralis* E
Red-billed Leiothrix *Leiothrix lutea* E
Bahama Mockingbird *Mimus gundlachii* C
Sage Thrasher *Oreoscoptes montanus* C
Curve-billed Thrasher *Toxostoma curvirostre* C
Common Myna *Acridotheres tristis* C
Jungle Myna *Acridotheres fuscus* E
Crested Myna *Acridotheres cristatellus* E
Hill Myna *Gracula religiosa* E
Yellow Wagtail *Motacilla flava* H
Bachman's Warbler *Vermivora bachmanii* X
Golden-cheeked Warbler *Dendroica chrysoparia* A
Townsend's Warbler *Dendroica townsendi* C
Kirtland's Warbler *Dendroica kirtlandii* C
MacGillivray's Warbler *Oporornis tolmiei* C
Painted Redstart *Myioborus pictus* A
Bananaquit *Coereba flaveola* C
Western Spindalis *Spindalis zena* C
Yellow-faced Grassquit *Tiaris olivacea* C
Black-faced Grassquit *Tiaris bicolor* C
Saffron Finch *Sicalis flaveola* E
Red-capped Cardinal *Paroaria gularis* E
Green-tailed Towhee *Pipilo chlorurus* C
Black-throated Sparrow *Amphispiza bilineata* A
Lark Bunting *Calamospiza melanocorys* C
Harris's Sparrow *Zonotrichia querula* C
Golden-crowned Sparrow *Zonotrichia atricapilla* A
Smith's Longspur *Calcarius pictus* C
Chestnut-collared Longspur *Calcarius ornatus* C
Snow Bunting *Plectrophenax nivalis* C
Black-headed Grosbeak *Pheucticus melanocephalus* C
Lazuli Bunting *Passerina amoena* C
Tawny-shouldered Blackbird *Agelaius humeralis* C
Western Meadowlark *Sturnella neglecta* C
Bronzed Cowbird *Molothrus aeneus* C
Troupial *Icterus icterus* E
Bullock's Oriole *Icterus bullockii* C
Montezuma Oropendola *Psarocolius montezuma* E
Red Crossbill *Loxia curvirostra* C
Common Redpoll *Carduelis flammea* C
European Goldfinch *Carduelis carduelis* E
Yellow-fronted Canary *Serinus mozambicus* E

Golden Sparrow *Passer luteus* E
Vitelline Masked Weaver *Ploceus velatus* E
Red Bishop *Euplectes orix* E
Yellow-crowned Bishop *Euplectes afer* E
Red-naped Widowbird *Euplectes laticauda* E
Red-cheeked Cordonbleu *Uraeginthus bengalus* E
Orange-cheeked Waxbill *Estrilda melpoda* E
Red Avadavat *Amandava amandava* E
Zebra Finch *Amandava subflava* E
Madagascar Mannikin *Lonchura nana* E
African Silverbill *Lonchura cantans* E
Nutmeg Mannikin *Lonchura punctulata* E
Chestnut Mannikin *Lonchura atricapilla* E
White-headed Mannikin *Lonchura maja* E
Pin-tailed Whydah *Vidua macroura* E

Appendix 2. Birding Sites in the Southeast

Directions are here provided to 189 of the best birding sites in the southeastern United States. Each is mentioned in one or more of the species accounts as being one of the best or, in some cases, the only place where a particular bird occurs in the region. I have tried to provide at least three such sites for each species. In compiling the list, I have leaned heavily on existing bird-finding guides—although responsibility for any errors is entirely mine.

When using the list, please keep in mind that mileages are estimates for the most part—designed to put you in the right vicinity. Consider roughly estimated mileages to be a challenge to your sense of adventure, and you will probably be happier. It is also helpful to have detailed maps.

In most cases, the bird-finding guides have more detailed information than I provide on the routes to take and what you are likely to find. The sources consulted for many of the sites in this list are as follows: *A Birder's Guide to Florida* edited by Bill Pranty (1996); *Birder's Guide to Alabama and Mississippi* by Ray Vaughan (1994); and *A Birder's Guide to Georgia* by J. R. Hitt and K. T. Blackshaw (1996).

The sites are listed alphabetically by states, except for pelagic sites, which are offshore from all of the states and so begin the list.

Abbreviations used in the descriptions are as follows:

I = Interstate Highway
AL = Alabama State Highway
FL = Florida State Highway
GA = Georgia State Highway
MS = Mississippi State Highway
FS = Forest Service Road
jct = junction
mi = miles
hq = headquarters
CR = County Road
SR = State Route
TR = Township Road

Pelagic

Pelagic or marine species seldom appear within sight of land, except after hurricanes, yet they can be quite common a few miles offshore. As mentioned in the caption for figure 18, cruise ships provide an excellent way to see pelagic species in some comfort. An added attraction of the cruise-ship method of bird-watching is that migrants often use the ships as resting platforms. During a recent October jaunt, we saw Gray Catbird, Ovenbird, Pine Warbler, Mourning Dove, Peregrine Falcon, Merlin, and Black-throated Blue Warbler at one time or another perched on various parts of the ship. Hardier souls can join one of the scores of deep-sea sport fishing boats that depart regularly from coastal areas throughout the region. Many are as happy to take bird-watchers along as paying customers as fishermen. Check the internet or local yellow pages for information.

Alabama (27)

Bladon Springs State Park

From the jct of US 84 and AL 17 at Bolinger, go east on US 84 about 6 mi to jct with CR 6. Turn right (south) on CR 6 and go about 3 mi to the park entrance on the left. Habitats include grasslands, hardwood forest, and pine woodlands.

Blakely Island

From I-10 east of Mobile take Exit 27 N onto US 90. Proceed north on US 90 about 2 mi to a gated dirt road that leads to dikes on the east side of the road. Park and enter. A permit is required in advance for entry. These may be obtained by writing to the General Manager, Administration, Alabama State Docks Dept., P.O. Box 1588, Mobile, AL 36633 (see Vaughan 1994:35 for additional details). Habitat is diked ponds, variously flooded or vegetated at different times.

Bon Secour National Wildlife Refuge

From the town of Gulf Shores (50 mi west of Pensacola, Florida), go west on AL 180 for 8 mi to the refuge Visitor Center on the right. Habitats include grasslands, fresh and saltwater marshes, swamp, pine forest, oak woodlands, dunes, and beach.

Cheaha State Park

Just east of Anniston, take Exit 191 off I-20 onto US 431. Go south on US 431 about 4 mi to jct AL 281 (Talladega Scenic Dr). Turn right on AL 281, and proceed about 12 mi to signs for the park entrance. Cheaha Mountain is the highest point in the State of Alabama at 2,407 feet. Habitat is highland deciduous forest.

Choctaw National Wildlife Refuge

From Coffeeville, at the jct of US 84 and AL 69, go west on US 84 about 9.5 mi to jct CR 21. Turn right (north) on CR 21 and go about 4 mi to jct with CR 14. Turn right on CR 14 and proceed about 4 mi to the town of Womack Hill. Turn right at Womack Hill (Lenoir Rd) and follow signs to the refuge. Habitats include bottomland forest, cypress bays, impoundments, and farmland.

Conecuh National Forest

From Andalusia, proceed south on US 29 about 10 mi to jct with AL 137. Go south on AL 137 to enter the national forest lands, which line both sides of the road all the way to the Florida-Alabama border. To reach Open Pond, go south from the jct of AL 137 and US 29 on AL 137 about 5.5 mi to jct with CR 24. Turn left (east) on CR 24. Go 0.3 mi to FR 336. Turn right (south) on FR 336 and proceed about 1 mi to the pond. Habitats include pine savanna, marsh, bottomland forest, and swamp.

Dauphin Island

From I-10 west of Mobile, take Exit 17A onto AL 193 S. Proceed south on AL 193 about 27 mi to the island. The Audubon Sanctuary is located at the east end of the island. Habitats include oak woodlands, freshwater marsh, jetties, beach, dunes, ocean, and bay.

DeSoto State Park

From I-59, take Exit 231 onto AL 117. Go east on AL 117 about 6 mi to the jct with Lookout Mountain Pkwy in Mentone. Turn right (south) onto the parkway and follow signs to the park hq. Habitat is highland deciduous forest.

Eufaula National Wildlife Refuge

From the town of Eufaula, proceed north on US 431 about 8 mi to jct with AL 165. Turn right (east) on AL 165 and go 1.5 mi to the refuge. Habitats include grasslands, croplands, forest, lake, and freshwater marsh.

Fairhope Park

From I-10 east of Mobile, take Exit 35 and follow US 98 south about 6 mi to where the road splits. Follow US 98 A into downtown Fairhope. The park is located downtown along the waterfront west of US 98 A. A pier extends well out into the bay. Habitat is open bay.

Fort Toulouse

From the jct of AL 157 and the Montgomery East Side By-Pass (East Blvd, US 231) on the northeast side of Montgomery, go 7.7 mi north on US 231 to jct with Ft. Toulouse Rd. Turn left (west) on Ft. Toulouse Rd and go 2.2 mi to the fort entrance. Habitats include open areas, hardwood forest, riparian bottomlands, river, and swamp.

Gulf State Park

East of Mobile, take Exit 44 off I-10 onto AL 59. Proceed south on AL 59 about 30 mi to jct with AL 180 in the town of Gulf Shores. Turn left on AL 180, go about 0.25 mi, then turn right (south) on AL 135 to enter the park. Habitats include fresh and saltwater marshes, dunes, beach, oak and pine woodlands, and scrub thickets.

Historic Blakeley State Park

From I-10 east of Mobile, take Exit 35 N on US98. Go north on US 98 about 0.7 mi to a "T" at Bridgehead. Turn right on US 31 and go about 0.3 mi to jct with AL 225. Turn left (north) on AL 225 and go about 5 mi to a left turn that will take you to the park.

Lagoon Park, Montgomery

At the jct of I-85 and AL 152 on the east side of Montgomery (Exit 6) go north on AL 152 about 4.3 mi to jct with US 231 at Madison Park. Exit southwest onto Dickinson Dr, and take the first left.

Lake Guntersville State Park

At the jct of US 431 and AL 227 in downtown Guntersville, turn left (east) on AL 227 and go about 6 mi to the park entrance on the left. Habitat is lake, grassland, lakeshore, pine forest, and deciduous woodlands.

Lakepoint Resort State Park

From the jct of US 82 and US 431 in downtown Eufaula, go north on combined US 82 and US 431 about 1.5 mi to where US 82 and US 431 split in Hoboken. Continue on the right fork (US 431) about 6 mi to signs for the park (on left side of road).

Lake Purdy

From the jct of I-20 and I-459 east of Birmingham, go south on I-459 about 2 mi to Exit 27. Take Exit 27 east onto Grants Mill Rd. Proceed east on Grants Mill Rd about 5 mi to the lake.

Little River Canyon National Preserve

From the jct of I-59 and AL 35 at Fort Payne, take Exit 218 onto AL 35 E. Proceed east on AL 35 about 7 mi through Ft. Payne to the preserve entrance. Principal habitat is deciduous forest.

Meaher State Park

From I-10 east of Mobile, take Exit 30 onto US 90/98 E. Proceed east on US 90/98 about 3 mi to the park entrance on the right (south). Habitats include woodlands, second growth, and marsh.

Moundville Archaeological State Park

From I-20 at Tuscaloosa, take Exit 71 onto AL 69 S. Proceed south on AL 69 about 13 mi to Moundville, and follow signs to the park. Habitats include grasslands, fields, and woodlands.

Oak Mountain State Park

From I-65 south of Birmingham, take Exit 246 west onto AL 119. Make an immediate left onto the State Park road, and proceed to the park entrance. Habitats include deciduous forest, fields, second growth, lake, and lakeshore.

Oakmulgee District, Talladega National Forest

From the town of Brent, go south on AL 25 about 5 mi to where AL 25 makes a right-hand turn to the west. Proceed west on AL 25 about 6 mi to FR 753. Park at the entrance to FR 753 and walk about 0.5 mi to mature pine savanna and Red-cockaded Woodpecker colony trees.

Pinto Pass Nature Observatory, Battleship Park

Just east of Mobile on I-10, take Exit 27 onto US 90 east and follow signs to the park and observatory.

Sipsey Wilderness, William B. Bankhead National Forest

From the jct of US 278 and AL 33 just west of Double Springs, go north on AL 33 about 12.6 mi to jct with CR 6. Turn left on CR 6 and go about 4 mi to the Sipsey River, wilderness trial heads, and picnic area. Habitats include mixed forest, river bottom, and river.

Tuskegee National Forest

From I-85 east of Tuskegee, take Exit 42 onto AL 186 S. The road enters the national forest in about 0.5 mi, and the forest lines the road for the next 4 mi or so. Continue about 2 mi from the interstate exit on AL 186 to Atasi Picnic Ground and access to Bartram Trail, which traverses a large section of the national forest. Habitats include pine forest, swamp, hardwood bottomlands, marsh, and various stages of second growth.

Weeks Bay National Estuarine Research Reserve

From I-10 east of Mobile, take Exit 35 onto US 98 S. Proceed south on US 98 about 18 mi to Barnwell. Turn left at Barnwell continuing on US 98 and go about 2.5 mi to a small parking lot for the reserve on the right (south) side of the road. Habitats include fields, second growth, mixed woodlands, marsh, and bay.

Wheeler National Wildlife Refuge

From I-65 just east of Decatur, take Exit 334 onto AL 67 W. Proceed west on AL 67 about 2.5 mi to the refuge Visitor Center. Habitats include lake, lakeshore, croplands, fields, old fields, second growth, impoundments, swamp, and woodlands.

Florida (76)

Apalachicola Municipal Airport

From the city of Apalachicola, go west about 1.8 mi on US 98 to signs for the airport. Turn right (north) and proceed about 0.7 mi to the terminal parking lot. Request permission to examine runway margins for grassland species.

Arbuckle Creek Road, Lorida

At the jct of US 98 and Arbuckle Creek Rd (FL 700A) in Lorida, go north on Arbuckle Creek Rd 1.2 mi and park along the road. Dry, overgrazed pasture suitable for Burrowing Owls, Cattle Egrets, Black Vultures, White-tailed Kites, etc., lines the west side of the road. Eurasian Collared-Doves frequent residential yards and casuarina trees (tall evergreens) in the area.

Archbold Biological Station

From the jct of US 27 and FL 70 about 35 mi west of the town of Okeechobee, go west on FL 70 about 1 mi to jct with old FL 8. Turn left (south) on old FL 8 and go 1.8 mi to the station entrance.

Arthur R. Marshal Loxahatchee National Wildlife Refuge

See Loxahatchee National Wildlife Refuge.

Avon Park Bombing Range

From the jct of US 98 and FL 64 in downtown Avon Park, go east on FL 64

(Main St) about 10 mi to the entrance of the bombing range. Ask directions to the Natural Resources Office at the gate kiosk, where you can sign in and obtain a visitor's permit and map. Habitats include marsh, dry prairie, hardwood forest, pine scrub, slash and longleaf pine woods.

Big Cypress Bend, Fakahatchee Strand Preserve State Park

From Carnestown at the jct of US 41 (Tamiami Trail) and FL 29, go west on US 41 about 7 mi to the Big Cypress Bend parking lot and boardwalk on the right (north) side of the highway. Habitat is spectacular old growth cypress bays.

Big Lagoon State Recreation Area

At the jct of US 98 and FL 293 about 5 mi west of Pensacola, go south on FL 293 about 5 mi until FL 293 runs into FL 292. Continue straight ahead from this intersection for another 1.5 mi or so to jct with FL 297. Turn left (east) on FL 297 and go about 0.5 mi to signs for the recreation area entrance. Habitats include beaches, salt marshes, thickets, slash pine stands, and swales.

Biscayne National Park

Proceeding south on the Florida Turnpike (FL 821) into Homestead, take Exit 6 onto Speedway Blvd. Turn left from the exit ramp onto Speedway Blvd and proceed to SW 328th St (North Canal Dr). Turn left, and continue to the end of the road (about 5 mi). Entrance to the park is on the left. Habitats include oak hammocks, mangroves, beach, dune, and lagoon.

Blackwater River State Park

From the town of Milton, go east on US 90 about 9 mi to the Harold exit. At Harold, exit north from US 90 and go north about 4 mi to signs for the park entrance. Habitats include pine forest, pine savanna, canebrakes, swamp, and bayou.

Buck Lake

From the jct of US 90 (Mahan Dr) and US 319 (Capital Circle) northeast of Tallahassee, go northeast on US 90 about 0.7 mi to jct with Buck Lake Rd. Bear right (east) on Buck Lake Rd and continue about 1 mi to Buck Lake on the left (north) side of the road. Habitat is lake and lakeshore.

Canal Overpass

From the jct of US 1 and SW 216th St (Hainlin Mill Dr) just north of Homestead, go east on SW 216th under the Florida Turnpike to the northbound service road. Turn left onto the service road and park on the right. SW 216th St crosses the canal where Cave Swallows often can be found just southeast of the parking area.

Canaveral National Seashore

From I-95 near Titusville, take Exit 80 onto FL 406. Follow FL 406 east through Titusville and out onto the barrier island about 6 mi to where the road splits. Take the right fork (FL 402) and continue another 5 mi or so to the park entrance. Habitats include coastal scrub, tidal marsh, bay, dune, beach, and ocean. Florida Scrub-Jays are very tame in the area marked "Jay Nesting Area" located just past the entrance kiosk, and easily photographed if you have a little trail mix or a few bread crumbs to hold their attention.

Castellow Hammock Preserve

From the jct of US 1 (Dixie Highway) and SW 216th St (Hainlin Mill Dr) just north of Homestead, go west on SW 216th St to jct with SW 162nd Ave. Turn left (south) on 162nd Ave (Farmlife Rd). The park is on your left. Habitat is mesic hammock.

Cedar Keys National Wildlife Refuge

From just southwest of Gainesville on I-75, exit onto FL 24 (Archer Rd) W. Follow FL 24 about 50 mi until it dead-ends at the town of Cedar Key. The refuge comprises 13 offshore islands accessible only by boat, with limits at certain times of the year to protect breeding wading birds. Habitats include coastal scrub, beach, and open Gulf. Seahorse Key has the largest colonial bird nesting site in North Florida.

Chassahowitzka National Wildlife Refuge

Proceeding south on US 19 into the town of Crystal River, turn right on SE Paradise Point Rd (which becomes Kings Bay Dr). The refuge hq is located next to Port Paradise Resort, while the refuge itself is accessible only by boat. Canoes are available for rent, and it is a 4 mi paddle to the refuge boundary from the launch area. Habitats include bay, saltwater marsh, hardwood swamp, and estuary.

Clewiston

Located at the southwest end of Lake Okechobee on FL 80, the town of Clewiston has several airboat operators providing rides to see Snail Kites—advertised prominently along the highway.

Corkscrew Swamp Sanctuary

From the jct of FL 29 and FL 846 in Immokalee, go south on FL 846 about 3.5

mi to where FL 846 makes a 90-degree turn to the W. Continue west on FL 846 about 7 mi to jct with FL 849. Turn right (north) on FL 849 and follow signs to the sanctuary entrance. Habitats include old growth cypress bays and swamp.

Crews Lake County Park

From the town of Gowers Corner at the jct of US 41 and FL 52, proceed west on FL 52 a little more than 2 mi to jct with Shady Hill Rd. Turn right (north) on Shady Hill Rd. Go north on Shady Hills Rd about 3 mi to the turn-off on the right for the park and lake (Crews Lake Rd). Habitats include lake, lakeshore, cypress swamp, sand hills, and oak scrub.

Curtiss Parkway, Miami

From the jct of Fl 826 (Palmetto Expressway) and NW 36th St just west of the Miami International Airport, go east on NW 36th St about 2 mi to jct with Curtiss Parkway. Turn left (north) on Curtiss Parkway and go about 1 mi to jct with Navarre Drive. Nursing home grounds and trees in the Curtiss Parkway median harbor several parrot species.

Driggers Road

From the jct of US 27 and FL 621 in Lake Placid, go east on FL 621 about 6 mi to Driggers Rd. Habitat is wet prairie.

Dry Tortugas National Park

Accessible only by boat or seaplane from the town of Key West. For information, contact the park hq at (305) 242-2587. Habitats include coastal scrub, beach, and open ocean.

DuPuis Management Area

From the jct of US 441/98 and FL 76 at Port Mayaca on the east shore of Lake Okechobee, go east on FL 76 3.4 mi to the visitor center on the right (south) side of the road. Habitats include grassland, pine savanna, and ponds.

Easterlin Park

From the jct of I-95 and FL 816 (Exit 31 of I-95) in Fort Lauderdale, go east on FL 816 to jct with 9th Ave. Turn left (north) on NW 9th Ave and proceed to jct with NW 38th St. Turn left to enter the park.

Everglades National Park

There are five major visitor centers in the park: Ernest F. Coe in Florida City; Royal Palm just off FL 9336 at the east entrance to the park; Flamingo on Florida Bay at the south end of FL 9336; Shark Valley on the Tamiami Trail (FL

41), and Gulf Coast, located south of the town of Everglades on FL 29 on the west side of the park. Habitats include pine forest, hardwood hammocks, wet sawgrass prairies, cypress swamps, and mangrove forest.

Florida Caverns State Park

From I-10 just east of the town of Marianna, take Exit 21 onto FL 71 and go north about 2 mi to jct with US 90/FL 10. Turn left (west) on US 90/FL 10 and go about 1.7 mi to jct with FL 71. Turn right (north) on FL 71 and go about 3 mi to jct with FL 166 (Caverns Rd). Turn left on FL 166 and proceed about 3 mi to park entrance on the right. Habitats include pine and mixed hardwood forest and swamp.

Florida Keys National Wildlife Refuges

Four refuges comprise the Florida Keys National Wildlife Refuge complex: Great White Heron, National Key Deer, Key West, and Crocodile Lake (closed to the public). To find the park hq, go to Big Pine Key on US 1. Just east of Mile Marker 30 at the light at the jct of US 1, Chapman St, and Key Deer Blvd, go north on Key Deer Blvd 0.1 mi and turn right into the shopping center. The refuge hq is located in the southeast corner of the shopping center (look for the American flag outside the door). Habitats include beach, mangroves, salt marsh, ocean, pine scrub, and ponds.

Fort Caroline National Memorial/Timucuan Ecological and Historic Preserve

Just north of Jacksonville on I-95, take Exit 126A onto FL 9A going E. Proceed about 10.3 mi on FL 9A to the Merrill Rd exit. Turn left on Merrill Rd (becomes Ft. Caroline Rd) and follow signs 4.3 mi from there to Ft. Caroline. Habitats include hardwood hammock, scrub, and saltmarsh.

Fort De Soto County Park

From the jct of I-275 and FL 682 (Pinellas Bayway) in southern St. Petersburg, go west on Pinellas Bayway about 2 mi to jct with Fl 679. Turn left (south) on FL 679 and proceed to park entrance. Beach habitat is good for migrating shorebirds while shrubs and tree plantings attracts migrant songbirds.

Freedom Lake Park, St. Petersburg

From the jct of US 19 (34th St) and FL 694 (Park Blvd heading west, Gandy Blvd heading northeast) in St. Petersburg, go northwest on US 19 about 1.8 mi to jct with 49th St (FL 611). Turn right on 49th St, and go 0.2 mi to Lake Blvd. Turn right on Lake Blvd, and then make an *immediate* right again on 102nd Ave. Proceed 0.4 mi to the park on the right.

Gulf Islands National Seashore

From the jct of US 98 and US 90 in downtown Pensacola, follow US 98 south across the Pensacola Bay Bridge to where US 98 and FL 399 split. Follow FL 399 to the right across another bridge onto Santa Rosa Island. Turn right and follow FL 399 into the Seashore. Habitats include open beaches, dunes, freshwater marshes, and woodlands.

Hobe Sound National Wildlife Refuge

From the jct of FL 708/707 and US 1 in the town of Hobe Sound, go east on FL 707 about 1 mi out onto Jupiter Island. Turn left, and go north abut 2 mi to enter the refuge. The refuge hq is located about 2 mi south of the town of Hobe Sound on US 1. Habitats on the refuge include pine-oak scrub, mangrove swamp, coastal dunes, and beach.

Honeymoon Island State Park

From the jct of US 19 and FL 60 in Clearwater, go north on US 19 about 6 mi to jct with CR 586 (Curlew Rd). Turn left (west) on Curlew Rd and proceed to the park.

Hugh Taylor Birch State Park

From the jct of I-95 and FL 838 (Exit 30) in downtown Fort Lauderdale, go east on FL 838 (Sunrise Blvd) and follow signs about 4 mi to the park (on the left). Habitats include mesic hammock and slough.

Huguenot Memorial City Park, Jacksonville

From the jct of I-95 and FL 105 (Heckscher Dr) just north of Jacksonville, go east on FL 105 about 15 mi to the ferry crossing for FL A1A. Continue north on combined FL 105/FL A1A about 0.8 mi to a blinking light. Turn right (east) and proceed to the park.

J. N. "Ding" Darling National Wildlife Refuge

From the city of Fort Myers, go south on FL 867 about 15 mi and across the causeway onto Sanibel Island. Turn right on Periwinkle Way and follow signs to the refuge. Habitats include ponds, swales, mudflats, and mangrove swamp.

Jay B. Starkey Wilderness Park

From the jct of US 19 and FL 54 (Elfers) in New Port Richey, go east on FL 54 about 4.1 mi to jct with Little Rd (CR 1). Turn left (north) on Little Road and go 1.4 mi to jct with River Crossing Blvd. Turn right (east) on River Crossing Blvd and proceed about 2 mi to the park.

Jaycee Park

From the jct of FL 70 and US 441 in Okeechobee, go south on US 441 about 3 mi to jct with FL 78 at the lake (US 441 and US 98 go left). To reach the park, turn right (west) on FL 78 and then make an immediate left at the signed entrance. Habitats include lake, lakeshore, and willow thickets. Birds include Boat-tailed Grackles, Ring-billed Gulls, American Coots, and Common Moorhens. Another option is to turn left at the light at the jct of US 441 and FL 78, and follow US 441 east and then south along the east shore of the lake. Look for Crested Caracaras and Bald Eagles in the air or perched along this route.

Jonathan Dickinson State Park

From the town of Stuart, go south on US 1 for 12 mi to the entrance. Alternatively, follow the signs from I-95 (Exit 87A) or the Florida Turnpike (Exit 116). Florida Scrub-Jays are common here.

Kaliga Park

From the jct of FL 500 (13th St) and FL 523 (Vermont Ave) in downtown St. Cloud, go north on FL 523 about 1 mi to Lakeshore Blvd. Turn right on Lakeshore Blvd and go about 0.6 mi to the park entrance on the left. Habitats include lake, lakeshore, and marsh.

Kingsley Plantation

From the jct of I-95 and FL 105 (Heckscher Dr) just north of Jacksonville, go east on FL 105 about 16 mi to jct with Palmetto Ave on Fort George Island. Turn left (north) on Palmetto Ave and go about 2 mi to the plantation. Habitats include second growth scrub, parklands and woodlands.

Lake Adair

From the jct of I-4 and FL 50 (Colonial Dr) in downtown Orlando, go west on FL 50 about 0.2 mi to Edgewater Dr Turn right on Edgewater, and proceed about 0.4 mi to the lake.

Lake Apopka Restoration Area (Zellwood Farms)

At the jct of US 441 (Orange Blossom Trail) and Jones Rd on the north side of the town of Zellwood, go west on Jones Rd about 0.2 mi. Turn left to enter farms. Habitat is muddy farm fields from July to September.

Lake Arbuckle Nature Trail, Avon Park Air Force Range

From the jct of US 98 and FL 64 in downtown Avon Park, go east on FL 64 (Main St) about 10 mi to the entrance of the bombing range. Ask directions to the Natural Resources Office at the gate kiosk, where you can sign in and obtain a visitor's permit and map. From the Natural Resources Office, go north on Frostproof Rd about 1.1 mi and turn left. Proceed to parking area for trail and observation tower. Habitats include cypress swamp, oak hammock, and lakeshore.

Lake George

From the jct of FL 19 and FR 43 at the north end of the town of Salt Springs in the Ocala National Forest, turn right (east) on FR 43 and proceed northeast about 7 mi to the lake. Habitats are lake, lakeshore, and swamp.

Lake Kissimmee State Park

From the jct of US 27 and FL 60 in Lake Wales, go east on FL 60 (Hesperides Rd) about 9 mi to jct with Boy Scout Camp Rd. Turn left (north) on Boy Scout Camp Rd and go about 3.7 mi to a "T" at Camp Mack Rd. Turn right on Camp Mack Rd and go about 5.5 mi to the park entrance on the right. Habitats include marsh, swamp, and woodlands.

Lake Woodruff National Wildlife Refuge

At the jct of US 17 and Retta St in DeLeon Springs, go west on Retta St. Proceed 1 blk to jct with Grand Ave. Turn left (south) on Grand Ave and go about 1 mi to the refuge hq. Habitats include wet sawgrass prairie, freshwater marsh, hardwood swamp, and pine forest.

Lanark Reef

The reef is located about 1 mi offshore from the town of Lanark Village, and reachable only by boat.

Lettuce Lake Regional Park

At the jct of I-75 and CR 582 A (Fletcher Ave) east of Tampa, go west on CR 582 A about 1 mi to the park on your right.

Lower Suwannee National Wildlife Refuge

From the town of Chiefland, go south on US 98/19 about 4.5 mi to jct with FL 347. Turn right (west) on FL 347 and go about 14 mi to Fowler Bluff. Continue on FL 347 for another 1.5 mi to the refuge hq. Habitats include freshwater marsh, bottomland hardwood swamp, and pine woodlands, much of which is accessible only by boat.

Loxahatchee National Wildlife Refuge

From the jct of FL 804 and I-95 (Exit 44) at Boynton Beach, go west on FL 804 to jct with FL 441. Turn left (south) on FL 441 and go to jct with Lee Road. Turn right (west) on Lee Rd and proceed to refuge entrance.

McKay Bay Nature Park

From I-4 in Tampa, take Exit 2 (40th St). Go south on 40th St (merges with 39th St) about 0.3 mi to 7th Ave. Turn right on 7th Ave and go 0.3 mi to 34th St. Turn left on 34th St and proceed 0.4 mi to the sign for the entrance to the park on the left (immediately after crossing under the crosstown expressway). Habitats include mangroves, mesic hammock, and bayshore.

Merritt Island National Wildlife Refuge

From I-95 near Titusville, take Exit 80 onto FL 406. Follow FL 406 east through Titusville and out onto the barrier island about 6 mi to where the road splits. Take the right fork (FL 402) and continue another 1 mi or so to the refuge hq and visitor center. Habitats include coastal scrub, pine forest, dunes, estuary, and marshland. Birds include Roseate Spoonbill, Wood Stork, Tricolored Heron, Pied-billed Grebe, Blue-winged Teal, and many others.

Miccosukee Indian Restaurant

On the Tamiami Trail (US 41) west of Miami, go west from the jct of US 41 and FL 997 about 18 mi to the restaurant (and everglades wet prairies).

Myakka River State Park

From the jct of I-75 and FL 72 just east of Sarasota, take Exit 37 onto FL 72 E. Proceed east on FL 72 about 9 mi to a left turn for the park. Habitat is oak/palm woodlands, marsh, and ponds.

Okaloosa County Holding Ponds

From the jct of US 98 and FL 393 just west of Fort Walton Beach, go north on FL 393 about 2.3 mi to the jct with FL 189 (Beal Pkwy). Turn left on FL 189, and proceed about 2.5 mi to the intersection with Roberts Blvd. Turn left on Roberts Blvd and proceed about 0.5 mi to the ponds on the right. Habitat is sewage ponds.

Orange County Eastern Water Reclamation Facility

From the jct of FL 50 and Alafaya Trail (FL 434) east of Orlando, go south on Alafaya Trail about 3.3 mi to the entrance of the facility. Check in at the Operations and Control Bldg. Habitats are ponds and pond borders.

Oscar Scherer State Park

From the jct of US 41 (Tamiami Trail) and FL 681 in the town of Laurel, go north on US 41 about 0.6 mi to the entrance to the recreation area on the right.

Palm Point Park

From the jct of US 441 (NW 13th St) and FL 26 (University Ave) in Gainesville, go east on FL 26 about 4.6 mi to a split, with FL 26 going northeast and FL 329B continuing east. Go straight on FL 329B, and follow it to the park entrance.

Paynes Prairie State Preserve

From the jct of US 441 and FL 26 (University Ave) in Gainesville, proceed east on FL 26 to SE 15th St. Turn right on SE 15th St and go about 3 mi to the hq building for the Preserve. Habitats include marsh, swamp, grasslands, and open ponds.

Pine Island County Park

From the jct of US 19 and FL 550/FL 50 (Cortez Blvd) in Weeki Wachee, go west on FL 550/FL 50 about 5 mi to jct with FL 595. Turn right (north) on FL 595 and go about 2.4 mi to the park. Habitats include salt marsh and ocean.

Reddington Beach

From the jct of I-275 and FL 694 (Gandy Blvd/Park Blvd) in St. Petersburg, go west on FL 694 to "T" with FL 699 at the beach. Turn left (south). Road travels along Reddington Beach.

Sanibel Island

See J. N. "Ding" Darling National Wildlife Refuge.

Sawgrass Lake County Park

From the jct of US 19 (34th St) and FL 694 (Park Blvd heading W, Gandy Blvd heading NE) in St. Petersburg, go south on US 19 about 0.7 mi to jct with 62nd Ave. Turn left on 62nd Ave, and go 0.6 mi to 25th St. Turn left on 25th and proceed to the park and lake. Habitats include lake, lakeshore, oak hammocks, and swamp.

Sebastian Inlet State Recreation Area

From the jct of US 1 and FL 510 at Wabasso, go east on FL 510 about 2.5 mi out onto Orchid Island and the "T" with FL A1A. Turn left (north) on FL A1A, and go 7 mi to the recreation area. Habitats include beach, ocean, and jetties.

St. Andrews Bay State Recreation Area

Proceed west from Panama City on US 98 across Hathaway Bridge. Turn left (south) after crossing the bridge on FL 3031 and go about 3 mi to signs on the right for the recreation area entrance. Habitats include pine scrub, dunes, beach, longleaf pine savanna, freshwater ponds and marshes, saltwater marsh, and mudflats.

St. George Island State Park

At the jct of US 98 and CR 300 at Eastpoint, go south on CR 300 5 mi to "T." Turn left at the "T" and proceed to the park entrance. Habitats include pine flatwoods, beach, and dunes.

St. Joseph Peninsula State Park

Just south of Port St. Joe, follow FL 30 west when US 98 turns east. Proceed on west on FL 30 about 6 mi to where the road ends in a "T." Follow the right turn (FL 30E) and go about 7 mi to the park entrance.

St. Marks National Wildlife Refuge

From the Tallahassee loop road (US 319/FL261) south of Tallahassee, exit onto FL 363 south and go about 12.5 mi to the jct with US 98. Turn left (east) on US 98 and go about 2.6 mi to jct with FL 59. Turn right (south) on FL 59 and go about 3.5 mi to the refuge entrance.

St. Vincent National Wildlife Refuge

At the jct of US 98 and Main Street in downtown Apalachicola, go north on Main Street to the hq and visitor center on the right. The refuge is on an island accessible only by boat about 500 yards offshore from Apalachicola.

Tall Timbers Research Station

From the jct of I-10 and US 319/FL 61 (Thomasville Rd) just north of Tallahassee, exit onto US 319/FL 61 and proceed north about 13 mi to jct with FL 12. Turn left on FL 12, and go about 2.7 mi to the entrance to the station. Habitats include fields, pine plantations, and hardwood forest.

Three Lakes Wildlife Management Area, Lake Marian Highlands

From the jct of FL 91 (Florida Turnpike) and FL 523, go west on FL 523 to the town of Lake Marian Highlands (about 1 mi). Continue on FL 523 (now Canoe Creek Rd) as it bends to the N, and go about 5 mi to enter the management area. For the next 7 or 8 mi through the management area, the road passes through wet prairies, pastures, swamps, and woodlands.

Tropical Audubon Society Office

From the jct of SW 57th Ave (Red Rd) and SW 72nd St (Sunset Dr) in Miami, go east on Sunset Dr and look for the office on the right (south) side of the street.

Upper Tampa Bay Regional Park

From the jct of I-275 and US 92 (Mabry Ave) in downtown Tampa, go north on

US 92 about 3.5 mi to jct with FL 580 (Hillsborough Ave). Turn left on Hillsborough Ave and go about 8.3 mi to jct with Double Branch Rd. Turn left (south) on Double Branch Rd and go about 0.5 mi to the park on the right.

Venice Beach

From Exit 195 off I-75, go west on Laurel Rd. Proceed 1.5 mi to jct with Albee Farm Rd. Turn left (south) onto Albee Farm Rd. Go 3.4 mi south on Albee Farm Rd (joins Venice Bypass en route) to jct with Venice Ave. Turn right (west) on Venice Ave and go 1.6 mi to the beach.

Vilano Beach Boat Ramp

From the jct of FL 5A (San Marco Ave) and FL A1A (May St) in St. Augustine, go east on A1A and watch for the boat ramp on your right. Habitats include mudflats and salt marsh.

Wakulla Springs State Park

From the Tallahassee loop road (US 319/FL261) south of Tallahassee, exit onto FL 61S and go about 10 mi to signs for the park entrance on the left.

Wekiwa Springs State Park

From the jct of I-4 and FL 434 north of Orlando, go west on FL 434 about 1 mi to a split in the road, with FL 434 going straight west and Wekiwa Springs Rd going northwest. Bear right on Wekiwa Springs Rd and continue about 3.7 mi to the park on your right.

West Beach Drive

From the jct of US 98 (18th St) and US Business Route 98 (Beck Ave) in downtown Panama City, go south on US Business Route 98 until it turns left and becomes West Beach Dr Park at James R. Asbell Park (The Salt Works) and scan the beach shore for shorebirds and the bay for ducks, grebes, terns, gulls, etc.

Georgia (45)

Altamaha River/Atkinson Tract

"Take US 341 north from Brunswick toward Jesup and, in the town of Everett (15 miles northwest of I-95, 20.3 miles southeast of Jesup), turn right onto Altamaha Road. A large sign, legible ONLY from the other side, reads 'Altamaha Fish Camp.' Altamaha Road leads to the Altamaha River, where an abandoned railroad trestle and tracks provide good trails. . . . To reach the Atkinson Tract, proceed as above but follow Altamaha Road for 3.1 miles, turning right on Pennick Road, a dirt road marked with a sign reading 'Atkinson Tract, GA

Game and Fish Management Area.'" (Hitt and Blackshaw 1996:17). Habitats include river bottomland, swamp, cypress bays, second growth, old fields, and farmland.

Arrowhead Public Fishing Area

From the jct of US 27 (Martha Berry Blvd) and GA 20 (Turner-McCall) in downtown Rome, go north on Martha Berry Blvd 11 mi to jct with GA 156 (Rosedale Rd). Turn right onto GA 156 and proceed 2.4 mi to jct with Floyd Springs Rd. Turn left on Floyd Springs Rd and go about 2 mi to the Arrowhead Public Fishing Area parking lot on the right. Habitats include dikes and ponds.

Beaverdam Wildlife Management Area

The Beaverdam Wildlife Management Area occurs in three separate blocks along the Oconee River. One section can be reached by going northwest from the jct of US 441 and US 80 in Dublin on US 441 about 4.4 mi to a "Y" where the road splits. US 441 is the left fork. Follow the right fork (Old Toomsboro Rd) about 7.5 mi to a road branching off to the right (northeast). Turn right and continue 1.5 mi to the entrance to the wildlife management area on the left. Habitat is hardwood swamp.

Blackbeard Island National Wildlife Refuge

Located about 18 mi from Shellman's Bluff, the refuge is accessible only by boat. Private boat launch available at Barbour River Landing, Harris Neck National Wildlife Refuge, or check at the hq of the Savannah Coastal Refuges office (tel. [912] 652-4415) for information on charter service. Habitats include oak forest, salt marsh, freshwater marsh, beach, bay, and ocean.

Black Rock Mountain State Park

From the jct of US 76 and US 441 in the northeast Georgia town of Clayton, go north on US 441 about 3 mi to the signed turnoff for the park to the left on Black Rock Mountain Parkway. Habitat is principally northern hardwood forest.

Brasstown Bald

From the jct of US 76 and US 19/US 129 in Blairsville, go south on US 19/US 129 about 9 mi to jct with GA 180. Turn left (east) on GA 180 and go about 9 mi to where GA 180 Spur goes off to the left, marked by a sign for Brasstown Bald. Take GA 180 Spur about 3 mi to the top of Brasstown Bald. Habitat is mixed deciduous and coniferous forest.

Chattahoochee River and Nature Center

From the jct of I-285 and US 19/GA400 north of Atlanta, go north on US 19/ GA 400 about 5 mi to the Northridge exit. Go west on Northridge about 0.5 mi until it meets Roswell Rd. Turn right (north) on Roswell and proceed 1.6 mi to jct with Azalea Dr. Turn left (west) on Azalea and proceed to jct with Willeo Rd. Turn left on Willeo and proceed to the nature center.

Chickamauga and Chattanooga National Military Park

The Chickamauga Visitor Center is located on US 27 in Fort Oglethorpe, Georgia. Habitats include pine, oak, and hickory forest, second growth, and grassland.

Cloudland Canyon State Park

From I-59 at the northwest Georgia town of Trenton, take Exit 2 onto GA 136 and go east about 8 mi to signs for the park entrance. The principal habitat is mixed hardwood–pine forest.

Crockford-Pigeon Mountain Wildlife Management Area

From the jct of GA 193 and US 27 BUS in LaFayette, go west on GA 193 about 3 mi to jct with Chamberlain Rd. Turn left (south) on Chamberlain Rd and go about 3.6 mi to a right turn that enters the wildlife management area.

Crooked River State Park

From the jct of I-95 and GA 40 at Kingsland, go east on GA 40 about 6 mi to left turn on GA 40 Spur. Turn left (north) on GA 40 Spur, and go about 7 mi to signs for the park entrance. Habitats include coastal woodlands, bayshore, tidal marsh, and open bay.

Cumberland Island National Seashore

From the jct of I-95 and GA 40 at Kingsland, go east on GA 40 about 8 mi to signs for the National Seashore visitor center in downtown St. Marys. Information can be obtained here about times and location for departure of the park service ferry to the island. Cumberland Island is located 7 mi east of St. Marys across the bay. Habitats include mudflats, oyster beds, beach, tidal marsh, freshwater marsh, and oak woodlands.

Fort Mountain State Park

From the town of Chatsworth in northwest Georgia, go east on GA 52 about 8 mi to signs for the park. Habitats include deciduous forest, lake, and lakeshore.

Fort Pulaski National Monument

From the Georgia coastal city of Savannah, follow US 80 east about 20 mi to signs marking the entrance of the national monument. Habitats include tidal marsh, bayshore, and bay.

Fort Yargo State Park

From the north-central Georgia town of Winder, go south 1 mi on GA 81 to signs for the park. Habitats include mesophytic deciduous forest, lake, and freshwater marsh.

George L. Smith State Park

From the town of Twin City in southeast Georgia, go south on GA 23 about 4 mi to signs for the park entrance. Habitats include cypress bays and ponds.

Grand Bay Wildlife Management Area

From I-75 in Valdosta, take Exit 16 onto US 84 East. Proceed east on US 84 about 2.4 mi to jct of US 84 and US 221. Turn left (north) on US 221 (Ashley St) and proceed 1.7 mi to where US 221 splits. Turn right to continue on US 221 north and go 8.2 mi to the signed entrance on the left for the wildlife management area. Habitats include hardwood and pine forest, swamp, and marsh.

Harris Neck National Wildlife Refuge

From I-95, take Exit 67 (South Newport) to US 17 S. Turn left and go 1 mi on US 17 to jct with Harris Neck Rd. Turn left (east) on Harris Neck Rd and go 6.4 mi to the refuge entrance. Habitats include saltwater marsh, freshwater impoundments, mixed deciduous forest, and open fields.

Jekyll Island

From I-95 south of Brunswick, exit east onto US 17/GA 520. Continue east about 5 mi to a split, with US 17 going north and GA 520 continuing southeast. Follow GA 520 (Jekyll Island Causeway) abut 6 mi to Jekyll Island. Habitats include beach, ocean, salt marsh, and mixed pine-oak woodland.

Lake Sidney Lanier

There are many access points to the lake following most roads leading north or west out of Gainesville (e.g., GA 53, GA 60, or US 129). Habitat is lake and lakeshore.

Laura S. Walker State Park

From the jct of US 82 and US 84 in Waycross, go east on US 82 about 8 mi to jct with GA 177. Turn right (south) on GA 177 and follow signs to the park entrance. Habitats include lake, lakeshore, farm fields, and pine forest.

Moccasin Creek State Park

From the jct of US 76 and US 441 in Clayton, go west on US 76 about 12 mi to jct GA 197. Turn left (south) on GA 197 and proceed to park entrance. Habitats include lake, lakeshore, and deciduous forest.

Newcomer Treatment Facility

"Follow US 129 south through downtown Fitzgerald (south-central Georgia), passing several restaurants and shopping centers. Turn right half a mile past the Wal-Mart, at the sign for the facility. Continue past the main building and treatment site and park on the side of the road." (Hopkins et al. in Hitt and Blackshaw 1996:99–100).

Newman Wetlands Center, Atlanta

On I-75 south of Atlanta, take Exit 77 south onto US 19/US 41 (Tara Blvd). Proceed south on US 19/US 41 about 8.2 mi to jct with Freeman Rd. Turn left on Freeman Rd and go about 2 mi to the wetlands center at 2755 Freeman Rd (Wed–Sun, 8:30–5). Habitats include woods, pond, wetland, and feeders.

Ocmulgee National Monument

From the jct of I-75 and I-16 in Macon, go east on I-16 to Exit 2 (Coliseum Exit) and follow signs for the monument about 1.6 mi to the entrance. Habitats include open fields, freshwater wetlands, swamps, canebrakes, oxbow lakes, and forests.

Okefenokee National Wildlife Refuge

From the town of Folkston, follow GA 121/23 south about 7 mi to jct with Okefenokee Parkway. Turn right (west) onto the parkway and follow signs to the visitor center.

Patterson Gap Road

From the jct of US 441 and Betty Creek Rd in the town of Dillard, go west on Betty Creek Rd about 3.5 mi to jct with Patterson Gap Rd. Turn left (south) on Patterson Gap Rd. Habitat is highland hardwood forest and second growth.

Piedmont National Wildlife Refuge

From I-75, 25 mi north of Macon take Exit 61 in Forsyth onto Juliette Rd. Proceed east on Juliette Rd 18 mi to the visitor center. Habitats include loblolly pine, mixed forest, bottomland forest, beaver swamp, freshwater impoundments, and streams.

Rabun Bald

At the jct of US 441 and GA 246 just north of the town of Dillard, go right on GA 246 and proceed about 4 mi to a 3–way intersection. Turn right toward Sky Valley resort. Go about 3 mi to jct with Old Rabun Bald Rd. Turn right onto Old Rabun Bald Rd, and proceed about 0.3 mi to pull-offs. The top of Rabun Bald is about a 1.5 mi walk from here continuing up the unimproved road.

Reed Bingham State Park

From I-75, take Exit 10 at Adel onto GA 37. Go west on GA 37 about 6 mi to signs for the park entrance. Habitats include longleaf pine savanna, cypress swamp, lake, lakeshore, pitcher plant bog, and sand dunes.

Rum Creek Wildlife Management Area

From I-75 just north of Macon, take Exit 55 N on US 23/GA 87. Continue north on US 23/GA 87 about 12 mi to Percale and the turnoff on the left for the management area. Habitats include fields, mixed forest, lake, lakeshore, marshes, and impoundments.

Sapelo Island National Estuarine Research Reserve

Accessible only by boat. Visitor center and ferry dock are located in the town of Meridian, 8 mi north of Darien on GA 99. Habitats on the barrier island include upland oak forest, salt marsh, bay, bayshore, dunes, and beach.

Savannah National Wildlife Refuge

From I-95 just north of Savannah, take Exit 109 onto GA 21/30. Go south (left) on GA 21/30 about 2.7 mi to where GA 30 turns left. Follow GA 30 left 0.8 mi into Port Wentworth and turn left at jct with GA 25 (Coastal Hwy). Follow GA 25 about 3.3 mi to the refuge (GA 25 becomes SC 170 when it crosses into South Carolina). Habitat is freshwater impoundments, freshwater marsh, tidal creeks, and bottomland hardwood forest and swamp.

Seminole State Park

From the jct of US 84 and GA 253 in Bainbridge, go southwest on GA 253 about 23 mi to the sign for the park entrance. Habitats include lake, lakeshore, grassland, and freshwater marsh.

Skidaway Island State Park

Take Exit 34 from I-16 in Savannah onto DeRenne Ave. Turn right on Waters Ave and proceed to Diamond Causeway. Follow Diamond Causeway to signs for the park entrance. Habitats include fresh and saltwater marshes, oak woodlands, and longleaf pine savanna.

South Brunswick River

From I-95 near the town of Brunswick, take Exit 29. Go west 0.3 mi on US 82 to jct with GA 303. Go north 1.1 mi on GA 303 to the South Brunswick causeway. Parking available on the left (west) side of the road.

Stephen C. Foster State Park

From the jct of US 441 and GA 177 in Edith, go north on GA 177 about 18 mi to the park entrance. Habitats include freshwater marsh, bayou, cypress bays, oak woodlands, and longleaf pine savanna.

St. Simons Island

"Start at the intersection of US 17 and the Torras Causeway [near Brunswick]. Pay a nominal toll fee at the booth and drive across the Torras Causeway about 4 miles to the island. Take the first right, King's Way. At the second traffic light, where the road becomes Ocean Boulevard, turn right onto Mallery Street. Park at the end of Mallery Street and walk to the picnic area on the left, where a colony of Gray Kingbird nests in the oaks during spring and summer." (Hitt and Blackshaw 1996:17–18). Habitats include oak forest, residential, dune, beach, ocean, bay, and bayshore.

Sweetwater Creek State Conservation Park

Proceeding west on I-20 from Atlanta, take Exit 12 at Thornton Rd. Turn left and go about 0.2 mi to Blairs Bridge Rd. Turn right on Blairs Bridge Rd, go about 2 mi, then left on Mount Vernon Rd, and proceed to signs for the park entrance. Habitats include lake, lakeshore, grassland, and deciduous woodland.

Tybee Island Beach

From the jct of I-16 and I-516 in Savannah, go east on I-16 to the GA 204 exit. Follow GA 204 (east on 37th St, then south on Abercorn) to jct with US 80 (Victory Dr). Turn left (east) on US 80 and go about 20 mi to its end on Tybee Island. Habitats are beach and ocean.

Unicoi Gap

From the north Georgia town of Helen, go north on GA 75 about 10 mi to the parking lot at the crest of the gap. Access to the Appalachian Trail can be gained here. Habitat is highland deciduous forest.

Vogel State Park

From the north Georgia town of Blairsville, go south on US 19/129 about 11 mi to signs for the park entrance. Habitats include highland deciduous forest, lake, and lakeshore.

Wassaw National Wildlife Refuge

Located about 10 mi southeast of Savannah and accessible only by boat. Contact the main office of the Savannah Coastal Refuges for information on marinas providing charters (1000 Business Center Dr, Suite 10, Savannah, GA 31405; tel. [912] 652-4415). Habitats include fresh and saltwater marshes, oak woodlands, beach, dunes, and ocean.

Watson Mill Bridge State Park

From the town of Comer, go east on GA 72 about 4 mi to a sign marking the turnoff on the right for the park. Habitat is bottomland forest.

Wolf Island National Wildlife Refuge

Located about 5 mi east of Darien and accessible only by boat. Contact the main office of the Savannah Coastal Refuges for information on marinas providing charters (1000 Business Center Dr, Suite 10, Savannah, GA 31405; tel. [912] 652-4415). Habitats include fresh and saltwater marshes, oak woodlands, beach, dunes, and ocean.

Mississippi (41)

Arkabutla Lake

From the jct of I-55 and CR 304 at Hernando, take Exit 280 west. Follow CR 304 about 10 mi to jct with CR 301 in Eudora. Turn left (south) on CR 301 and proceed to jct with Pratt Rd. Turn left (east) on Pratt Rd., and go to lake. Habitats include lake, grassy margin, deciduous woodlands, and beaver swamp.

Black Creek Trail

From the town of Wiggins, go northeast on MS 29 about 12 mi to Janice Landing on the north side of the MS 29 bridge across Black Creek. The Black Creek trailhead is located off MS 29 about 0.5 mi south of the Black Creek bridge. There is a parking area there as well.

Bogue Chitto National Wildlife Refuge

From the jct of I-10 and I-59 at Slidell, Louisiana, go north on I-59 for 3 mi to jct with LA 41. Go north on LA 41 and access the refuge at locks 1, 2, or 3. Habitat is bottomland hardwoood and mixed forest, sloughs, and bayous along the Pearl River, which here forms the border between Louisiana and Mississippi.

Buccaneer State Park

From Gulfport, go west on US 90 about 19 mi to Waveland, and follow signs about 2 mi west from there to the park. Though the area is developed, there are some habitat remnants that include small areas of beach, tidal marsh, and woodlands.

Chewalla Lake, Holly Springs National Forest

From the jct of MS 349 and US 78 in Potts Camp, go west on US 78 about 5.4 mi to Exit 37 onto GA 178, and follow signs to Chewalla Lake. Habitats are lake, lakeshore, and bottomland hardwoods.

Clarkco State Park

From Meridian, proceed south on US 45 about 20 mi to a sign marking the turnoff for the park. Principal habitats are lake and lakeshore.

Clear Springs Lake, Homochitto National Forest

From the town of Bude, go west on US 84 about 7 mi to a sign marking the turnoff for Clear Springs Lake. Turn left (south) on CR 104 and go 3.8 mi to the lake. Habitats include lake, lakeshore, and pine forest.

Cypress Swamp, Natchez Trace Parkway

The scenic parkway runs from Natchez (Mile 0) on the Mississippi River north through Jackson and Tupelo to Nashville, Tennessee. Habitats include farm fields, upland pine and mixed forest, bottomland hardwoods, and cypress swamps. Cypress Swamp is at Mile 122.0 near Jackson.

Dahomey National Wildlife Refuge

From the jct of MS 8 and US 61 in Cleveland, go south on US 61 about 3 mi to the jct of MS 446 and US 61 in Boyle. Turn right (west) on MS 446 and proceed 10 mi to the refuge, which lines both sides of MS 446 for about 3 mi. Habitats include bottomland hardwood forest, farm fields, and second growth.

Donivan Slough, Natchez Trace Parkway

The scenic parkway runs from Natchez (Mile 0) on the Mississippi River north through Jackson and Tupelo to Nashville, Tennessee. Habitats include farm fields, upland pine and mixed forest, bottomland hardwoods, and cypress swamps. Donivan Slough is at Mile 283.3 near Tupelo.

Freedom Hills Overlook, Natchez Trace Parkway

The scenic parkway runs from Natchez (Mile 0) on the Mississippi River north through Jackson and Tupelo to Nashville, Tennessee. Habitats include farm fields, upland pine and mixed forest, bottomland hardwoods, and cypress swamps. Freedom Hills Overlook is at Mile 317.0 near Tishomingo in the northeast corner of the state.

Grand Bay National Wildlife Refuge

Located about 10 mi east of Pascagoula, take I-10 to exit 75 and go south on Franklin Creek Rd for 1.7 mi. Turn left to cross railroad tracks. Then turn right onto Bayou Heron Rd and go about 1 mi to the refuge hq at 6005 Bayou Heron Rd.

Gulf Islands National Seashore

From the town of Ocean Springs, proceed east on US 90, and follow signs to the Seashore Visitor Center. Mainland habitats include bayous and salt marshes. The Gulf islands are available by boat. Inquire at the visitor center for fees and departure sites and times. Island habitats include, beach, dune, salt marsh, and woodlands.

Gulf Marine State Park

Going west on US 90 across the bridge from Ocean Springs, turn left (south) at the first light west of the bridge onto Myrtle St. Follow Myrtle St. to the bay.

Hillside National Wildlife Refuge

From Yazoo City, go north on US 49E about 13 mi to the refuge, located on the east side of the road. Habitats include farm fields and bottomland hardwoods interspersed with cypress-tupelo pools.

Hugh White State Park

From the jct of I-55 and MS 8 at Grenada, take MS 8 about 5 mi east to the park entrance. The park provides access to Grenada Lake.

J. P. Coleman State Park

From the jct of US 72 and MS 25 south of Iuka, go north on MS 25 about 15 mi to the turnoff for the park. Principal habitats are lake and lakeshore (the Pickwick Lake reservoir on the Tennessee River).

John W. Kyle State Park

From the jct of I-55 and MS 315 (Exit 252) at Sardis, exit east onto MS 315 and follow signs to the park.

Leaf Wilderness, De Soto National Forest

On US 98, about 35 mi northwest of Mobile, exit onto MS 198 to McClain (following signs for MS 57S). Follow MS 198 1.6 mi (through McClain) to the turn-off for MS 57S. Proceed south on MS 57 about 7 mi to parking lot on the left for the Leaf River Wilderness Trailhead. Habitats include upland pine and mixed hardwood forest, bottomland hardwoods, swamp, and river.

Legion State Park

From the town of Louisville, take North Columbus Ave (Old Hwy 25) north about 2 mi to the turnoff for the park. Habitats include lake, lakeshore, and pine forest.

Mathews Brake National Wildlife Refuge

From the jct of US 82 and US 49E in Greenwood, go south on US 49E to Sidon. Turn left (east) at Sidon and proceed about 3 mi to the refuge. Habitats include an oxbow lake and bottomland hardwoods.

Mississippi Sandhill Crane National Wildlife Refuge

Proceeding east on I-10 from Biloxi, take the next exit (61, Gautier-Van Cleave Rd), and go north about 0.5 mi to the turnoff for the Visitor Center. Habitats include pine savanna, scrub, forested bottomlands, and tidal marsh.

Morgan Brake National Wildlife Refuge

From the jct of US 82 and US 49E in Greenwood, go south on US 49E about 21 mi to the refuge (east side of road). Habitats include farm fields, sloughs, cane-brakes, and bottomland hardwoods.

Natchez State Park

From the jct of US 65 and US 61 in Natchez, go north (actually northeast) on US 61 about 10 mi to the turnoff for the park (east side of road). Main habitats are lake and lakeshore with some surrounding hardwood forest.

Natchez Trace Parkway

The scenic parkway runs from Natchez (Mile 0) on the Mississippi River north through Jackson and Tupelo to Nashville, Tennessee. Habitats include farm fields, upland pine and mixed forest, bottomland hardwoods, and cypress swamps.

Noxubee National Wildlife Refuge

From Starkville, follow MS 12 to Oktoc Road. Turn south on Oktoc, and follow signs for 17 mi or so to the refuge hq. Habitats include pine savanna, farm fields, bottomland hardwoods, cypress-tupelo bays, lakes, and streams.

Panther Swamp National Wildife Refuge

From Yazoo City, proceed northwest on 49W about 2 mi to River Rd. Turn left (south) on River Rd and go about 6 mi to the refuge hq. Habitats include bottomland hardwood forest, cypress bays, and farm fields.

Pearl River Waterfowl Refuge

From the jct of I-55 and the Natchez Trace Parkway just north of Jackson, go north on the parkway 13 mi to jct with MS 43. Turn right (east) on MS 43 to enter the refuge, which is located on the north side of MS 43, on the west side of Ross Barnett Reservoir. Refuge habitats include impoundments, lake, marsh, and lakeshore.

Pharr Mounds, Natchez Trace Parkway

See instructions for Natchez Trace Parkway. Pharr Mounds is located at Mile 286.7 along the parkway. Habitat is open grassland.

Roosevelt State Park

From the jct of US 20 and MS 481 south of Morton, exit north onto MS 481 and follow signs to the park.

Shepard State Park

From Pascagoula, proceed about 3 mi west on US 90 to Ladnier Road. Turn left (south) on Ladnier and follow signs to park. Habitats are pine-oak woodlands and salt marsh.

St. Catherine Creek National Wildlife Refuge

From Natchez, proceed south on US 61 about 10 mi to York Rd. Turn right (west) on York Rd, and go 2 mi to the refuge entrance. Habitats include cypress bays, bottomland hardwoods, farm fields, second growth, and beaver swamp.

Tallahatchie National Wildlife Refuge

Bear Lake Unit

From Grenada, go west on MS 8 about 19 mi to the Grenada/Tallahatchie county line. The refuge lines MS 8 for the next 2 mi, going west. Habitats include old fields, farmland, bayous, and hardwood bottomland forest.

Black Bayou Unit

From the jct of MS 32 and MS 35 in Charleston, go north on MS 35 about 2 mi to Paducah Wells Rd. Turn left (west) on Paducah Wells Rd and proceed to a "T" at the Panola-Quitman Floodway Levee Rd. Turn right (north) on the levee road and go 3 mi. The refuge lies along the west side of the levee.

Tenn-Tom Waterway, Natchez Trace Parkway

The scenic parkway runs from Natchez (Mile 0) on the Mississippi River north through Jackson and Tupelo to Nashville, Tennessee. Habitats include farm fields, upland pine and mixed forest, bottomland hardwoods, and cypress swamps. The Tenn-Tom Waterway is at Mile 293.2, about 30 mi northeast of Tupelo.

Tombigbee State Park

In the town of Tupelo, take the Veterans Blvd exit from US 78. Proceed south on MS 6 about 5 mi, following signs to the park turnoff. Turn and go about 3 mi to the park entrance. Principal habitats are lake, lakeshore, and upland hardwoods.

Trace State Park

From Tupelo, proceed west on MS 6 about 10 mi to the turnoff (to the north) for the park on CR 65. Habitats are lake, lakeshore, and woodlands.

US 90 between Gulfport and Biloxi

The beach bordering the highway on its southern side is home to a variety of shorebirds.

Vicksburg National Military Park

From I-20, take Vicksburg exit 4B and follow Clay St (US 80) west 0.2 mi to the park entrance. Habitats include hardwood forest, riparian forest, second growth, river, and open fields.

Wall Doxey State Park

From the town of Holly Springs, go south on MS 7 about 6 mi to signs for the park entrance. Habitats include cypress swamp, lake, lakeshore, beaver swamp, and bottomland hardwood forest.

West Ship Island

The island is accessible only by boat. A ferry can be taken from Gulfport Yacht Harbor (jct of US 90 and US 49 in the town of Gulfport) (see Vaughan 1994:112 for details). Habitats include fresh and saltwater marshes, ponds, and beaches.

Yazoo National Wildlife Refuge

From Greenville, proceed south on MS 1 about 22 mi to the signed turnoff to the left (east) for the refuge hq. Habitats include bottomland hardwoods, farm fields, and cypress bays.

Credits

Photographers' names are followed by the species for which they provided photos.

Vernon E. Grove Jr.: Fulvous Whistling Duck, Greater White-fronted Goose, Brant, Tundra Swan, Mallard, Mottled Duck, Northern Shoveler, Northern Pintail, Ruddy Duck, Ruffed Grouse, Wild Turkey, Northern Bobwhite, Pied-billed Grebe, Eared Grebe, Brown Booby, Northern Gannet, Anhinga, American Bittern, Yellow-crowned Night-Heron, Great Blue Heron, Great Egret, Snowy Egret, Little Blue Heron, Tricolored Heron, Cattle Egret, White Ibis, Roseate Spoonbill, Wood Stork, Turkey Vulture, Osprey, Bald Eagle, Swainson's Hawk, Red-tailed Hawk, King Rail, Sora, Purple Gallinule, Common Moorhen, American Coot, Sandhill Crane, Whooping Crane, Black-bellied Plover, American Golden-Plover, Snowy Plover, Semipalmated Plover, Killdeer, American Oystercatcher, American Avocet, Lesser Yellowlegs, Spotted Sandpiper, Whimbrel, Long-billed Curlew, Marbled Godwit, Ruddy Turnstone, Short-billed Dowitcher, Common Snipe, Wilson's Phalarope, Red-necked Phalarope, Great Black-backed Gull, Caspian Tern, Royal Tern, Sandwich Tern, Black Skimmer, Rock Pigeon, Smooth-billed Ani, Barn Owl, Great Horned Owl, Burrowing Owl, Barred Owl, Short-eared Owl, Common Nighthawk, Belted Kingfisher, Red-headed Woodpecker, Red-bellied Woodpecker, Eastern Phoebe, Vermilion Flycatcher, Eastern Kingbird, Scissor-tailed Flycatcher, Horned Lark, Loggerhead Shrike, Barn Swallow, Marsh Wren, Eastern Bluebird, Northern Mockingbird, European Starling, Vesper Sparrow, Savannah Sparrow, White-crowned Sparrow, Red-winged Blackbird, Brewer's Blackbird, Eastern Meadowlark, Common Grackle, Brown-headed Cowbird, Evening Grosbeak, House Sparrow

David F. Parmelee: Long-tailed Duck, Red-throated Loon, Red Knot, Least Sandpiper, White-rumped Sandpiper, Baird's Sandpiper, Pectoral Sandpiper, Stilt Sandpiper, American Woodcock, Red Phalarope, Glaucous Gull

John H. Rappole: Black-bellied Whistling Duck, Muscovy Duck, Gadwall, American Black Duck, Blue-winged Teal, Canvasback, Bufflehead, Common Goldeneye, Common Merganser, Plain Chachalaca, Double-crested Cormorant, Magnificent Frigatebird, Reddish Egret, Black Vulture, Swallow-tailed Kite, White-tailed Kite, Red-shouldered Hawk, Crested Caracara, Wilson's Plover, Piping Plover, Willet, Upland Sandpiper, Sanderling, Buff-breasted Sandpiper, Laughing Gull, Ring-billed Gull, Gull-billed Tern, Forster's Tern, Sooty Tern, Brown Noddy, Eurasian Collared-Dove, White-winged Dove, Groove-billed Ani, Chimney Swift, Ruby-throated Hummingbird, Black-chinned Hummingbird, Rufous Hummingbird, Downy Woodpecker, Hairy Woodpecker, Eastern Wood-Pewee, Acadian Flycatcher, Great Crested Flycatcher, Florida Scrub-Jay, American Crow, Fish Crow, Common Raven, Purple Martin, Tree Swallow, Northern Rough-winged Swallow, House Wren, Carolina Chickadee, Tufted Titmouse, White-breasted Nuthatch, Brown-headed Nuthatch, American Robin, Cedar Waxwing, Pine Warbler, Eastern Towhee, American Tree Sparrow, Grasshopper Sparrow, Song Sparrow, White-throated Sparrow, Dark-eyed Junco, Bobolink, Boat-tailed Grackle, Purple Finch, House Finch, American Goldfinch

Barth Schorre: Snow Goose, Canada Goose, Wood Duck, American Wigeon, Green-winged Teal, Redhead, Ring-necked Duck, Hooded Merganser, American White Pelican, Brown Pelican, Green Heron, Black-crowned Night-Heron, Greater Flamingo, Black-necked Stilt, Greater Yellowlegs, Herring Gull, Black-legged Kittiwake, Least Tern, Ringed Turtle-Dove, Mourning Dove, Common Ground-Dove, Yellow-billed Cuckoo, Eastern Screech-Owl, Pileated Woodpecker, Alder Flycatcher, White-eyed Vireo, Bell's Vireo, Yellow-throated Vireo, Blue-headed Vireo, Warbling Vireo, Red-eyed Vireo, Blue Jay, American Bittern, Carolina Wren, Veery, Gray-cheeked Thrush, Swainson's Thrush, Hermit Thrush, Wood Thrush, Gray Catbird, Brown Thrasher, Blue-winged Warbler, Golden-winged Warbler, Tennessee Warbler, Nashville Warbler, Northern Parula, Yellow Warbler, Chestnut-sided Warbler, Magnolia Warbler, Yellow-rumped Warbler, Black-throated Green Warbler, Blackburnian Warbler, Yellow-throated Warbler, Prairie Warbler, Palm Warbler, Bay-breasted Warbler, Blackpoll Warbler, Cerulean Warbler, Black-and-white Warbler, American Redstart, Prothonotary Warbler, Worm-eating Warbler, Ovenbird, Northern Waterthrush, Louisiana Waterthrush, Kentucky Warbler, Mourning Warbler, Common Yellowthroat, Hooded Warbler, Wilson's Warbler, Canada Warbler, Yellow-breasted Chat, Summer Tanager, Scarlet Tanager, Western Tanager, Chipping Sparrow, Clay-colored Sparrow, Lark Sparrow, Lincoln's Sparrow, Northern Cardinal, Rose-breasted Grosbeak, Blue Grosbeak, Indigo Bunting, Painted Bunting, Dickcissel, Yellow-headed Blackbird, Orchard Oriole, Baltimore Oriole, Pine Siskin

VIREO (Academy of Natural Sciences): G. Armistead, Audubon's Shearwater; S. Bahrt, Black Scoter; G. Bailey, Black-throated Blue Warbler; R. & N. Bowers,

Greater Scaup, Franklin's Gull, Whip-poor-will, Yellow-bellied Flycatcher, Sprague's Pipit; J. Cameron, Bachman's Sparrow; B. Chudleigh, Bridled Tern; H. Clarke, Red-breasted Merganser, Black Rail, Cave Swallow; P. Craig-Cooper, Glossy Ibis; H. Cruickshank, Least Bittern; R. Curtis, Horned Grebe, Virginia Rail, Monk Parakeet, Black-hooded Parakeet, Lesser Nighthawk, Black-whiskered Vireo, Golden-crowned Kinglet, Henslow's Sparrow, LeConte's Sparrow; J. Dunning, Solitary Sandpiper, Yellow-chevroned Parakeet, Connecticut Warbler, Shiny Cowbird; S. Faccio, Bicknell's Thrush; C. H. Greenewalt, Budgerigar, Red-whiskered Bulbul; B. Henry, Brown Creeper; S. Holt, Mississippi Kite, Red-crowned Parrot; M. Hyett, Gray Kingbird; K. Karlson, Orange-crowned Warbler; J. Lang, Common Loon, Willow Flycatcher, Field Sparrow; F. Lanting, Peregrine Falcon; Greg W. Lasley, Cory's Shearwater, Sooty Shearwater; P. La-Tourrette, Western Kingbird; S. Maka, Red-cockaded Woodpecker; G. McElroy, American Pipit; A. Morris, Lesser Scaup, Merlin, Northern Flicker, Parasitic Jaeger, Lesser Black-backed Gull, Roseate Tern, Black Tern, Cape May Warbler, Rusty Blackbird; A. & E. Morris, Ash-throated Flycatcher; J. P. Myers, Pomarine Jaeger; J. P. O'Neill, Red-masked Parakeet; T. Pederson, White-winged Parakeet; R. L. Pitman, Greater Shearwater, Leach's Storm-Petrel, Band-rumped Storm-Petrel; M. J. Ruzon, Sooty Tern; R. Saldino, Black-capped Petrel, White-crowned Pigeon; C. R. Sams, II, Yellow Rail; K. Schafer, Black Noddy; F. K. Schleicher, White-tailed Tropicbird; J. Schuman, Black-billed Cuckoo; R. & A. Simpson, Philadelphia Vireo; Brian E. Small, Surf Scoter, White-winged Scoter, Clapper Rail, Olive-sided Flycatcher, Least Flycatcher, Brown-crested Flycatcher, Sedge Wren, Black-throated Gray Warbler, Nelson's Sharp-tailed Sparrow; H. P. Smith, Jr., Sharp-shinned Hawk; M. Smith, Purple Sandpiper; B. Sorrie, Red-footed Booby; M. Stubblefield, Semipalmated Sandpiper, Yellow-bellied Sapsucker, Ruby-crowned Kinglet, Swamp Sparrow; D. Tipling, Manx Shearwater; T. Vezo, Pectoral Sandpiper, Common Tern, Winter Wren, Salt-marsh Sharp-tailed Sparrow; D. Wechsler, Western Sandpiper, Long-billed Dowitcher, Mangrove Cuckoo, Seaside Sparrow, Lapland Longspur; B. K. Wheeler, Snail Kite, Broad-winged Hawk, Short-tailed Hawk, Golden Eagle; J. Williams, Spot-breasted Oriole; T. J. Witt, Antillean Nighthawk; J. R. Woodward, Blue-gray Gnatcatcher, Fox Sparrow; D. & M. Zimmerman, Masked Booby, Cooper's Hawk

Kevin Winker: Swainson's Warbler

References

Abbey, E. 1968. *Desert solitaire*. Simon and Schuster, New York.

Aldrich, J. W., and J. S. Weske. 1978. Origin and evolution of the eastern House Finch population. *Auk* 95:528–536.

American Ornithologists' Union [A.O.U.]. 1998. *Check-list of North American birds*, 7th ed. American Ornithologists' Union, Lawrence, Kans.

———. 2000. Forty-second supplement to the American Ornithologists' Union's *Check-list of North American birds*. *Auk* 117:847–858.

———. 2002. Forty-third supplement to the American Ornithologists' Union's *Check-list of North American birds*. *Auk* 119:897–906.

———. 2003. Forty-fourth supplement to the American Ornithologists' Union's *Check-list of North American birds*. *Auk* 120:923–981.

———. 2004. Forty-fifth supplement to the American Ornithologists' Union's *Check-list of North American birds*. *Auk* 121:985–995.

Audubon, J. J. 1832. Letter to the editor. *Monthly American Journal of Geology and Natural Science* 1:529–537.

Bartram, W. 1928. *Travels of William Bartram*. Dover Publications, New York.

Clark, W. S., and B. K. Wheeler. 1987. *A field guide to hawks: North America*. Houghton Mifflin, Boston.

Clement, P., A. Harris, and J. Davis. 1993. *Finches and sparrows: an identification guide*. Princeton University Press, Princeton, N.J.

Curson, J., D. Quinn, and D. Beadle. 1994. *New World warblers*. A&C Black, London.

DeGraaf, R. M., and J. H. Rappole. 1995. *Neotropical migratory birds: natural history, distribution, and population change*. Cornell University Press, Ithaca, N.Y. 676 pp.

DeGraaf, R. M., V. E. Scott, R. H. Hamre, L. Ernst, and S. H. Anderson. 1991. Forest and rangeland birds of the United States: natural history and habitat use. Forest Service, United States Department of Agriculture, Agriculture handbook 688.

Dunne, P., and C. Sutton. 1989. *Hawks in flight: flight identification of North American migrant raptors*. Houghton Mifflin, Boston.

Edwards, E. P. 1972. *A field guide to the birds of Mexico*. E. P. Edwards, Sweet Briar, Va.

Grant, P. J . 1982. *Gulls: a guide to identification*. Poyser, Calton, Stoke on Trent, U.K.

Greenlaw, J. S. 1993. Behavioral and morphological diversification in Sharp-tailed Sparrows (*Ammodramus caudacutus*) of the Atlantic coast. *Auk* 110:286–303.

Harrison, G. H. 1976. *Roger Tory Peterson's dozen birding hot spots*. Simon and Schuster, New York.

Harrison, P. 1983. *Seabirds: an identification guide*. Houghton Mifflin, Boston.

Hayman, P., J. Marchant, and T. Prater. 1986. *Shorebirds: an identification guide to the waders of the world*. Houghton Mifflin, Boston. 412 pp.

Hemingway, E. 1970. *Islands in the stream*. Charles Scribner's and Sons, New York.

Hines, R. W. 1985. Ducks at a distance: A waterfowl identification guide. U. S. Fish and Wildlife Service, Washington, D.C.

Hitt, J. R., and K. T. Blackshaw (eds.). 1996. *A birder's guide to Georgia*, 5th ed. Occ. Publ. 13, Georgia Ornithological Society, Cartersville.

Howell, A. H. 1928. Birds of Alabama. Dept. of Game Fish., Birmingham, Ala.

———. 1932. *Florida bird life*. Coward-McCann, New York.

Hunt, C. B. 1967. *Physiography of the United States*. W. H. Freeman, San Francisco. 480 pp.

———. 1974. *Natural regions of the United States and Canada*. W. H. Freeman, San Francisco.

Imhof, T. A. 1976. *Birds of Alabama*, 2nd ed. University of Alabama Press, Tuscaloosa.

Johnsgard, P. A. 1979. *A guide to North American waterfowl*. Indiana University Press, Bloomington. 274 pp.

King, B. F., and E. C. Dickinson. 1975. *A field guide to the birds of south-east Asia*. Collins, London.

King, J. 1953. *Telling trees*. William Sloane, New York.

Lanier, S. 1916. *Poems of Sidney Lanier*. University of Georgia Press, Athens.

Lanyon, W., and J. Bull. 1967. Identification of Connecticut, Mourning, and MacGillivray's warblers. *Bird-Banding* 39:187–194.

Loughlin, M. H., J. C. Ogden, W. B. Robertson, Jr., K. Russell, and R. W. March. 1991. *Everglades National Park: bird checklist*. Florida National Parks and Monuments Association, Homestead.

National Geographic Society. 1987. *Field guide to the birds of North America*, 2nd ed. National Geographic Society, Washington, D.C. 464 pp.

Oberholser, H. C. 1974. *The bird life of Texas*. Univ. Texas Press, Austin.

Peterson, R. T. 1980. *A field guide to the birds: a completely new guide to all the birds of eastern and central United States*, 4th ed. Houghton Mifflin, Boston.

Phillips, A. R. 1975. Semipalmated Sandpiper identification, migration, summer and winter ranges. *Amer. Birds* 29:799–806.

———. 1986. *The known birds of North and Middle America. Part I: Hirundinidae to Mimidae; Certhiidae*. Privately published, Denver, Colo. 259 pp.

———. 1991. *The known birds of North and Middle America. Part II: Bombycillidae; Sylviidae to Sturnidae; Vireonidae*. Privately published, Denver, Colo. 259 pp.

Rising, J. D. 1996. *A guide to the identification and natural history of the sparrows of the United States and Canada*. Academic Press, New York.

Robbins, C. S., B. Brunn, and H. S. Zimm. 1983. *Birds of North America: a guide to identification*, rev. ed. Golden, New York. 340 pp.

Sibley, C. G., and B. L. Monroe, Jr. 1990. *Distribution and taxonomy of birds of the world*. Yale University Press, New Haven, Conn.

Sibley, D. A. 2000. *The Sibley guide to birds*. Alfred A. Knopf, New York.

Stevenson, H. M., and B. H. Anderson. 1994. *The birdlife of Florida*. University Press of Florida, Gainesville.

Stiles, F. G., and A. F. Skutch. 1989. *A guide to the birds of Costa Rica*. Cornell University Press, Ithaca, N.Y. 511 pp.

Stokes, D. W., and L. Q. Stokes. 1996. *Stokes field guide to birds: eastern region*. Little, Brown, Boston.

Toups, J. A., and J. A. Jackson. 1987. *Birds and birding on the Mississippi coast*. University Press of Mississippi, Jackson.

Vaughan, R. 1994. *Birder's guide to Alabama and Mississippi*. Gulf Publishing, Houston, Tex.

Index

Numbers in **boldface** refer to species accounts; numbers in *italics* refer to illustrations.

Gaviiformes, 44

Geologic provinces, 3; Appalachian Plateau, 4; Blue Ridge, 4; Coastal Plain, 4; Interior Low Plains, 4; Piedmont, 4; Ridge and Valley, 4

Geopelia cuneata, 275

George L. Smith State Park (Ga.), 62, 69, 186, 197, 300

Geothlypis trichas, **236**

Geotrygon: chrysia, 275; *montana*, 275

Gnatcatcher, Blue-gray, **202**

Godwit: Bar-tailed, 275; Black-tailed, 275; Hudsonian, 275; Marbled, **109**

Goldeneye, Common, **98**

Goldfinch: American, **270**; European, 278

Goose: Bean, 273; Canada, **22**; Egyptian, 273; Greater White-fronted, **20**; Greylag, 273; Orinoco, 273; Ross's, 273; Snow, 13, **21**; Swan, 273

Goshawk, Northern, 274

Grackle: Boat-tailed, **263**; Common, **263**

Gracula religiosa, 278

Grand Bay National Wildlife Refuge (Miss.), 60, 306

Grand Bay Wildlife Management Area (Ga.), 92, 105, *107*, 114, 164, 180, 231, 245, 300

Grassquit: Black-faced, 278; Yellow-faced, 278

Grebe: Clark's, 274; Eared, **47**; Horned, **47**; Pied-billed, **46**; Red-necked, 274; Western, 274

Grosbeak: Black-headed, 278; Blue, 176, **256**; Evening, 230, **271**; Rose-breasted, 8, 14, 230, **255**

Ground-Dove. *See* Dove

Ground-Hornbill, Abyssinian, 277

Grouse, Ruffed, **42**, 230

Gruidae, 95

Gruiformes, 88

Grus: americana, **96**; *antigone*, 274; *canadensis*, **96**

Guineafowl, Helmeted, 274

Gulf Islands National Seashore (Fla.), 55, 59, 65, 108, 112, 151, 161, 206, 216, 245, 291

Gulf Islands National Seashore (Miss.), 40, *45*, 47, 57, 74, 87, 89, 90, 91, 94, 99, 110, 113, 117, 119, 127, 129, 132, 134, 135, 136, 138, 144, 199, 227, 249, 264, 306

Gulf Marine State Park (Miss.), 126, 133, 306

Gulf State Park (Ala.), 55, 88, 90, 91, 93, 111, 138, 179, 210, 284

Gull: Band-tailed, 275; Black-headed, 275; Bonaparte's, **126**; Franklin's, **126**; Glaucous, **130**; Great Black-backed, **130**; Heermann's, 275; Herring, **128**; Iceland, 275; Laughing, **125**; Lesser Black-backed, **129**; Little, 275; Ring-billed, **127**; Sabine's, 275; Thayer's, 275

Habitat, 5; agriculture/residential, 11, 13; Appalachian oak forest, 8, 9; broadleaf deciduous and mixed forest, 8, 9; freshwater wetlands, 7; grassland and dry prairies, 7, 8; marine, coastal waters, and shoreline, 6; mesic hammocks, 10, 11; pine forest and savanna, 10; southern floodplain forest, 11, 12

Haematopodidae, 102

Haematopus palliatus, **102**

Haliaeetus leucocephalus, **77**

Harrier, Northern, **78**, 245

Harris Neck National Wildlife Refuge (Ga.), 21, 28, 34, 59, 70, 94, 99, 105, 110, *112*, 132, 138, 198, 206, 212, 226, 249, 252, 300

Hawk: Broad-winged, 13, **81**; Cooper's, **80**; Ferruginous, 274; Red-shouldered, 8, **80**; Red-tailed, **83**; Rough-legged, 274; Sharp-shinned, **79**; Short-tailed, 10, 11, **82**; Swainson's, **83**

Helmitheros vermivorum, **231**

Heron: Black-crowned Night, **67**; Great Blue, **61**; Great White, **61**, 150; Green, **67**, 120; Little Blue, 7, **64**, 120; Tricolored, 7, **64**; Yellow-crowned Night, 11, **68**, 150

Hillside National Wildlife Refuge (Miss.), 78, 209, 306

Himantopus mexicanus, **103**

Hirundo rustica, **191**

Historic Blakeley State Park (Ala.), 191, 284

Histrionicus histrionicus, 274

Hobe Sound National Wildlife Refuge (Fla.), 68, 81, 100, 101, 105, 107, 110, 113, 114, 117, 119, 134, 135, 144, 184, *185*, 186, 291

Honeymoon Island State Park (Fla.), 101, 126, 291

Howell, A. H., 3, 42

Hugh Taylor Birch State Park (Fla.), *11*, 64, *266*, 267, 291

Hugh White State Park (Miss.), 188, 306

Huguenot Memorial City Park, Jacksonville (Fla.), 116, 291

Hummingbird: Allen's, 277; Anna's, 277; Black-

307. *See also* Cypress Swamp; Donivan Slough; Freedom Hills Overlook; Pharr Mounds; Tenn-Tom Waterway

Neochen jubata, 273

Netta peposaca, 274

Newcomer Treatment Facility (Ga.), 246, 301

Newman Wetlands Center, Atlanta (Ga.), 271, 301

Nighthawk: Antillean, 77, **157**; Common, **157**; Lesser, **156**

Night-Heron. *See* Heron

Noddy: Black, 6, **139**; Brown, 6, 137, **138**

Nomonyx dominicus, 274

Nothura, Spotted, 273

Nothura maculosa, 273

Noxubee National Wildlife Refuge (Miss.), 29, 32, 39, 48, 59, 69, 73, 79, 104, 113, 121, 155, 167, 196, 219, 224, 228, 233, 243, 246, 247, 263, 307

Numenius: *americanus*, **109**; *arquata*, 275; *phaeopus*, **108**

Numida meleagris, 274

Nuthatch: Brown-headed, 10, **194**; Red-breasted, **193**; White-breasted, **194**

Nyctanassa violacea, **68**

Nycticorax nycticorax, **67**

Nymphichs hollandicus, 276

Oak Mountain State Park (Ala.), 73, 78, 153, 158, 160, 185, 197, 201, 204, 206, 215, 236, 245, 253, 269, 285

Oakmulgee District, Talladega National Forest (Ala.), 167, 169, 255, 285

Oceanites oceanicus, **51**

Oceanodroma: *castro*, **52**; *leucorhoa*, **52**

Ocmulgee National Monument (Ga.), 81, 163, 178, 202, 210, 215, 232, 233, 244, 255, 257, 271, 301

Odontophoridae, 43

Oenanthe oenanthe, 278

Oglethorpe, James, 1

Okaloosa County Holding Ponds (Fla.), 48, 115, 248, 249, 254, 294

Okefenokee National Wildlife Refuge (Ga.), 29, 39, 59, 64, 68, 71, 72, 75, 96, 121, 144, 149, *166*, 167, 195, 201, 217, 242, 301; Minnie's Island, 224

Oporornis: *agilis*, 235; *formosus*, **234**; *philadelphia*, 235

Orange County Eastern Water Reclamation Facility (Fla.), 212, 294

Oreoscoptes montanus, 278

Oriole: Baltimore, 8, **267**; Bullock's, 278; Orchard, **265**; Spot-breasted, **266**

Orlando (Fla.), 236

Oropendola, Montezuma, 278

Ortalis vetula, **41**

Oscar Scherer State Park (Fla.), 184, 294

Osprey, **74**, 245

Otus flammeolus, 277

Ovenbird, 8, 11, **232**, 282

Owl: Barn, **152**; Barred, **154**; Burrowing, 8, **154**, 286; Eastern Screech, 10, 120, **152**; Flammulated, 277; Great Horned, 10, **153**; Long-eared, 277; Northern Saw-whet, 277; Short-eared, **155**; Snowy, 277; Spectacled, 277

Oxyura jamaicensis, **41**

Oystercatcher, American, 6, **102**, 128

Palm Point Park (Fla.), 215, 295

Palm-Swift, Antillean, 277

Pandion haliaetus, **74**

Panther Swamp National Wildlife Refuge (Miss.), 25, 29, 41, 43, 46, 62, 78, 208, 308

Parakeet: Black-hooded, **146**; Blossom-headed, 276; Brown-throated, 276; Carolina, 276; Crimson-fronted, 276; Dusky-headed, 276; Green, 276; Green-cheeked, 276; Hispaniolan, 276; Maroon-bellied, 276; Mitred, 276; Monk, 13, **145**; Orange-chinned, 276; Orange-fronted, 276; Peach-fronted, 276; Plum-headed, 276; Red-masked, **146**; Rose-ringed, 276; Scarlet-fronted, 276; Tui, 276; White-eyed, 276; White-winged, **147**; Yellow-chevroned, 3, **147**

Paridae, 192

Paroaria gularis, 278

Parrot: Burrowing, 2, 276; Eclectus, 276; Gray, 276; Hispaniolan, 276; Lilac-crowned, 276; Maroon-fronted, 276; Mealy, 276; Orange-winged, 276; Red-crowned, 11, **148**; Red-lored, 276; Red-spectacled, 276; Rueppell's, 276; Senegal, 276; Turquoise-fronted, 276; White-crowned, 276; White-fronted, 276; Yellow-crowned, 277; Yellow-headed, 277; Yellow-naped, 277

Parula, Northern, 7, **217**

Sipsey Wilderness, William B. Bankhead National Forest (Ala.), 159, 170, 172, 285; Sipsey Fork, *161*

Siskin, Pine, 230, **269**

Sitta: canadensis, **193**; *carolinensis*, **194**; *pusilla*, **194**

Sittidae, 193

Skidaway Island State Park (Ga.), 225, 228, 236, 249, 302

Skimmer, Black, 7, **139**

Skua, South Polar, 275

Snipe, Wilson's, **120**

Somateria: mollissima, 274; *spectabilis*, 274

Sora, **91**

South Brunswick River (Ga.), *92*

Sparrow: American Tree, **243**; Bachman's, 10, **242**; Black-throated, 278; Chipping, **243**; Clay-colored, **244**; Field, **244**; Fox, 250; Golden, 279; Golden-crowned, 278; Grasshopper, **247**; Harris's, 278; Henslow's, **247**; House, 12, 17, **272**; Lark, **246**; LeConte's, **246**; Lincoln's, **251**; Nelson's Sharp-tailed, **248**; Saltmarsh Sharp-tailed, **249**; Savannah, **246**; Seaside, **250**; Song, **251**; Swamp, **252**; Vesper, **245**; White-crowned, **253**; White-throated, **252**

Sphyrapicus varius, **164**

Spindalis, Western, 278

Spindalis zena, 278

Spiza americana, **258**

Spizella: arborea, **243**; *pallida*, **244**; *passerina*, **243**; *pusilla*, **244**

Spoonbill, Roseate, 7, **70**, 71, 150, 294

St. Andrews Bay State Recreation Area (Fla.), 78, 86, 91, 94, 99, 127, 129, 136, 140, 188, 198, 209, 219, 232, 245, 246, 253, 256, 267, 271, 295

Starling, European, 12, **211**

St. Augustine (Fla.), 1

St. Catherine Creek National Wildlife Refuge (Miss.), *12*, 76, 80, 167, 218, 239, 308

St. Catherine's Island (Ga.), *10*

Stelgidopteryx serripennis, **189**

Stellula calliope, 277

Stephen C. Foster State Park (Ga.), 62, 63, 66, 68, 74, 158, 303

Stercorarius: longicaudus, 275; *maccormicki*, 275; *parasiticus*, **125**; *pomarinus*, **124**

Sterna: anaethetus, **137**; *antillarum*, **136**;

caspia, **132**; *dougallii*, **134**; *elegans*, 275; *forsteri*, **135**; *fuscata*, **137**; *hirundo*, **135**; *maxima*, **133**; *nilotica*, **133**; *pardisea*, 275; *sandvicensis*, **133**

St. George Island State Park (Fla.), 57, 296

Stilt, Black-necked, **103**, 112

St. Joseph Peninsula State Park (Fla.), 79, 202, 296

St. Marks National Wildlife Refuge (Fla.), 21, 25, 36, *98*, 99, 106, 153, 155, 163, 173, 175, 189, 198, 229, 244, 248, 251, 296

Stork: Black-necked, 274; Wood, 7, **71**

Storm-Petrel: Band-rumped, **52**; Leach's, **52**; White-bellied, 274; Wilson's, **51**

St. Petersburg (Fla.), 13, 24, 142, 145, 146

Streptopelia: chinensis, 275; *decaocto*, **142**; *risoria*, **141**; *rosegrisea*, 142; *turtur*, 275

Streptoprocne zonaris, 277

Strigidae, 152

Strigiformes, 152

Strix varia, **154**

St. Simons Island (Ga.), 136, *176*, 303

Sturnella: magna, **260**; *neglecta*, 278

Sturnidae, 211

Sturnus vulgaris, **211**

St. Vincent National Wildlife Refuge (Fla.), 35, 151, 172, 182, 296

Sula: dactylatra, **54**; *leucogaster*, **54**; *sula*, **55**

Sulidae, 53

Surfbird, 275

Swallow: Bahama, 277; Bank, **189**; Barn, **191**; Cave, **190**; Cliff, **190**; Northern Rough-winged, **189**; Tree, **188**

Swamphen, Purple, 274

Swan: Black, 273; Mute, 273; Tundra, **23**; Whooper, 273

Sweetwater Creek State Conservation Park (Ga.), 34, 41, 164, 303

Swift: Chimney, **159**; White-collared, 277

Sylviidae, 202

Tachornis phoenicobia, 277

Tachycineta: bicolor, **188**; *cyaneoviridis*, 277

Tadorna ferruginea, 274

Talapoosa River, 209

Talladega National Forest. *See* Oakmulgee District, Talladega National Forest (Ala.)

Tallahatchie National Wildlife Refuge (Miss.), 85, 93, 201, 232, 245, 263, 271, 308

Tall Timbers Research Station (Fla.), 44, 80, 144, 155, 160, 192, 207, 225, 296

Tamiami Trail (Fla.), 224

Tanager: Scarlet, 8, 14, **240**; Stripe-headed, 266; Summer, **239**; Western, **241**

Teal: Blue-winged, **29**; Cinnamon, 274; Green-winged, **30**; Hottentot, 274; Ringed, 274

Tenn-Tom Waterway, Natchez Trace Parkway (Miss.), 190, 191, 309

Tern: Arctic, 275; Black, **138**; Bridled, 6, **137**; Caspian, **132**; Common, **135**; Elegant, 275; Forster's, **135**; Gull-billed, 7, **131**; Least, 6, 128, **136**; Roseate, **134**; Royal, 6, **133**; Sandwich, **133**; Sooty, **137**; White-winged, 275

Thalassarche melanophris, 274

Thrasher: Brown, **210**; Curve-billed, 278; Sage, 278

Thraupidae, 239

Three Lakes Wildlife Management Area, Lake Marian Highlands (Fla.), 85, 97, 197, 242, 247, 296

Threskiornithidae, 69

Thrush: Bicknell's, **205**; Gray-cheeked, **204**; Hermit, **206**; Swainson's, **206**; Varied, 278; Wood, 8, 176, 203, **207**

Thryomanes bewickii, 277

Thryothorus ludovicianus, **196**

Tiaris: bicolor, 278; *olivacea*, 278

Titmouse, Tufted, 9, **192**

Tombigbee State Park (Miss.), 159, 163, 204, 309

Toucan: Citron-throated, 277; Toco, 277

Touraco, Violet, 277

Towhee: Eastern, 8, 176, **241**; Green-tailed, 278

Toxostoma: curvirostre, 278; *rufum*, **210**

Trace State Park (Miss.), 257, 309

Trichoglossus: chlorolepidotus, 275; *haematod*, 275; *ornatus*, 275

Tringa: flavipes, **105**; *melanoleuca*, **104**; *solitaria*, **106**

Trochilidae, 160

Troglodytes: aedon, **197**; *troglodytes*, **197**

Troglodytidae, 196

Tropical Audubon Society Office (Fla.), 146, 296

Tropicbird: Red-billed, 274; White-tailed, 6, **53**, 137

Troupial, 278

Tryngites subruficollis, **118**

Turdidae, 203

Turdus migratorius, **208**

Turkey, Wild, **43**

Turnstone, Ruddy, **110**

Turtle-Dove. *See* Dove

Tuskegee National Forest (Ala.), 45, 157, 163, 164, 174, 224, 231, 237, 285

Tybee Island Beach (Ga.), 45, 98, 107, 111, 113, 116, 133, 303

Tyrannidae, 168

Tyrannus: caudifasciatus, 277; *couchii*, 277; *dominicensis*, **176**; *forficatus*, **177**; *melancholicus*, 277; *savana*, 277; *tyrannus*, **175**; *verticalis*, **175**; *vociferans*, 277

Tyto alba, **152**

Tytonidae, 152

Unicoi Gap (Ga.), 222, 240, 303

Upper Tampa Bay Regional Park (Fla.), 296

Uraeginthus bengalus, 279

US 90 between Gulfport and Biloxi (Miss.), 100, 140, 309

Valdosta (Ga.), 107

Vanellus: chilensis, 275; *vanellus*, 274

Vaughan, Ray, 161

Veery, 8, **204**, 256

Venice Beach (Fla.), *63*

Vermivora: bachmanii, 278; *celata*, **216**; *chrysoptera*, **214**; *peregrina*, **215**; *pinus*, **214**; *ruficapilla*, **216**

Vicksburg National Military Park (Miss.), 21, 26, 67, 84, 144, 160, 185, 193, *194*, 215, 244, 245, 251, 253, 269, 270, 309

Vidua macroura, 279

Vilano Beach Boat Ramp (Fla.), 132, 297

Vireo: Bell's, **179**; Black-whiskered, **182**; Blue-headed, **180**, 256; Philadelphia, **181**; Red-eyed, 8, 176, **182**; Thick-billed, 277; Warbling, **181**; White-eyed, 7, **178**; Yellow-green, 277; Yellow-throated, **180**

Vireo: altiloquus, **182**, 183; *bellii*, **179**; *crassirostris*, 277; *flavifrons*, **180**; *flavoviridis*, 277; *gilvus*, **181**; *griseus*, **178**; *olivaceous*, **182**; *philadelphicus*, **181**; *solitarius*, **180**

Vireonidae, 178

Vogel State Park (Ga.), **194**, **196**, 303

Vulture: Black, **72**; King, 274; Turkey, **73**

Vultur sacra, 3

John H. Rappole is a senior research scientist in ornithology and conservation biology at the Smithsonian Conservation and Research Center in Front Royal, Virginia. He is author or coauthor of eleven books, including *Birds of the Southwest: Arizona, New Mexico, Southern California, and Southern Nevada* (2000), *Birds of the Mid-Atlantic Region and Where to Find Them* (2002), and *The Ecology of Migrant Birds* (1995), as well as 130 professional publications.

Related-interest titles from the University Press of Florida

Death in the Everglades: The Murder of Guy Bradley, America's First Martyr to Environmentalism
Stuart B. McIver

A Field Guide and Identification Manual for Florida and Eastern U.S. Tiger Beetles
Paul M. Choate Jr.

Florida Butterfly Caterpillars and Their Host Plants
Marc C. Minno, Jerry F. Butler, and Donald W. Hall

Florida's Fragile Wildlife: Conservation and Management
Don A. Wood

Florida on Horseback: A Trail Rider's Guide to the South and Central Regions
Cornelia Bernard Henderson

Guide to the Great Florida Birding Trail: East Section
Julie A. Brashears and Susan Cerulean

Journeys Through Paradise: Pioneering Naturalists in the Southeast
Gail Fishman

Miami's Parrot Jungle and Gardens: The Colorful History of an Uncommon Attraction
Cory H. Gittner

Rare and Endangered Biota of Florida: Volume 5, Birds
James A. Rodgers Jr., Herbert W. Kale II, and Henry T. Smith

The Wild East: A Biography of the Great Smoky Mountains
Margaret Lynn Brown

Wild Orchids of the Southeastern United States, North of Peninsular Florida
Paul Martin Brown with drawings by Stan Folsom

For more information on these and other books, visit our website at www.upf.com.